Entrepreneurial Music Education

"This is a terrific contribution to innovative practices in music education, and makes a profound connection with the musical world outside the classroom."
— Emerita Professor Lucy Green, *UCL Institute of Education, UK*

"Entrepreneurial skills are essential for aspiring musicians, artists and composers in the contemporary music economy. The question is how to design a learning experience where young musicians are able to develop such skills. In this important book, Dr Kelman reports on her successful approach to this challenge. Dr Kelman's entrepreneurial education model that allows students grow their own business venture provides crucial insights for music industry educators around the world."
— Professor Patrik Wikstrom, *Queensland University of Technology, Australia*

Kristina Kelman

Entrepreneurial Music Education

Professional Learning in Schools and the Industry

Kristina Kelman
Queensland University of Technology
Kelvin Grove, QLD, Australia

ISBN 978-3-030-37128-9   ISBN 978-3-030-37129-6   (eBook)
https://doi.org/10.1007/978-3-030-37129-6

Cover image: © Daisy Godwin

This Palgrave Macmillan imprint is published by the registered company Springer Nature Switzerland AG
The registered company address is: Gewerbestrasse 11, 6330 Cham, Switzerland

Acknowledgements

I have been a music educator and professional musician since 1992, and over that time I have observed the changing needs and demands of my students. In 2007 I was appointed to an exciting position as a foundation music teacher in a selective arts high school, where the aims were to nurture and encourage the next generation of creative entrepreneurs and knowledge workers. It was an exciting time for me to consider how I might complement the existing academic curriculum with a new learning design that might foster the development of entrepreneurial attributes in my students, as well as directly interfacing them with the music industry.

The journey started as a learning and teaching experiment, which soon gained enormous momentum and visibility within our city. It became clear to me that this learning environment should be captured through the students' voices, and distilled into a practical set of design principles for teachers and academics as a doctoral project, and now condensed into this book.

The project presented many risks for the school. I am grateful to the principal at the time, John Jose who trusted the students and I with an ambitious set of objectives including the staging of large-scale music festivals, and a regular all-ages music venue. The project would not have been possible without his support. To all the industry folk that generously gave of their time to mentor and support my students, thank you.

To my Ph.D. supervisors, Catherine Doherty and Andy Arthurs, thank you for guiding me and supporting me on this academic journey, and helping me to reframe my teaching practice as research. Thank you to Daniel Pratt for coming on board this year as a research assistant. Your industry and educator eyes were incredibly valuable in helping me to transform the project into this publication. To Tom Dick and my family, thank you for your support and patience during these intense and busy years.

Lastly, and most importantly, thank you to my students, who are now out making their mark on the world. It is their voices that have created this work. They showed endless enthusiasm for their enterprise, and worked tirelessly for over four years to create and build a supportive youth music scene in Brisbane, Australia. There are many students who were involved over that time, but a special acknowledgement must go to the foundation members of YMI, Gonzalo Rodino, Harrison Prouse, Hannah Anderson Cook, Stephen J. Smith, Ella Bailey, Sam Ryan, Amir Rezaee, Lucas Price, and Benjamin Hovav.

Contents

1 Introduction   1

2 Making a Case for an Entrepreneurial Music Education
   in Schools   9

3 Current Approaches to Education—But What About
   the Music Industry?   23

4 Building the Emerging Professional Learning Model   63

5 Designing an Entrepreneurial Learning Project   93

6 Developing Social Skills for Entrepreneurship
   in the Music Industry   117

7 Learning About Project Management
   for Entrepreneurship in the Music Industry   143

8   Acquiring Domain Knowledge for Entrepreneurship
    in the Music Industry   167

9   Design Principles to Plan Entrepreneurial Learning
    in Music Education   207

Index   243

Abbreviations

CoP   Community of Practice
CoPs   Communities of Practice
DBR   Design-based research
YMI   Youth Music Industries

List of Figures

Fig. 4.1	The emerging professional learning model	86
Fig. 5.1	Development approach to IT research (Reeves, 2000, p. 9)	96
Fig. 6.1	Reflection Box 1: timetables and time management	120
Fig. 6.2	Reflection Box 2: students meet teachers	121
Fig. 6.3	Reflection Box 3: real world meets school world	124
Fig. 6.4	Reflection Box 4: school workload versus real world workload	125
Fig. 6.5	Reflection Box 5: school culture versus industry culture	128
Fig. 7.1	Poster: *Four Walls Festival* (Phase 1) illustration by Ken Smith	147
Fig. 7.2	*Four Walls Festival* poster: initial sketch (Phase 2) illustration by Ken Smith	148
Fig. 7.3	Poster: *Four Walls Festival* (Phase 2) illustration by Ken Smith	151
Fig. 7.4	Reflection Box 6: teacher leadership and student limitations	152
Fig. 7.5	Reflection Box 7: emergence of leaders	154
Fig. 7.6	Reflection Box 8: risk management realities	158
Fig. 7.7	Reflection Box 9: learning my boundaries	159
Fig. 8.1	Reflection Box 10: risks of 'real world' learning	170
Fig. 8.2	Reflection Box 11: growing beyond the school walls	178
Fig. 8.3	YMI governance model, Phase 3	195
Fig. 8.4	Reflection Box 12: succession planning	196
Fig. 9.1	Design principle 1: networking	214

Fig. 9.2   Design principle 2: goals   216
Fig. 9.3   Design principle 3: interpersonal skills   219
Fig. 9.4   Design principle 4: reflection   221
Fig. 9.5   Design principle 5: domain knowledge   224
Fig. 9.6   Design principle 6: professionalism and industry standards   226
Fig. 9.7   Design principle 7: sustainability   228

List of Tables

Table 4.1   The evolution of CoPs—stages and elements   73
Table 4.2   Social capital mobilised through CoP development
            and learning   83
Table 4.3   Entrepreneurial competencies   85
Table 5.1   Summary of design-based research design phases
            and interventions used in this study   106
Table 6.1   Learning about networking across the three phases   131
Table 6.2   Learning about interpersonal skills across the three phases   139
Table 7.1   Learning about setting goals and completing tasks across
            the three phases   160
Table 7.2   Learning about reflection across the three phases   165
Table 8.1   Learning about the music business across the three phases 174
Table 8.2   Learning about music industry expectations across
            the three phases   180
Table 8.3   Learning about music and musicians across
            the three phases   186
Table 8.4   Learning about sustainability across the three phases   203
Table 9.1   Summary and description of design principles   230

1

Introduction

My principal role for the last 17 years has been that of secondary school music educator. I have taught in a variety of schools in Australia, ranging from a small co-educational private school to a boys' grammar school and, more recently, to a selective and innovative public school. I have worked as a classroom teacher and Head of Department, and as director of various ensembles and choirs. Throughout this time, I have also balanced my teaching career with a freelance career as a professional musician, a practice that is not unusual for music educators. This dual practitioner/educator role has been a major influence on my educational philosophy, and has convinced me of the need to provide my students with connections to the music industry. This connection has also highlighted and modelled the multiplicity of skills needed to sustain a career in the industry.

At the beginning of my career, I was thrilled to have my students eagerly hang off my every word. I brought my formal, disciplined past into the classroom, believing that if I had learned that way, then my students should and could as well. The musical training, I received throughout my undergraduate degree involved learning and developing the skills and dispositions of Western classical music. For the most part,

© The Author(s) 2020
K. Kelman, *Entrepreneurial Music Education*,
https://doi.org/10.1007/978-3-030-37129-6_1

this was a very solitary journey where I spent four hours a day at the piano in a practice room. This was the approach I first brought to the music classroom as a young teacher.

The educational needs and demands of my students have since changed. We are now living in a profoundly digital world where the foundations of knowledge are constantly shifting (Loader, 2007). My students are increasingly self-sufficient learners and can acquire specific skills and knowledge through other channels, such as informal learning in garage band contexts, tutorials on YouTube, music programmes at their church, and part-time employment. I began to ask myself what it means to be a music teacher today. How might I respond to this emerging context? These questions motivated me to revisit past assumptions and to seek an updated approach to my teaching practice. While I was exploiting the latest trends in music technology and ensuring that learning experiences were collaborative, I still found that students were disengaged. This is because the international curriculum offered at my school, was designed to feed students into a performance-oriented conservatorium or tertiary course. This project, on the other hand, is underpinned by the premise that if young musicians are to enter music industry careers and prosper, they need a broader set of skills that are not currently addressed in the official music syllabi.

In 2007, I was appointed as music teacher to a new and selective arts-focused high school in Australia. This position offered a unique opportunity to create an innovative music programme that could supplement the conventional music curriculum.

The School

The school in which this research was conducted was designed as part of a government strategy to develop selective specialist senior secondary schools in the public sector in an effort to stem the drift of students to the private sector (Doherty, 2009). The school aims to nurture and encourage the next generation of creative entrepreneurs and knowledge workers, to enhance excellence in the arts and build social cohesion in a global and multicultural society. The school's vision resonates strongly with the creative industries' agendas profiled above. The school believes that there must be aligned action and shared vision among the government, the education sector, and industry artists. The Queensland Government's Smart State Strategy report (2008) acknowledges the contribution that arts can make to our schools and artists. To achieve an aligned vision, schools should be drawn into the wider arts and cultural community and into creative industries while, at the same time, the arts and cultural community and creative industries should be drawn into schools. The challenge is to realise the necessary conditions for such dynamic arts and education partnerships.

This ambitious and innovative vision conflicts with the more conservative overarching curriculum chosen for the school. While the school that is the context of this study promotes a creative and innovative pedagogical environment, there is an intensified focus on academic results in order to maintain and enhance a public image. The international curriculum was implemented as a point of difference in the market, and in this curricular market, returns to a more traditional, disciplined curriculum. The chosen curriculum offers a rigorous and structured course that is heavily content-based and time-intensive. Corbett's (2007) interview with teachers teaching the same curriculum, concluded that 'the courses are so packed with content, there is little room for critical self-reflective teaching and learning on a day-to-day basis' (p. 31).

By the nature of its assessment, the music curriculum privileges the more formally trained musician with a high level of music literacy. For example, students over the course of two years are expected to recognise and analyse music covering the last five hundred years of the Western Art music tradition, as well as contemporary pop, jazz and Non-Western musical styles. This work culminates in a three hour externally assessed exam of seven essays. Five of these are based on score and audio excerpts, and two are based on two set works from Western Art Music. Musical analysis comprises 50% of the subject. The remaining assessment is a twenty-minute solo recital focusing on technical skill and stylistic awareness, and a composition folio that demonstrates technical skill and proficient development of musical ideas. This prescriptive curriculum sits in stark contrast to the local curriculum offering set out by the Queensland Core Curriculum Authority, (QCCA) which was designed to allow greater flexibility and adaptability, recognising the importance of developing twenty-first century skills.

As opposed to the rigorous assessment regime prescribed by the school's chosen curriculum, the QCCA music curriculum assesses students on four summative tasks selected out of ongoing assessment in a two-year period: a composition developed in any style or genre and communicated in any format; a performance including solo or ensemble playing, accompanying or conducting; a multimodal integrated project combining a musicological investigation which informs either a performance or composition; and an external exam requiring an extended response to any style of music. These tasks can be negotiated by the student, based on student-interest, and assessment can be updated and improved on throughout the two-year course (Queensland Government, Queensland Curriculum and Assessment Authority, 2019).

Many of my students were highly talented, though informally trained, and typically collaborated with others in the popular 'singer-songwriter' genre. In contrast, the focus of the chosen music curriculum is more about an individual pathway, with students being assessed largely on solo performance and academic work. Kamin, Richards, and Collins (2007) found that popular musicians are positively influenced by peer learning; however, this is difficult to design in the chosen music curriculum due to the nature of its assessment. The mismatch between student aspirations and the curriculum has contributed to an attenuated environment, where student retention has been quite poor. Each year, some students withdrew from the subject 'Music', which had initially been the primary reason for their enrolment at the school.

The impetus for this study came about after many informal discussions with my students about whether they should remain enrolled in this selective school or return to their former schools. They expressed a desire for a meaningful, relevant and industry-connected experience. They wanted to develop the skills and confidence to engage directly with the music industry and to build sustainable careers.

I became interested in the concept of entrepreneurial learning and how being connected with others is a core component of entrepreneurialism. Given the more contemporary musicians in my classroom, I also began some preliminary research into how popular musicians learn. Following her research into the more informal and peer-learning processes of popular musicians, Green asked music teachers to initially stand back and observe, offering help only after students had organised themselves into groups, chosen music, and started a process of aural learning (2002, 2008). She noted that when students' performance deteriorated, teachers were surprised to find that they often managed to improve in the early stages without input. A quote from one of the teachers in Green's study encapsulates her experience: 'In a normal class I am working so hard, I am just making such an effort; they're not working nearly as hard as I am. In this class, they are doing the work' (Green, 2006, p. 109).

I similarly aimed to develop a pedagogical approach that would nurture self-directed learners who could transition to careers beyond high school and tertiary institutions. Given the nature of the industry and the scarcity of employment for musicians, young people will need to consider self-employment and freelance work. While the development of entrepreneurial skills, such as opportunity recognition, risk-taking behaviour, creativity and networking skills are key to this transition (Rae, 2005), I questioned how these skills could be developed in a conventional classroom environment. I could design activities that simulated contexts, however, the benefit of authentic experience with industry networks and adult work settings was my preferred option. The students and I also wanted to create a meaningful project that would have outcomes beyond our own learning, and benefit young musicians and audiences across Queensland.

In 2010, I read an article in the local newspaper that discussed the dearth of music venues where under-age musicians could go to gain performance experience, and to hear the music of their peers. I made copies of the article and distributed them to my students the next day. I met with a core group of nine students (typically 15–17 year olds from Years 10 and 11) who were interested in responding to the article and we created Youth Music Industries (YMI). In less than a year, the students had started their own business, with an ambitious set of objectives that would normally be considered to be well beyond the scope of such young people. Their aim was to provide a framework within which young musicians could perform, record, publish, and broadcast their music.

The students enacted this vision by establishing and operating under-age venues. At these venues, they hosted monthly *Emerge* nights, which gave youth musicians an opportunity to perform their original music. Over the three years of this study, they held a youth music festival each year, the *Four Walls Festival*, which was a full day, three-stage festival showcasing emerging talent alongside Australian headliners. In the second year, they developed and formalised partnerships with QMIA, (the Queensland government music industry development association) and the Queensland Music Festival. They have also co-designed and hosted *Little Big Sound*, a youth music conference in conjunction with QMIA's premier industry event, *Big Sound*. This development allowed YMI to expand its membership to industry professionals, and to benefit from greater exposure and support. At the end of the first year, I successfully sourced $50,000 in government grants to further support the work of YMI. In addition, we won two awards over the next two years; $25,000 and $35,000, in recognition of the success of our school-industry partnership with QMIA.

YMI continued to host events after the study had finished, with the addition of 'Meet ups', where young people meet and share their expertise around various music industry topics. They have also expanded their work into regional Queensland by taking their *Emerge* events to towns such as Cairns in North Queensland, Gympie in South-East Queensland, and Coolangatta on the Gold Coast.

This project was generated to develop educational principles for entrepreneurial learning, based on empirical evidence of how students learn in highly networked and authentic music industry contexts. The project was deliberately engineered to foster collaboration with grounded, realistic opportunities. While there is a wide range of literature surrounding communities of practice, creative industries, and entrepreneurship education, it is rare to find practical and theorised exemplars of secondary school students learning through engagement in their own authentic, music industry organisation. Thus, this project sought to understand how the design of YMI developed entrepreneurial qualities, and identified opportunities for further improvement of that design. In this way, the study sought to offer pedagogical principles for orchestrating entrepreneurial learning for high school students in the creative industries. I therefore sought to explore the following questions:

1. What skills (related to social interaction and project management) do students acquire through an education designed to foster entrepreneurial capacity in the music industry?

   a. How do students acquire these skills?

2. What music industry knowledge do students learn in an environment designed to foster entrepreneurial capacity in the music industry?

   b. How does this learning unfold?

In terms of a learning opportunity, there are several unique aspects to YMI:

- The students and I had never run a music industry enterprise and, thus, we were all learning together;
- The learning environment was an authentic organisation functioning in the public domain, and run by young people for young people;
- YMI was designed by teacher and students in an ongoing iterative process;
- My interventions as a teacher were not made explicit in a conventional manner, but rather were embodied as seeds or questions from which students were able to form their own ideas.

The students' attitudinal changes and sustained motivation have been of particular interest to me over this process, and have inspired me to use YMI as a case study learning design for this book.

References

Corbett, A. C. (2007). Learning asymmetries and the discovery of entrepreneurial opportunities. *Journal of Business Venturing, 22*(1), 97–118. https://doi.org/10.1016/j.jbusvent.2005.10.001.

Doherty, C. (2009). The appeal of the International Baccalaureate in Australia's educational market: A curriculum of choice for mobile futures. *Discourse: Studies in the Cultural Politics of Education, 30*(1), 73–90.

Green, L. (2002). From the Western classics to the world: Secondary music teachers' changing attitudes in England, 1982 and 1998. *British Journal of Music Education, 19*(1), 5–30.

Green, L. (2006). Popular music education in and for itself, and for 'other' music: Current research in the classroom. *International Journal of Music Education, 24*(2), 101–118. https://doi.org/10.1177/0255761406065471.

Green, L. (2008). Group cooperation, inclusion and disaffected pupils: Some responses to informal learning in the music classroom. Presented at the RIME Conference 2007, Exeter, UK. *Music Education Research, 10*(2), 177–192.

Kamin, S., Richards, H., & Collins, D. (2007). Influences on the talent development process of non-classical musicians: Psychological, social and environmental influences. *Music Education Research, 9*(3), 449–468. https://doi.org/10.1080/14613800701587860.

Loader, D. (2007). *Schools for the 21st century* [podcast radio interview by Richard Aedy on *Life Matters*, ABC Radio National, 9 August]. Retrieved from http://www.abc.net.au/radionational/programs/lifematters/schools-for-the-21st-century/3233878.

Queensland Government. (2008). *Smart State strategy, Queensland's smart future, 2008–2012.* Retrieved from http://bit.ly/1p7aY6r.

Queensland Government, Queensland Curriculum and Assessment Authority. (2019). Retrieved from https://www.qcaa.qld.edu.au/senior/senior-subjects/the-arts/music.

Rae, D. (2005). Entrepreneurial learning: A narrative-based conceptual model. *Journal of Small Business and Enterprise Development, 12*(3), 323–335. https://doi.org/10.1108/14626000510612259.

2

Making a Case for an Entrepreneurial Music Education in Schools

Setting the Scene

Youth Music Industries (YMI) was a business venture co-created by myself, as teacher-researcher, and my high school students. The venture was established to create a learning environment that would equip students with the knowledge and skills required for successful participation in the music industry. YMI was an innovative and complex educational setting where the students were invited to run their own youth music organisation. The study responds to arts policies within both the Australian and United Kingdom creative industries sectors that acknowledge that the future of their sectors depends on nurturing the next generation of arts and cultural workers, producers, managers, and creative entrepreneurs. This chapter first explores the current creative industries landscape and the implications of this landscape for teaching and learning.

While young people might be more educated than ever before, the world before them is much more complex, the risks are higher, and there are fewer secure landmarks. Barrington-Leach, Canoy, Hubert, and Lerais (2007) acknowledge that life decisions are more complex

© The Author(s) 2020
K. Kelman, *Entrepreneurial Music Education*,
https://doi.org/10.1007/978-3-030-37129-6_2

than in the past, that they require skills as well as knowledge, and that these skills will be acquired through investment in both human and social capital. Arguably, schools as learning environments are not well equipped to support these shifting requirements of passage. Freire (1968) likened the education system to a bank, viewing the passive student as an empty account to be filled by the teacher. Forty years later, Siemens (2005, p. 9) makes the same critique, observing that, 'our institutions are primarily set up to *fill* learners'. This study explores a different approach to knowledge building that foregrounds the process of learning, rather than the product.

A conventional curriculum determines and packages a specific body of knowledge to be assessed, and syllabi are typically not revised frequently enough to keep pace with the 'half-life' of knowledge (Wenger, MacDermott, & Snyder, 2002, p. 6). This has implications for the relevance and currency of the knowledge being imparted. For example, the chosen international music curriculum at my school, emphasises a strong tradition of Western art music, requiring an extensive accumulation of disciplinary knowledge. Students are assessed through a lengthy external written examination, a solo performance, and a composition folio. Without downplaying the importance of formal music education, I argue the need for a broader, more twenty-first century suite of skills and knowledge that aligns with the music industry in particular, and with the creative industries more generally.

The learning design developed in this study seeks to challenge the conventional music curriculum, and suggests that we need to establish a more creative and entrepreneurial curriculum that encourages problem-solving, risk-taking, innovation, and flexibility. The research does not focus on the teaching of music, but rather on the development of a young person's capacity to work collaboratively, flexibly, and with an entrepreneurial mindset (Bridgstock, 2013, 2017; Haynie, Shepherd, Mosakowski, & Earley, 2010; Kriewall & Mekemson, 2010). This capacity, in turn, nurtures the skills and qualities needed for success in the 'cultural and entrepreneurial economy' (Leadbeater & Oakley, 1999, p. 43).

The Creative Industries

The concept of 'Creative Industries' originated in the United Kingdom in the mid-1990s. Reports from both the UK and Australia describe the creative industries as being concerned with the generation of creative intellectual property that has the potential to be commercialised (Australian Government, Attorney-General's Department, Ministry for the Arts, 2011; Newbigin, 2010). The creative industries include

- music and performing arts;
- film, television, and radio;
- advertising and marketing;
- software development, computer animation, web design and interactive content;
- writing, publishing and print media; and
- architecture, design (industrial, urban, and fashion) and visual arts.

In his report to the UK government, *Nurturing Creativity in Young People*, Roberts (2006) argues that the creative industry sector had grown twice as fast as the overall economy in the last decade. It employed two million people and accounted for one-twelfth of the economy. More recently, the *Creative Industries Economic Estimates Report* (Department for Culture, Media and Sport, 2016) revealed that creative industries accounted for 5.2% of the United Kingdom's total employment and contributed 6% to the gross domestic product (GDP). In Australia, the report *The Creative Economy in Australia* (QUT Digital Media Research Centre, 2016) reveals that creative industries accounted for 5.5% of Australia's total employment. Creative Industries contributed 6.4% to GDP in the 2016–2017 financial year (Australian Government, Bureau of Communications and Arts Research, 2018). According to the *Creative Skills for the Future Economy Report*, creative occupations in Australia are also growing at twice the rate of other occupations, and they are under less threat from automation because creativity is non-routine cognitive work (Australian Government, Department of Communications and the Arts, 2019).

While the creative industries sector is flourishing within the Australian and UK economies, jobs for musicians are scarce. The Creative Industries Innovation Centre report (2013) also identifies that music and performing arts make up only 3% of the total employment within the creative industries. According to the report *Employment in Culture* (Australian Bureau of Statistics, 2011) aspiring musicians face small creative incomes and uncertain career prospects. Many adopt 'portfolio' careers, and leverage their skills in arts-related industries such as music teaching. The report reveals that the median creative income from creative work is $7000 for practising professional musicians. In 2010–2011, the census showed that over 500,000 Australian adults were involved in writing songs, composing, and mixing, and 950,000 adults were involved in singing or playing an instrument. However, very few actually earned a wage or salary for their engagement, and those who did earned less than 25% of their total income in this way. Only 7900 adults were in a full-time music occupation.

Given this conflicting scenario—where the creative industries make a significant contribution to GDP, but career prospects for musicians are limited—my work in music education addresses the need for a new learning design that prepares students for the realities of a music industry career, without deterring their passion for such a career. The design also aims to help music students to imagine other career possibilities within the creative industries.

Roberts (2006) argues that it is imperative to give young people creative experience—both to develop a personal identity and confidence, and to understand and prepare for a twenty-first-century society. He argues that:

- community cohesion is dependent on shared cultures;
- there is the means for mass participation in art and culture;
- creativity offers the means of new levels of personalised learning for, and commitment by, young people; and
- culture and creativity will increasingly provide our livelihoods (2006, p. 12).

Roberts also refers to the potential of the 'Building schools for the future' (BSF) project, which was effective during the 2000s but scrapped in 2010. BSF was an investment in buildings and ICT, which aimed to renew every secondary school in the UK over a 10–15 year period. While the project was never completed, its vision was a catalyst for imagining new approaches to teaching and learning and for encouraging the use of school facilities by local communities. The project aimed to provide creative experience for students, and supported both formal and informal learning that would open the school to the community and creative practitioners. In his recommendations to the government, Roberts (2006) also proposed that one-third of all high schools and half of all primary schools remain open from 8 a.m. to 6 p.m. to allow more freedom and flexibility, and to develop creativity through stronger connections and networking between specialist schools and creative practitioners. This study takes a reimagined approach to music education that similarly blurs the boundary between school and the external community and, in particular, the music industry.

For a creative industries approach to music education, I explore the idea of creating a learning community that encompasses not only students and teachers but also practitioners within the wider music industry. According to Wenger:

> Ultimately, (learning) belongs to the real world of experience and practice. It follows the negotiation of meaning; it moves on its own terms. It slips through the cracks; it creates its own crack. (1998, p. 225)

Wenger's (1998) notion speaks to the fundamental difference and dynamic relationship between formal and informal, or more experiential learning. While exploring young people's engagement with formal in-school music programmes, Temmerman (2005) argues that most secondary school students have more positive experiences with music outside the classroom; that is, in informal learning settings. Temmerman (2005) suggests that creating opportunities for students to engage with the real professional world—through live performances, festivals, and contact with professional musicians—has a positive impact on students' attitudes towards school music.

Education has a role to play in fostering collaborative learning environments where students can gain a better understanding of the industry they will inhabit in the future. The report *Restoring Our Edge in Education* (Business Council of Australia, 2007) argues the need for communication, teamwork, problem-solving, ongoing learning, creativity, cultural understanding, entrepreneurship, and leadership for collaboration in the workplace. In addition, the *Pathways to Technological Innovation* report (The Parliament of the Commonwealth of Australia, House of Representatives, Standing Committee on Science and Innovation, 2006) reveals a need to foster an entrepreneurial culture. In Queensland, the *Creative Workforce for a Smart State* Report similarly highlights that 'schools and teachers should foster the development of project management and entrepreneurship as core skills' (Oakley, 2007, p. 9).

Linking diverse communities of practice that lie beyond schools through the construction of communities of practice in music education could be one way to empower practitioners and expand school music education programmes in entrepreneurial directions (Froehlich, 2009). Expanding students' networks to include industry professionals could foster an appropriate environment in which to develop new innovative products and ideas. This initiative would also contextualise and situate learning in an industry context.

The argument for a more community-focused approach to learning, where students have opportunities to integrate with industry practitioners, presents challenges for educational institutions, teachers, and conventional models of learning. Leadbeater and Oakley (1999) argue that institutions need to be more flexible and modular in the way they engage students in learning. They suggest that rather than 'bricks and mortar and courses', educational institutions should be constructed as 'sets of relationships and flows of people' where informal, network-based practices encourage collaboration and risk-taking (p. 42). They work on the premise that cultural entrepreneurs learn on demand, learn from experience, and, quite often, learn from their peers.

In preparing for the creative industries workforce, students are most likely to find themselves self-employed, working for a small to medium enterprise, or freelancing (Ball, 2003). This prospect requires a diversity of skills. As I am a teacher who prepares students for the creative workforce, my project explores learning that prioritises students' individual expertise and prior knowledge. McWilliam and Haukka (2008) argue the importance of a shift from 'Sage on Stage' and 'Guide on the side' to 'Meddler in the middle' (p. 21). This shift would reposition the teacher and student as co-directors of learning, in an environment where the teacher becomes a risk-taker, a designer, an editor, an assembler, and a collaborative critic and authentic evaluator. While teachers might incorporate some of McWilliam's suggestions for 'Meddler in the Middle' in their pedagogy, this is not an easy undertaking when working with a demanding syllabus that prescribes strict objectives, time constraints, and assessment regime. McWilliam (2008) goes on to suggest that teachers need to work shoulder to shoulder with their students, modelling mutual engagement and learning through the mistakes of the student 'beside them' (p. 266). This suggests a shift in values away from transmission of knowledge towards pedagogical exchange as a form of value creation (McWilliam, 2008). This study explores the potential of such reconstructed teacher–student roles, where objectives and learning experiences are co-created by students, teachers, school administration, and industry practitioners.

Preparing students for careers in the creative industries—in particular, the music industry—is not simply about developing musicianship and talent. The creative industries context is more demanding, requiring workers to participate in a symbiotic relationship between creativity and enterprise. Schools and universities are not equipped to respond to the need for young people to be creative, flexible, adaptive, and innovative. Hartley (2005) acknowledges that while the modernisation of twentieth-century education through the expansion of formal institutions and regulated performance targets has strengthened the education system, it has also had negative impacts on the types of knowledge imparted and on the 'wider social desire to learn' (p. 5).

The YMI study proposes a learning design that provides meaningful opportunities for students to learn about the music industry, and to develop the necessary skills and attributes required for sustainable music careers. The design is based on authentic projects requiring collaboration with industry practitioners. I aim for a design to be a 'distributed system, dedicated to creativity, innovation and customised needs and networked across many sites from the family kitchen to the business breakfast as well as the classroom, café and workplace' (Hartley, 2005, p. 5).

Significance of the Study

Much secondary school education is still underpinned by what Robinson (2010) refers to as an industrial model, whereby schools are set up to 'manufacture' students. The school in this study offers a different kind of potential. As an arts-based school, it places great value on the arts and boasts an impressive physical environment that supports students' engagement in the arts. However, while the highly technological and creative spaces open up more opportunities for active and collaborative learning and a high-level of artistic product, aspects of the curriculum and assessment framework do not. With respect to current systems of education, Robinson writes:

> We are generating cultural and social circumstances within which the old processes of rationalism in themselves are increasingly inadequate. ... we need new structures of learning for a different type of future. ... subjects should be taught in ways that reflect their intimate connections in the world beyond education. (2001, p. 197)

Robinson (2001) makes explicit the view that creative environments give people room to experiment, to fail, to try again, to ask questions, to discover, to play, and to make connections; however, these environments are only enabled by new and innovative ways of thinking about knowledge and learning. While universities are coming to terms with the concept of creative industries and their difference from other discipline areas, this is only a very recent development at the high school level. This study is significant, therefore, because it (i) pursues a creative industries approach in the secondary school context; and (ii) because students develop entrepreneurial skills through being entrepreneurial, as opposed to learning about entrepreneurship. This experiential shift is considered the central logic in a creative industries education.

Entrepreneurship education can be too simplistically linked with profit-making activity. In contrast, Rae (2005) argues that learning is a fundamental and integral part of the entrepreneurial process in which the human, social, and behavioural activities are of as much concern as the economic aspects. In this way, entrepreneurialism is a space for creativity:

> Entrepreneurship in these sectors means to have creative ideas and to pursue them in a commercial way, with the purpose to make a profit. However, the profit alone is not the driver; it is the creativity and the possibility to build something, the self-fulfilment or being able to pursue your own creative interests. There is a mix between the entrepreneurial side and the creative side. (Hogeschool vor de Kunsten Utrecht, HKU, 2010, p. 10)

While issues of financial sustainability were important factors for the YMI students, their passion, interests, and future aspirations were equally crucial to their developing entrepreneurialism. These values and attitudes provide the momentum and energy required for a start-up venture. This project is significant in understanding how the fields of music and entrepreneurship might merge in a productive synergy.

Gibb (1996) argues that while education can provide cultural awareness, and the knowledge and skills of entrepreneurship, the 'art' of entrepreneurial practice is not practised in a heuristic educational environment; rather, it is learnt experientially in business. Entrepreneurial learning must be explored as contextualised and active, rather than as an isolated educational process. This study can inform the teaching and learning process in schools and other educational organisations, by exploring the role that schools and industry partners might play in preparing young people with the entrepreneurial skills and attributes necessary to sustain careers in the music industry and in creative industries more broadly.

Overview of the Research Design

The case under study comprises a group of nine students who were aged between 15 and 16 years at the commencement of the study. These students formed the core committee of YMI and most of them were involved in the initial stage of the enterprise. Placing the students at the nexus of the research added a layer of risk to the project. However, this was balanced by the depth and richness of the data gathered in their Facebook interactions over time.

The research was conducted by the teacher, as participant-observer (Jorgensen, 1989), extracting both the teacher and participant perspectives through observations of face-to-face meetings; workshops and Facebook meetings; and semi-structured interviews. These perspectives informed the iterative design of the interventions to develop students' entrepreneurial capacity.

A design-based research (DBR) methodology was adopted to reflect the purpose of the research and to fulfil its aims. DBR understands the 'messiness' of real-world practice, where context is a core part of the story, rather than an extraneous variable to be controlled. It involves flexible design revision and the capture of social interaction. Most importantly, and key to this study, is that participants are not research subjects; rather, they are treated as co-participants in the research design (Barab & Squire, 2004). The design methodology, according to Sandoval and Bell (2004), was developed as a method of studying innovative learning environments in classroom settings.

Overview of This Book

Chapter 3 reviews the literature relevant to the field of enquiry such as studies that have examined peer-learning environments in the conservatorium setting, the informal learning of popular musicians, and the learning that occurs in online social networks. The review also considers relevant studies related to entrepreneurial learning and work-integrated learning. Chapter 4 develops an integrated theoretical framework. It draws on theories of social learning and social capital. The theoretical framework is then explained in terms of how these theories are underpinned by a pragmatist philosophical position. Following Chapter 4's review of the literature and identification of the theoretical framework, Chapter 5 presents the research methodology and aims to tell the story of how the research, and subsequently learning design was developed. Chapters 6, 7, and 8 detail the findings of the study. Chapters 6 and 7 address the first research question, revealing the skills that students learned in relation to social interaction and project management, and the way in which these skills were acquired. Chapter 8 addresses research question 2, detailing the specific music industry knowledge that the students attained, and the way in which it was acquired. The analysis is presented in light of the theoretical framework underpinning the study.

In conclusion, Chapter 9 reviews the major findings of the project and provides recommendations for practitioners and other researchers in cognate fields. It distills the design principles that emerge from the project and their possible applications in other fields. The book concludes with future research questions that could extend this line of enquiry.

A New Approach to Education

The YMI project offers a new approach to music education—an approach that highlights the role that schools, teachers, and industry partners can play in equipping young people with the transferrable skills and knowledge needed for careers in the creative industries. The study also aims to better inform music teaching and learning processes in schools and other educational contexts.

References

Australian Bureau of Statistics. (2011). *Employment in culture Australia 2011*. Retrieved from http://www.ausstats.abs.gov.au/ausstats/subscriber. nsf/0/24CE26B099300AF2CA257ADA00132646/$File/62730_2011.pdf.

Australian Government, Attorney-General's Department, Ministry for the Arts. (2011). *Creative industries, a strategy for 21st century Australia*. Retrieved from Australian Government, Attorney-General's Department, Ministry for the Arts Website. http://arts.gov.au/creative.

Australian Government, Bureau of Communications and Arts Research. (2018). Retrieved from https://www.communications.gov.au/departmental-news/economic-value-cultural-and-creative-activity.

Australian Government, Department of Communications and the Arts. (2019). *Creative skills for the future economy*. Retrieved from https://www. communications.gov.au/departmental-news/creative-skills-future-economy.

Ball, L. (2003). *Future directions for employability research in the creative industries*. ADM (The Higher Education Academy Subject Centre for Arts, Design and Media). York: The Higher Education Academy.

Barab, S., & Squire, K. (2004). Introduction: Design-based research: Putting a stake in the ground. *The Journal of the Learning Sciences, 13*(1), 1–14. https://doi.org/10.2307/1466930.

Barrington-Leach, L., Canoy, M., Hubert, A., & Lerais, F. (2007). *Investing in youth: An empowerment strategy*. Bureau of European Policy Advisers (BEPA).

Bridgstock, R. (2013). Not a dirty word: Arts entrepreneurship and higher education. *Arts and Humanities in Higher Education, 12*(2–3), 122–137. https://doi.org/10.1177/1474022212465725.

Bridgstock, R. (2017). The university and the knowledge network: A new educational model for twenty-first century learning and employability. In *Graduate employability in context* (pp. 339–358). London: Palgrave Macmillan.

Business Council of Australia. (2007). *Restoring our edge in education—Making Australia's education system its next competitive advantage*. Retrieved from http://www.bca.com.au/publications/2007-reports-and-papers.

Creative Industries Innovation Centre. (2013). *Valuing Australia's creative industries final report December 2013*. Retrieved from https://www.sgsep. com.au/assets/Valuing-Australias-Creative-Industries-Final-Report.pdf.

Department for Culture, Media and Sport. (2016). *The creative industries economics estimates report*. Retrieved from https://assets.publishing. service.gov.uk/government/uploads/system/uploads/attachment_data/

file/523024/Creative_Industries_Economic_Estimates_January_2016_Updated_201605.pdf.

Freire, P. (1968). *Pedagogy of the oppressed*. New York: Continuum.

Froehlich, H. (2009). Music education and community: Reflections on "Webs of Interaction" in school music. *Action, Criticism, and Theory for Music Education, 8*(1), 85–107.

Gibb, A. A. (1996). Entrepreneurship and small business management: Can we afford to neglect them in the twenty-first century business school? *British Journal of Management, 7*(4), 309–322. https://doi.org/10.1111/j.1467-8551.1996.tb00121.x.

Hartley, J. (2005). *Creative industries*. Malden, MA: Blackwell.

Haynie, J. M., Shepherd, D., Mosakowski, E., & Earley, P. C. (2010). A situated metacognitive model of the entrepreneurial mindset. *Journal of Business Venturing, 25*(2), 217–229. https://doi.org/10.1016/j.jbusvent.2008.10.001.

Hogeschool vor de Kunsten Utrecht, HKU. (2010). *The entrepreneurial dimension of the cultural and creative industries*. Utrecht School of the Arts, Netherlands. Retrieved from http://www.creativwirtschaft.at/document/11_StudyontheEntrepreneurialDimensionoftheCulturalandCreativeIndustries.pdf.

Jorgensen, D. L. (1989). *Participant observation: A methodology for human studies* (Vol. 15). Newbury Park, CA: Sage.

Kriewall, T. J., & Mekemson, K. (2010). Instilling the entrepreneurial mindset into engineering undergraduates. *The Journal of Engineering Entrepreneurship, 1*(1), 5–19.

Leadbeater, C., & Oakley, K. (1999). *The independents: Britain's new cultural entrepreneurs*. London: Demos.

McWilliam, E. (2008). *The creative workforce: How to launch young people into high-flying futures*. Sydney: University of NSW Press.

McWilliam, E., & Haukka, S. (2008). Educating the creative workforce: New directions for twenty-first century schooling. *British Educational Research Journal, 34*(5), 651–666. https://doi.org/10.1080/01411920802224204.

Newbigin, J. (2010). *The creative economy: An introductory guide*. London: The British Council.

Oakley, K. (2007). *Educating for the creative workforce: Rethinking arts and education*. Australia Council for the Arts. Retrieved from http://bit.ly/1xLDDB1.

QUT Digital Media Research Centre. (2016). *The creative economy in Australia*. Retrieved from https://research.qut.edu.au/dmrc/wp-content/uploads/sites/5/2018/03/Factsheet-1-Creative-Employment-overview-V5.pdf.

Rae, D. (2005). Entrepreneurial learning: A narrative-based conceptual model. *Journal of Small Business and Enterprise Development, 12*(3), 323–335. https://doi.org/10.1108/14626000510612259.

Roberts, P. (2006). *Nurturing creativity in young people: A report to government to inform future policy*. Media and Sport: Department for Culture.

Robinson, K. (2001). Balancing the books. In J. Hartley (Ed.), *Creative industries*. Malden, MA: Blackwell.

Robinson, K. (2010). *Changing education paradigms*. RSA Animate, The Royal Society of Arts, London. Retrieved from http://www.youtube.com/watch.

Sandoval, W. A., & Bell, P. (2004). Design-based research methods for studying learning in context: Introduction. *Educational Psychologist, 39*(4), 199–201. https://doi.org/10.1207/s15326985ep3904_1.

Siemens, G. (2005). Connectivism: A learning theory for the digital age. *International Journal of Instructional Technology and Distance Learning, 2*(1), 3–10.

Temmerman, N. (2005). Children's participation in music: Connecting the cultural contexts—An Australian perspective. *British Journal of Music Education, 22*(2), 113.

The Parliament of the Commonwealth of Australia, House of Representatives, Standing Committee on Science and Innovation. (2006). *Pathways to technological innovation report*. Retrieved from the Parliament of Australia Website. https://www.aph.gov.au/Parliamentary_Business/Committees/House_of_Representatives_Committees?url=scin/pathways/report.htm.

Wenger, E. (1998). *Communities of practice: Learning, meaning, and identity*. Cambridge, UK: Cambridge University Press.

Wenger, E., MacDermott, R. A., & Snyder, W. M. (2002). *Cultivating communities of practice: A guide to managing knowledge*. Boston: Harvard Business School Press.

3

Current Approaches to Education—But What About the Music Industry?

Teaching and Learning in the Twenty-First Century

Education needs to respond not only to societal changes—in particular, to the emergent conditions of creative and knowledge economies (Florida, 2000; Leadbeater, 2000a)—but also to the changing needs of today's learners. There are a number of research studies that are relevant to the development of the YMI design. The YMI design is an innovative approach to engaging young music students in learning environments to facilitate the development of skills and attributes. These facilities enable them to more effectively negotiate entrepreneurial careers within the creative industries. This chapter expands on the critique of the traditional music education system from the previous chapter and examines the new approaches to teaching and learning for the music industry. I review various contributions that advocate a new direction in twenty-first century education. These contributions include research into informal learning, network learning, online learning and school–corporate/community partnerships in education.

© The Author(s) 2020
K. Kelman, *Entrepreneurial Music Education*,
https://doi.org/10.1007/978-3-030-37129-6_3

Setting the Scene

Despite nineteen years of discourse surrounding the rise of the digital economy and education (Baskakova & Soboleva, 2019; Leadbeater, 2000a; Oakley, 2007; Williamson, 2013) the arguments for new educational directions remain unchanged. The only recent exception to this is New Zealand's removal of national standardised testing (Buchanan, 2018). Leadbeater (2000a) asserts that 'the real assets of the modern economy come out of our heads, not out of the ground: imagination, knowledge, skills, talent and creativity' (p. 18). This sentiment is echoed by Harris and Temmermann (2016) who argues that 'creative skills and capacities are emerging as a central focus of twenty-first century education economies' (p. 103). According to the literature in both business and economic policy, the demand for creativity continues to increase in the workplace, which needs workers who are able to think creatively and imaginatively, and to generate ideas (Suarta, Suwintana, Sudhana, & Hariyanti, 2017). Since 1999, Blackwell and Harvey report that employers in the modern world are eager for new ideas, and are thus seeking risk-takers, lateral thinkers, and creative problem-solvers. Creativity is necessary for adapting and responding to the environment, which is constantly changing due to the rapid flow of information (D'Andrea, 2012). Indeed, as far back as 2000 Bauman argued that the modern world as 'liquid' where 'change is the only permanence and uncertainty the only certainty' (p. viii).

These uncertainties challenge educators today and have created a weakened relationship between formal education and the workforce. While formal education providers are concerned with knowledge acquisition, employers are disgruntled at the lack of skills in graduates (Stewart, 2016). While schools still operate on overly prescriptive curriculum mandates, employers want people who can suggest solutions without requiring a full set of information upon which to base their decisions. Furthermore, the knowledge required today is likely to be irrelevant tomorrow, and this places heavy responsibility on educators to rethink and reconsider their approach to learning and knowledge, as well as their approach to teaching.

Finally, new economies are demanding different work patterns, and entry-level jobs that presume a linear career path are no longer guaranteed for the twenty-first-century graduate. Graduates today are more likely to engage with a diversity of work situations, including freelance and small enterprises (Bridgstock, 2013).

Re-thinking Teaching and Learning

Formal education is still typically designed around classrooms and campuses, where a central instructor or teacher is 'powering' the learning experience (Siemens, 2008, p. 14). However, given the development of communication technologies and the ability to digitise resources, students are now more capable of being autonomous and self-directed learners. Despite the opportunities that this development provides, schools and universities are still perpetuating the model of instruction where knowledge is passed down hierarchically. McWilliam's (2005) conceptual critique of teaching and learning habits explains that we perpetuate this tradition by re-enacting patterns, such as the habitual preparation and review of curriculum to ensure wide coverage, and the compromising of assessment practices to ensure transparency. She also points out that these pedagogical habits are suitable for a world that is linear, predictable and stable. However, given the social reality of the modern digital world, these habits could be impediments to success. McWilliam (2005) identifies the 'seven deadly habits of pedagogical thinking' (p. 5) as:

1. The more learning the better
2. Teachers should know more than students
3. Teachers lead, students follow
4. Teachers assess, students are assessed
5. Curriculum must be set in advance
6. The more we know our students, the better
7. Our disciplines can save the world.

McWilliam's critique of these habits is relevant because she offers useful points to consider when designing new learning environments that might better prepare young people for the modern economies.

Habit 1—The More Learning the Better

In response to Bauman's 'liquid' study, McWilliam (2005) argues that 'forgetting or de-learning becomes as important as learning' (p. 7). In didactic education, emphasis is still placed on memory and the ability to recall facts. For example, the curriculum that operates in the school resonates with neo-conservative values through its design of 'canonical knowledge, disciplinary study, traditional pedagogies, high stakes external exams and prescriptive curriculum and pedagogy' (Doherty, Luke, Shield, & Hincksman, 2012, p. 11). McWilliam argues that, given that knowledge, technology and information is changing so rapidly, it might be just as useful to be able to forget in order to learn what is useful in a given set of circumstances.

Habit 2—Teachers Should Know More Than Students

Public policy thinker, Charles Leadbeater (2000b) weighs up the pedagogic value of knowledge and ignorance to challenge the presumption that teachers should know more. While both students and teachers believe that there is still an expectation that the teacher should be a step ahead of their students, Leadbeater explains that there is value in pedagogy when the teacher is 'usefully ignorant' (p. 4). Being usefully ignorant according to Claxton (2004) is about knowing what to do when you do not know what to do. He argues that the ability to take risks is becoming more valuable in a rapidly changing world where knowledge is not fixed and there are fewer templates or roadmaps. This position encourages teachers to take a risk in designing learning environments where they too can be usefully ignorant. This, in turn, has great potential for teachers and students to co-construct new pedagogical experiences better suited to new contexts.

Habit 3—Teachers Lead, Students Follow

Conventional learning environments uphold the notion that teachers should know more than their students (McWilliam, 2005). As introduced in Chapter 2, McWilliam (2008) argues that the challenge for teachers is to spend less time being 'sage on the stage' and/or 'guide on the side' and begin to take on the role of 'meddler in the middle' (p. 21). This premise is similar to Hearn's (2005) 'value ecology thinking', which highlights the shift from a generation of passive consumers, to a new generation of 'prod-users' who value-add to the product they consume (p. 1). McWilliam (2005) suggests how students can be 'prod-users' of disciplinary and interdisciplinary knowledge, as opposed to consumers of teacher knowledge.

This critique of didactic education is not new. In *Education and Experience* (1938), Dewey advocated a similar form of progressive education. Dewey argued that learning should be designed out of experience and within the capacity of students, and that the experience should 'arouse in the learner an active quest for information and for production of new ideas' (p. 79). These new ideas, in turn, become the grounds for further experiences, and create new possibilities for learning. Dewey referred to this iterative process as the 'experience continuum' (p. 79), whereby the students actively participate and set the social conventions for learning, as opposed to the teacher enforcing control.

Habit 4—Teachers Assess, Students Are Assessed

In an ideal setting, where students and teachers have co-created the learning, McWilliam (2005) questions the ethics of assessing co-edited work. She also argues that while assessment in schools and higher education is highly individualistic, students are then expected to work effectively in workplace teams. Peer-learning and peer-assessment offer one response to this issue; however, McWilliam reports that many students are reluctant to embrace this approach given their negative experience of working in groups, and their need for quality assurance and legitimation from an objective, more experienced other.

Habit 5—Curriculum Must Be Set in Advance

When pedagogy is conceived as co-creation of value, then curriculum cannot be planned or prescribed in advance. McWilliam (2005) notes that this co-creation of pedagogical value goes against the very nature of a national curriculum, as instituted in both the UK and Australia. She argues that the nature of curriculum planning must change, from 'fixed and immutable' to 'content for meddling with' (p. 14). Designing a learning environment that appropriately aligns with the uncertainties of the modern world does not validate a lack of preparedness; it does validate, however, a process of emergence that accommodates a culture of experimentation where the curricular outcomes are not necessarily known or guaranteed.

Habit 6—The More We Know Our Students, the Better

McWilliam (2005) reports the experience of asking her masters and doctoral students what they thought was the purpose of education. 'Raising self-esteem' and 'helping one reach their full potential' were typical responses, indicating the importance of educating the whole person. McWilliam suggests that pedagogy and personal therapy are conflated to the detriment of students. It creates an attenuated environment where the goal is for risk-taking and unlearning, while at the same time protecting students from damaging personal experiences. In response, McWilliam questions just how much we should know about our students in order to teach them. She recommends that we revert to a culture that 'respects students enough to challenge them by messing things up with and for them' (p. 18).

Habit 7—Our Disciplines Can Save the World

McWilliam (2005) offers a critique of the overly neat knowledge categories contained within disciplinary boundaries. She argues that in a more experimental, co-created learning environment, learners will be reminded that there are things that they don't know and need to find out. This might entail the need to know something beyond one's main discipline. McWilliam (2005) contrasts disciplinary structures with the 'cut and paste' strategy of the creative assembler (p. 19). The latter strategy has implications for depth of disciplinary knowledge; however, as discussed above, knowledge is constantly changing, and learning will need to be negotiated on a 'need to know' basis. Sometimes, indeed, it might be necessary to forget or unlearn something altogether.

So far, I have argued for a new model of teaching and learning that is better suited to the knowledge conditions of the twenty-first century. I presented arguments for designing a learning environment that can break the inherited habits of formal education, in favour of a more experiential learning culture. In doing so, I suggest that teachers should be prepared to co-create learning with their students, and facilitate opportunities for not knowing and for making mistakes. As a body of scholarship, the literature does not offer any empirical evidence to support how the designs it advocates might play out, for better or for worse. The thinking also fails to acknowledge that educational institutions are averse to radical change. This book, on the other hand, not only engages with the ideas and designs advocated in this literature, it also tests them in an iterative and authentic context.

Investigating New Approaches to Teaching and Learning

This section reviews literature that offers fresh approaches to teaching and learning, in particular, network learning, online social networking, learning communities and partnerships, and learning in authentic contexts. The common thread emerging across these approaches is learning in collaboration with others.

Network Learning

Networks have altered or 'flattened' much of society, enabling access to content, experts, and global connections with fellow learners. Friedman's (2005) conceptual analysis, *The World Is Flat*, has become a popular and accessible metaphor for how globalisation has created a level playing field. He interviewed many employers and educators and asked them to describe the kind of education young people will need to prepare for jobs in the new global economy. He reports: 'What they shared with me were not specific courses you should take, but rather certain skill sets and attitudes that will be important' (p. 302). He lists five skill sets that were deemed important for succeeding in the 'flat' world of networks:

Ability to Learn How to Learn

Friedman (2005) describes the 'ability to learn how to learn' as the ability to absorb and teach oneself new ways of doing old things, or new ways of doing new things.

Possession of Passion and Curiosity

In a flat world, where information is everywhere, simply having knowledge is not enough. Success will be governed by the passion and curiosity that a person brings to a new job, subject area, or hobby. He explains this as an equation: 'CQ(curiosity quotient) + PQ(passion quotient)>IQ(intelligence quotient)' (p. 304).

Plays Well with Others

Friedman (2005) found that while having good people skills has always been an asset, it is even more so in the flat world where jobs require personalised interactions that can never be automated or outsourced.

Exercises the Right-Brain Stuff

Friedman (2005) concludes: 'The abilities that matter most are now closer in the spirit to the specialities of the brain's right hemisphere – artistry, empathy, seeing the big picture and pursuing the transcendent' (p. 307).

While Friedman's popular (2005) text presents a neo-liberal economically driven narrative, the five skills that he highlights were of particular interest to me in considering a collaborative approach to learning.

If knowledge resides in networks, learning how to form and navigate these networks play a crucial role in the design of a new learning environment that can better prepare students for the flat world of the modern economies. Working from the premise that knowledge exists in networks, Siemens (2008) observes that learners now have greater access to information, experts, and peer learners. Dede (2005) refers to these learners as 'millennial learners' and explains that due to their digital lifestyles, they expect education environments to be participative, engaging, and active.

To design a new learning environment, it is important to have a greater understanding of the skills required for working in the 'flat world' which is premised on network navigation and inter-connectivity. The new flat world environment is largely attributed to the expansion of digital technologies and advancements in communication. The concept of the network is central to the YMI project, ensuring that students can use and acquire the skills necessary for participation. As a result, the learning will evolve through opportunities and resources accessed through networks.

Online Learning and Social Media Technologies

For the learning design developed in this current study, I was interested in online social networking to develop young people's competence in peer culture communities both inside and outside school hours. Ito et al. (2013), in their proposal for a 'connected learning' approach (p. 5), point out that participants in online communities have the ability to learn, create good work and exercise leadership, thus increasing the capacity and value for others in their community and beyond. With classrooms based on standardised metrics and individual competitiveness, Ito et al. (2013) argue that:

> The classroom experience does not elevate culture at large or expand a valuable social network if the activity ends at the classroom walls. Further, when individual competence is assessed based on grades, test scores, and other standardised and summative metrics, one student's success highlights another student's failure. (p. 48)

Given the contrast in learning environments, how can formal education harness the empowerment experienced in online communities? Connecting classrooms with interest-driven communities by creating links to academic relevance would be one way of achieving this. Further extending the social networks to include industry practitioners might be another way to support and enhance further student learning. This would also create an opportunity to open up new interests and to connect with career and work goals.

Regan and Steeve's (2010) study of young internet users argues that surveillance is an important aspect of social network learning as it allows for feedback and reflection and, if enabled with the appropriate conditions, surveillance can empower rather than control. In turn, it offers enormous possibilities for reflection, which is a key principle of entrepreneurial learning. Social media networks allow participants to record and watch their lives unfold over time, a practice often referred to as 'life-logging' (Moenk, 2007).

Regan and Steeve's idea of surveillance has also been discussed in terms of transparency. In a study of cooperative online learning in a distance education program, Dalsgaard and Paulsen (2009) emphasise the importance of online network transparency. In this regard, they argue that members and their activities are visible to fellow students and teachers within a learning environment; this, in turn, makes participants available to each other as resources for their learning activities. They suggest that transparency has three positive effects on quality:

- *Preventive quality improvement*: We are prone to provide better quality when we know that others have access to the information and contributions we provide.
- *Constructive quality improvement*: We might learn from others when we have access to their data and contributions.
- *Reactive quality improvement*: We might receive feedback from others when they have access to our data and contributions.

Transparency might reduce the number of low-quality contributions and make high quality work more accessible, thus enhancing the experience for all involved and perpetuating the learning community.

For the learning design developed in the YMI project, social network platforms provided students with greater ownership of their learning. The transparency inherent in online networks can also enable members to learn from each other, thus creating greater accountability and momentum for learning. Ito et al. (2013) suggest that the openness, accessibility and open standards experienced in online communities can inform a more open-door policy in physical learning spaces, encouraging them to extend beyond the physical boundaries of the school and to allow greater access to resources and wider connection to other institutions and communities.

Browne (2003) reported on a case study carried out in a UK university that offered an online masters' degree. Groups communicated using conferencing and e-mail systems, and were able to share files via online communication. Browne investigated how learning manifested when individuals communicated and tested ideas with one another. With regard to interactivity, Browne (2003) reported positive outcomes for the first year of the online masters' degree, in that a learning community had been successfully established. This was evidenced through the interactions of staff and students who supported each other in both academic and personal terms.

The sharing through online communication established a culture of openness and accessibility to new ideas. However, Discussion was not always harmonious, and one community member had commented that she had become effective in the art of people management. To resolve any potential issues, the community established a code of conduct before the start of each new cohort. This type of code is referred to by Mann and Stewart (2000) as 'netiquette' (p. 14).

With regard to reflectivity, the asynchronous facilities that feature in online networks were considered advantageous because they provide the opportunity for reflection and analysis. Students who felt more hesitant about committing their thoughts in public found it easier to respond in their own time. Staff also found the quality of student responses to be much higher, given the additional time for consideration and depth. As a support network, students were able to offer suggestions for solutions to problems.

The design developed in the YMI project differs from Browne's design in a number of ways. As the teacher, for example, I did not interact or instruct in the online space; rather, I left students to develop their own processes of 'netiquette' and communication. Creating a learning environment for the flat world required me to develop self-directed learners who could solve highly complex problems within their own network. Browne's (2003) study, while requiring students to be motivated, independent learners, still utilised aspects of a top-down or hierarchical approach. The YMI project utilised a flat, lateral network approach in order to nurture student autonomy and ownership of learning. Browne's programme was also achieved entirely online, with no face-to-face interaction. On the other hand, I am concerned with a broader learning ecology of online learning driven by peer culture, with academic and career relevance supported by schools and other institutions.

Lastly, Browne's report does not offer empirical evidence of explicit knowledge gained by the students. It is important for the YMI project to report not only on how students learned, but also on what they learned.

Learning Communities and Partnerships

Tinto (2000) argues that for some students, learning is very much a 'spectator sport' (p. 1), especially in higher education. This has led researchers to reconceptualise educational infrastructure, practices and curricular designs to more actively involve students in learning. Educational institutions are moving to facilitate stronger connections between schooling and the world of work (Radinsky, Bouillion, Lento, & Gomez, 2001). This has included the establishment of programs such as tech-prep, school-to-work (Kazis, 1993), a wide variety of corporate–school partnerships (Gurn, 2016), and work-integrated learning (WIL) programs in higher education (Jackson, 2015).

In the following section, I move from online learning communities to face-to-face learning communities to develop the concept of a 'learning community'. This is followed by a discussion of three studies related to learning communities: Tinto's (2000) study of three American colleges that employ cross-subject learning communities; Freudenberg, Brimble and Vyvyan's (2010) study of a WIL initiative; and Kisiel's (2010) study of a school–aquarium partnership.

Common to these three studies is the collaborative pedagogy that underpins them. Learning communities are operationalised through collaboration, cooperation and/or partnerships. Community members work together based on shared goals and interests, with the potential for generating new knowledge (Radinsky et al., 2001). Knowledge construction can be a shared and collaborative community outcome. The following three studies provide further insight into the design of learning community environments and consider the positive and negative aspects of such learning. It is also important to note that much of the research in this area has emerged from research in higher education contexts rather than in school settings.

The Impact of Community

Tinto (2000) explores the impacts of learning community programs on academic and social behaviours and on the retention of new students at three universities in the USA. The learning community programs were based on linked classrooms. That is, the students were grouped across different disciplines, but connected by an organising theme that gave meaning to their linkage. Small groups of 20–30 students were linked throughout the year and met several times a week, while still participating in lectures of 200–300 people. Comparative survey and qualitative research methods were employed in Tinto's (2000) research. Questionnaires, interviews and observations of student interactions were used to understand the impact of the design across the three colleges. While limited in scope, Tinto explains that, as a starting point, this research did yield some important insights into the impacts of communities on student learning and retention.

This brief article was framed within the stance that students learn through social interaction. Drawing similar conclusions to Browne's (2003) virtual-ethnographic study, it shows how the students formed their own self-support groups, which were crucial to their perseverance. Tinto found that students became more actively involved in classroom learning than students in the traditional curriculum. Furthermore, they were engaging after class, thus learning and making friends at the same time. They revealed that the more time they spent together, the more they learned, and that by learning together their knowledge and understandings were richer.

Teaching staff also reported that there was an improvement in the quality of student learning. In addition to these outcomes, the students asserted a greater sense of responsibility for both their own learning and the learning of others. Tinto's study also evidenced greater student retention, with a 25% increase in retention rate compared to previous cohorts in the conventional curriculum.

Work-Integrated Learning Improving Student Learning

Research studies within the UK, USA, and Australia reveal that WIL programs influence student satisfaction with their study in higher education, and successfully lead to employment outcomes (Hansen & Hoag, 2018; Harvey, Moon, Geall, & Bower, 1997). Freudenberg et al. (2010) argue that education should involve the integration of theory and practice, but that this is not always successfully done. They explain that the danger of keeping theory and practice separate can lead to the problem of 'inert knowledge' (p. 45), which makes it difficult for students to transfer their knowledge from the educational setting to the workplace. Freudenberg et al. (2010) believe that the key benefit of WIL programs is that they can assist in the transferability of skills and knowledge from the university to the workplace. This study followed students who planned and executed a conference with industry partners.

Students responded to their work in the study by stating that the stakes in this context were higher, thus providing motivation to work harder. They appreciated the authenticity of their assessment, the ability to network with the industry, and the potential to be noticed for future employment. However, some students found the pressure of preparing for an industry conference added stress to the assessment task.

Nevertheless, evidence from the one-off event showed that the authentic experience facilitated student learning and motivation.

Initiatives that involve collaboration with industry form a significant aspect of the YMI project. While the outcomes in Freudenberg et al.'s (2010) study resulted in students being motivated to work harder and receive industry feedback, the literature suggests that there is even greater potential in the networking capacity of such an initiative. For the YMI project, I aimed to create opportunities for students to develop ongoing meaningful relationships with industry partners, and to collaborate on authentic projects. Unlike the students in Freudenberg et al.'s (2010) conference initiative, YMI students learned through collaboration with professionals, and then applied new knowledge to design their own events. A learning community designed in this way has potential benefits for everyone involved—industry, teachers, students, and the wider youth community.

A School–Aquarium Collaboration

In 2010, Kisiel reported on the outcomes of a school-aquarium partnership. The aims of this collaborative project were to use aquarium resources to enhance science education at a neighbouring elementary school. Both aquarium instructors and teachers at the school reported that while the new partnership did take time away from the development or maintenance of other programs, it also provided another outlet for new and more creative educational approaches. The friction between institutional practices and innovative practice is a reality that is often overlooked in the imagined pedagogies advocated by Leadbeater and McWilliam. The potential for new and creative ideas provided the impetus for all parties involved to commit time and effort to the partnership.

Although understated in this particular study, this collaboration provided outcomes for the students. Teachers explained how it provided students with new opportunities and enthusiasm for learning science, by being exposed to authentic experiences and industry professionals. The 'hands on' nature of the learning experience provided a layer of understanding that students would not have received in a classroom. It also gave some students a new passion and interest in science, evidenced through their regular visits to the aquarium outside of school time.

Kisiel (2010) argues that when embarking on school–industry collaborations, it is necessary to identify commonalities and constraints early, so that collaborative strategies can be identified and negotiated. While this current study does not examine the impacts of such collaboration on partners and teachers, it does share an interest in the challenges that arise in bringing two very distinct communities together. One aspect of this research, therefore, is its investigation of the learning that occurs when students collaborate with industry.

To conclude this review of previous literature, and to contextualise the project, I will briefly discuss Radinsky et al. (2001) study of authentic learning, and Mitra's (2005) study of minimally guided learning.

Authentic and Minimally-Guided Learning

The previous section reviewed studies of the affordance of social media, and the application of learning communities and industry partnerships to students' learning. Central to this group of studies is the horizontal 'flat-world' network approach, where learners encounter a range of knowledge and opportunities for learning. The concept of authenticity is a feature of the designs that have been described. Here, I use the term 'authenticity' to describe learning experiences that have 'real-world' relevance. Radinsky et al. (2001) describe two types of authenticity, 'simulation' and 'participation':

> Simulation refers to the designing of materials, tools, assignments and interactions that map to the activity of a professional community. Simulated authenticity uses an instructional approach, where a particular domain is represented in the classroom, where the students are "enculturated into the ways of knowing of the target domain". (p. 406)

The three previous studies; the conference reported on by Freudenberg et al. (2010), the cross-subject learning community study reported on by Tinto (2000) and Kisiel's (2010) study of a school–community partnership, are all simulated approaches. In contrast, a participation approach to authenticity occurs by creating opportunities for students to engage in the actual ongoing work of a professional community. A participation approach maximises opportunities for incidental learning in the educational environment. This incidental or vicarious learning cannot be captured in simulated contexts in the conventional classroom. This stance on learning resonates with McWilliam's (2005) suggestions for 'unlearning pedagogy', in particular, the fixed curriculum approach.

Reeves, Herrington, and Oliver (2002, p. 564) reflect on the authentic activities described by various researchers and provide the following ten characteristics of authentic learning environments.

- Authentic activities have real-world relevance.
- Authentic activities are ill-defined, requiring students to define the tasks and sub-tasks needed to complete the activity.
- Authentic activities comprise complex tasks to be investigated by students over a sustained period.
- Authentic activities provide the opportunity for students to examine the task from different perspectives, using a variety of resources.
- Authentic activities provide the opportunity to collaborate.
- Authentic activities provide the opportunity to reflect.
- Authentic activities can be integrated and applied across different subject areas and lead beyond domain-specific outcomes.
- Authentic activities are seamlessly integrated with assessment.
- Authentic activities create polished products valuable in their own right rather than as preparation for something else.
- Authentic activities allow competing solutions and diversity of outcome.

There will always be tension when considering whether instructor versus learner control is best suited to particular learning activities. For example, some researchers believe that minimal guidance is not as effective as guided instruction, claiming that students 'labour under misconceptions' (Siemens, 2008, p. 12). However, Mitra (2005), known for his 'hole-in- the-wall' experiment, found that children aged 6–12 years, with minimal education and limited English, were able to browse the Internet and perform tasks within days of their first encounter with a computer. He concludes that children do not require direct instruction to acquire basic computer literacy skills. While I am similarly interested in the notion of minimal guidance for my learning design, and take the idea of trusting the learner from Mitra's work, I am more interested in establishing a very clear set of objectives aimed at developing a particular body of industry knowledge in students.

Final Thoughts on Teaching and Learning in the Twenty-First Century

Part one of this chapter reviewed the literature that grapples with the contextual demands and affordances of modern economies and their possible implications for teaching and learning. The sources reviewed argue for a new kind of learning environment founded on a network approach to learning. This kind of learning both exploits and responds to the essence of Friedman's 'flat world' to better prepare students for their future in ever-changing and more uncertain 'liquid' social settings. Within a networked, learning community approach to learning, there is no hierarchical transmission of knowledge or fixed curriculum; rather, knowledge is accessed, remixed and created within the network. The learning community recognises that teachers, students, and stakeholders are all network actors on an increasingly level playing field and, as such, bring their own knowledge and expertise to the community.

This networked approach informed the development of the YMI project which is concerned with engineering authentic learning contexts and experiences; specifically, students were responsible for running their own music industry organisation. They collaborated with a range of people, set their own tasks, and identified their own gaps in knowledge. This design for 'in-demand' knowledge is highly appropriate to a world where knowledge and skills that are relevant today might no longer be relevant tomorrow. This section also considered studies of the benefits of virtual learning communities. The transparency of online learning enables students to be accountable to the community and produce high quality work, as well as enabling them to establish a culture of trust and reciprocity.

While the researchers represented so far, offer innovative, imagined learning environments suited to twenty-first-century learners, their models and approaches are attenuated by the current and binding conditions of formal education. Given the competition in the current job market, neo-liberal marketisation strategies are giving parents more choices in selecting a school that will give their child the best chance. This sits in strange combination with neo-conservative values where formal education is deemed more important than ever before (Apple, 2004), with a return to highly rigorous, disciplined approaches to curriculum and pedagogy.

Empirical studies related to new teaching and learning approaches offer some useful findings for an innovative creative industries learning environment. These empirical studies have relied on either large sets of self-assessed surveys or interview data, rather than on evidence of what and how students have learned in these environments. The lack of empirical research highlights how small-scale, deeply descriptive accounts of student learning, such as the YMI project, could inform an important way forward for education.

Teaching and Learning for the Music Industry

The second section of this chapter describes how the music industry has undergone a major shift since the late 1990s. Technological disruption has changed the nature of the industry, creating more opportunities for musicians to make and sell their music. This has affected the role of the musician, who now assumes a diverse range of responsibilities other than performing. Researchers in this area argue that survival in this industry requires musicians to be multi-skilled. As a result, educational institutions need to rethink practices in music teaching and learning. This section investigates various models and approaches proposed by music educators to develop this wider suite of skills for musicians.

In the late 1990s, the music industry was transformed by the emergence of technological innovations such as the MP3 and peer-to-peer networks, which 'induced the digitalisation of the record industry' (Moyon & LeCocq, 2013, p. 2). Moyon and LeCocq (2013) explains that by the late 1990s, the music industry had become a very profitable business, with annual global sales over $40 billion. The main record labels (BMG, EMI, Sony, Universal and Warner) were vertically integrated, that is, from artist detection to record distribution. This business model involved the record company being responsible for discovering the talent, producing and marketing the artist, and manufacturing and packaging the tapes, records and, eventually, CDs. Moyon and LeCocq (2013) point out that under this model, artists were the record industry's fundamental resources. The industry was also a copyright industry and, as such, was able to create value and make profits.

The emergence of the digital era posed enormous challenges for the prevailing music industry model. Despite these 'disruptive' innovations, new opportunities appeared to develop alternative distribution channels and to sell music differently (Moyon & LeCocq, 2013, p. 2). New business models have also changed the role of consumers, who now play an important role in the music that is produced.

In Australia, the music industry has been described as being two-tiered (Benner & Waldfogel, 2016; Ninan, Hearn, & Oakley, 2004). The first tier represents the major record label business model which administers commercially successful artists who attract significant sales. The second tier involves predominantly independent music activity. This grassroots industry largely consists of independent musicians, sound engineers, and producers, and creates value through networking and creative entrepreneurialism. The second tier does not follow the linear supply chain model of the first tier, but is more in line with Hearn's (2005) 'value-ecology thinking' discussed earlier in the chapter.

Second-tier musicians are able to sell their work independently of the major labels, and opportunities for financial gain have opened up due to 'Do it Yourself (DIY) technology' (Cox, Ninan, Hearn, Roodhouse, & Cunningham, 2004, p. 4). This technology makes it easier for new, emerging artists and bands to record their own albums in low-cost home studios (Goold, 2018; Homer, 2009; Pras et al., 2013). They now also do their own band management and preparation for live shows, including marketing and promotion. Rogers, Ninan, Hearn, Cunningham, and Luckman (2004) explain that, in Queensland, the onus for marketing products and achieving visibility on the local, national and international music scene lies increasingly with the artist or band themselves.

Ninan et al. (2004) conclude that if artists and bands do not get assistance, they look to alternative careers. Many of the participants in Ninan et al.'s study reported looking to formal education to address the absence of the 'right kind of knowledge and skills', but also asserted that 'formal training is good, but it has to go hand in hand with personal training' (p. 33). In their opinion, this training should occur in the formative years, even before they arrive at university or technical colleges. This merging of formal knowledge/technique and 'street smart' know-how is a major challenge for the creative sectors. One studio owner in Ninan et al.'s study confirmed, 'training including practical and street skills into curricula and working on sowing the seeds way ahead of the university level of education is where it all begins ... the curriculum has to change' (p. 34).

Rogers et al. (2004) explored how second-tier practices, such as the reliance on social media and DIY culture, offer alternative methods for 'doing music' and generating value in the creative industries (p. 1). They conducted a mixed-method, rigorous study of the Queensland music industry, through the administration of 357 questionnaire surveys across a wide range of music industry representatives, and the conduct of twenty qualitative in-depth interviews. From their analysis, they conclude that educational organisations need to place greater emphasis on tacit experience, and that Queensland musicians require a better understanding of 'business-industry-audience relationships' (p. 20). While there has been no in-depth study since these 2004 publications, they still provide a detailed context within which to challenge the current education paradigm. It was out of the scope of this report to consider how these practices rub against formal education.

The music business is volatile due to 'constantly changing technologies, legal frameworks, social behaviours, economic conditions and the transient tastes of the listening public' (Bruenger, 2015, p. 101) and it is difficult to speculate what is going to happen next. In this sense, the main concern for music industry education is its ability to stay current. To better understand how industry education can adapt to the evolving industry, Chase and Hatschek (2010) held a meeting with industry executives to ask the question 'what skills and competencies should a newly hired employee possess in order to succeed in today's music business?' Responses included, looking for potential employees that had emotional, social, intellectual, and musical competence. Other industry representatives deemed the ability to interpret the nuances of the industry as vital for success, along with personalities that can collaborate with artists at a mature and productive level. Chase and Hatschek then questioned traditional education methods in much of American higher education, suggesting that the lecture-essay-examination model, would not equip students with the knowledge, skills and experiences required for a successful music industry career. Bruenger (2015) advocates for a curriculum that reflects the evolving complexity of the music industry, and argues for the development of adaptive capacity in students.

Rethinking Education for Musicians

While the studies reviewed above specifically consider the contemporary music industry, the issues raised should be regarded as applicable to musicians across all styles of music, whether classical or contemporary. In this regard, Forrest (2001) offers a broader definition of the music industry:

> The music industry included those aspects of work concerned with the performance and presentation of live and recorded music in the market place. The market place could include a concert hall, a pub, a recording (or garage) studio. The music industry also includes administration, management, marketing and entrepreneurship within the broad music and performing arts field. (p. 82)

All musicians are vying for a place in the professional world; however, scholars in this field argue that the skills and knowledge required for success are now much broader. Creech et al. (2008) conducted in-depth interviews with 27 classical musicians who were in the early stages of their professional careers in the United Kingdom. They found that the competitive nature of the industry presented several challenges for newcomers to the music profession. These included finding time for professional development and self-promotion and dealing with self-doubt, fear, frustration and financial constraints. Similarly, Bennett (2007) in her detailed study of musicians, artists, arts workers and educators from across Australia, Europe, and the USA between 2005 and 2007 found that most musicians wanted business skills and opportunities to learn about the profession in their formal training years. The participants in her study consider that sustaining a practice is like sustaining a small business, and reported that most musicians work across different capacities within the profession, such as teaching, composing, performing, and directing. Thus, Bennett concludes that in addition to performance skills, musicians require the skills to run a small business; the confidence to create new opportunities; communication skills for use in educational, ensemble, and community settings; and industry knowledge and strong professional networks.

Similar to Ninan et al.'s (2004) study of musicians moving into unrelated careers, Bennett's study found that many musicians take on unrelated low-skill and low-income jobs in order to sustain a living (Bennett, 2004, 2007; Bennett & Bridgstock, 2015). She argues that if these musicians had a better skill set there would be other opportunities for a more satisfying, wider range of higher paying jobs within the creative industries as a secondary or alternative position. Bennett (2007) notes that within formal education, students are not necessarily supplied with these skills, and recommends that they at least be made aware of the business management skills required for professional careers, and the resources and education available to them. In another study in which musicians were asked to consider their careers retrospectively, Bennett (2004) found that they considered the absence not only of business skills, but also of marketing skills, a disadvantage. These musicians also added entrepreneurship, professional networks, technology skills and community development to the list of requisites for professional careers.

Coulson (2012) used a biographic narrative approach, interviewing 17 musicians. By finding out how practising musicians in the north east of England were supported and made a living, she aimed to investigate what could be learnt from musicians' understanding of entrepreneurship. The biographic approach allowed the participants to give an uninterrupted account of their life, with the interviewer asking questions arising from the narrative. As Bennett (2004) did, Coulson highlights networking as crucial for musicians. She found that musicians were dependent on relationships with other musicians for exchange of ideas, moral support, and performance relationships. The findings also show that performance opportunities are often created through engagement with peer networks.

While these studies make recommendations for improving the education of musicians, there are limited studies of learning environments that are designed for this purpose, and which could test their claims. Bennett (2004), for example, assumes that institutions cannot teach all of these skills, and suggests that music students simply be made aware of the professional world and the resources available to them. Bennett also suggests that students should acquire business skills, but provides no recommendations on how this is to be done, or when.

The YMI project is chiefly concerned with a design that enables students to develop 'street knowledge' skills. Are these skills 'teachable' in a didactic sense? Can they be developed through abstract lessons that occur outside of the industry context, for example, in separate business classes? Can networks comprising peers, teachers and industry not only provide the sharing of knowledge and expertise, but also the lifelong connections that will be beneficial for a successful career?

Bennett's (2004) argument—that if musicians are able to acquire this broader set of skills, then they will be able to apply these skills in other satisfying creative careers—provides a valuable point of departure. Throsby and Zednik (2011) suggest that aspiring professional practitioners, whether by choice or necessity, will adopt a 'portfolio' approach to their career, and that institutions need to prepare students for this career path. In this vein, the learning design required students to work across a diversity of roles, including project and event management, marketing, talent research, administration, and stakeholder management. The aim was to demonstrate the multiple career pathways in the music industry, and to show students how they could apply their creative skills. My research thus actively responds to the agendas mapped out by the industry career studies discussed above.

The following section investigates initiatives that have been developed by music educators to better prepare their students for the music industry, and the modern economy in general. In these studies, many of the approaches that were discussed in the first part of the literature review are now applied to a music context. These approaches include learning in communities, online learning, and informal and peer learning.

New Approaches to Music Education

According to Forrest (2001), music industry education has expanded since the 1990s, with offerings at both the university and technical and further education (TAFE) levels. Forrest points out that one of the main criticisms of existing higher education courses is the lack of direct industry-related training and education, which could give young musicians an awareness of the ways in which to use their artistry to gain meaningful employment. This also highlights the importance of industry interface and formative teaching, as outlined in the Queensland music industry studies discussed in the previous section. Direct connection with the industry, therefore, provides an essential component of a new learning design for music education. However, I also contend that these connections must be made before higher education begins. Therefore, I will first address learning innovations reported in school settings, before examining some current practices reported in higher education settings.

Sloboda's (2001) review of various studies from within the United Kingdom aims to raise broad issues around the nature and purpose of music education. He argues that classroom music, as currently conceptualised and typically organised in schools, might be an inappropriate vehicle for mass music education (p. 252), given the diverse range of music resources available beyond the school environment that might be able to provide a more effective source of music education. Lamont, Hargreaves, Marshall, and Tarrant (2003) conducted a detailed study of student and teacher attitudes to school music in the United Kingdom. They conducted questionnaires with 1479 students aged between 8 and 14, interviews with 42 music teachers, and focus groups with 134 students from the same sample. As did Sloboda (2001), they argue that the challenge for school music is to develop the interests the students have in music beyond the classroom. They suggest that creating opportunities for contact with professional musicians and events such as music festivals, would have an impact on their attitude towards school music.

While school music education now covers a broader range of styles than previously, Sloboda (2001) explains that the great classical works are still prioritised as, 'the pinnacle of musical value [and] deeper appreciation and understanding of such artworks is the most important (and universally applicable) aim of music education' (p. 249). He does not dismiss school music but, rather, sees it as an 'anchor-point where diverse experiences might be reflected upon, integrated and coordinated' (p. 253). This popular music versus classical music debate has occupied many researchers over the last decade (Folkestad, 2006; Green, 2002; Jaffurs, 2004; Westerlund, 2006). In contrast, my learning design focuses on the broader set of skills and knowledge that musicians can develop in authentic contexts, regardless of musical genre or preference.

Much research has focused on the inclusion of popular music in schools. I visit this work in the next section of this chapter, not because of its choice of musical content or repertoire, but because of its interest in the process by which popular musicians typically learn, and because of the way in which it seeks to connect the music curriculum with students' interests in music outside of school.

Informal Learning

Sefton-Green (2006) argues that developments in, and uses of technology, and recent speculation about the new or changing nature of the 'knowledge economy' have created an interest in 'out-of-school' learning (p. 2). He also points out that modern education systems need to make provision for young people in complex societies by considering issues of diversity, workplace learning, social inclusion, media culture, and school-to-work transition. Thus, Sefton-Green's (2006) research contributes to the theory relating to out-of-school or non-formal education, and aims to show how these forms of learning could become part of a wider ecology of educational provision for young people.

Sefton-Green (2006) defines 'non-formal learning' as projects, programs, and activities that are organised outside of statutory education systems, in structured, non-compulsory forms. He includes after-school clubs, such as the school play, film clubs and fashion shows as types of non-formal learning. Sefton-Green goes on to define 'informal learning' as learning that might happen casually, or in unplanned, disorganised or 'accidental' ways (p. 2). He acknowledges that there are no absolute distinctions between formal and non-formal learning, especially given that informal learning can happen in the school classroom, and that highly formal teaching can result in non-formal learning.

The sharp binary that is highlighted in the literature discussed above raises the important questions: Can the power of informal modes of learning be harnessed by formal education? If so, would its power be destroyed in the process? There is a body of research in music education that addresses these questions, and asks whether schools would benefit from the influence of the more informal learning that occurs in everyday musical contexts. In this regard, rock band musicianship has gained special recognition as a viable model for music education (Green, 2006; Westerlund, 2006). The garage rock band has been studied and characterised as a more collective, creative, spontaneous, informal and open musical education process than the more teacher-governed, disciplined, formal processes that are adopted in schools. Two studies of the informal rock band music education model—(Green, 2008) and Lindgren and Ericsson (2010)—are explored below.

Green's (2008) highly cited study *Music, Informal Learning and the School* tested a new classroom pedagogy, a national initiative implemented between 2002 and 2006. This pedagogy focused on the nurturing of musicianship and aimed to transfer the informal learning processes of rock and pop bands to the school music context. In Green's study, informal principles were applied in a systematic way across a range of schools in the greater London area.

At the start of the project, the informal strategies implemented in classrooms across the UK and observed by Green (2005, p. 2), included:

- learning based on students' personal choice, enjoyment, identification and familiarity with the music, as distinct from their being introduced to new and often unfamiliar music
- recorded music as the principal aural means of musical transmission and skill-acquisition, as distinct from notated or other written or verbal instructions and exercises
- self-teaching and peer-directed learning, as distinct from adult supervision and guidance, curricula, syllabi or external assessment
- the assimilation of skills and knowledge in haphazard ways according to musical preferences, rather than through a heuristic progression from simple to complex
- integration of listening, performing, improvising, and composing throughout the learning process, as distinct from the increasing differentiation of these elements.

Green reported that the students' levels of musical knowledge rose when they were given the opportunity to work informally. Green's study illustrated that informal learning strategies can assist students to develop skills required for the modern world (teamwork, communication, creativity). The formal school curriculum, on the other hand, does not allow students to experience a broader set of music-related activities in authentic, networked practice.

Lindgren and Ericsson (2010) report on the Swedish context, where pop and rock music have been placed at the centre of the curriculum for decades. Thus, Swedish music education is dominated today by singing and playing in pop and rock bands, while Western classical music, jazz, folk music, and music from other cultures are only marginally represented in the music classroom. Lindgren and Ericsson's (2010) perspectives on the informal approach in the Swedish context is in stark contrast to Green's (2006) perspectives on the British context.

Lindgren and Ericsson observed 9th Grade music classes at eight schools for a semester. Their research questioned the rock band context privileged in music education in Swedish schools in relation to governance and knowledge formation. They observed that leaving insufficiently skilled students to their own devices was problematic and resulted in their being incapable of executing their musical tasks. They found that even though the students had freedom, they had to account for their time and productivity. In this sense, Lindgren and Ericsson (2010) question the meaningfulness of incorporating non-school practices—such as authenticity, creativity, and collective learning—into the controlled, regulated and disciplined school environment.

There are risks of buying into the extremes of any argument by constructing a polarised binary; that is, that one position is better than the other. It is too simplistic a view. It is also too simple to suggest that informal learning takes place out of school, and formal learning in school. Folkestad (2006) reviews several international music education research studies that focus on formal and informal learning, and argues that the boundaries are often blurred. For example, he concludes that formal learning is pre-sequenced and arranged by someone who leads and carries out the activity. This person could be a teacher, or another student. Informal learning then, is the process of interaction of participants in the activity; however, as soon as one of the participants directly teaches another, then the learning that occurs is considered formal. Folkestad suggests that the two forms of learning are not dichotomous, but dialectical; that is, new forms of learning are generated through the awareness of the two forms of learning.

This section provided a variety of perspectives on informal and formal learning, and argues for an approach that considers them in a dialectical, rather than binary, way. Furthermore, while Folkestad's (2006) review of formal and informal studies briefly touches on how informal music practices achieve more than simply music education outcomes, such as administration and management skills, there is little research that considers the way in which young musicians acquire the skills and knowledge required for participation in the music industry. I suggest, therefore, that the learning environments discussed in the literature above, can provide a starting point for the design of a new 'music industry' education.

Music Education Through Social Online Networks

Salavuo's (2006, 2008) studies report on the influences and potential of online networks for pedagogical change in music learning. His (2006) research on online music communities reports on the educational benefits that stem from engaging in online social network platforms. He conducted a web-based survey of a Finnish online musical community (mikeseri.net), which has over 50,000 registered users, in order to better understand the motivation of these users to share their music, and contribute to the community. This research showed that users were more interested in their peer appreciation than in national or worldwide recognition through record deals. Other significant reasons that members gave for their participation were a chance to receive feedback; to gain and advance knowledge; to gain friendships, and to exchange information. Salavuo also reports that, in cases where users are already familiar with the metaphors and interface, online music communities offer 'on-demand' learning, He argues that participation, presence and ownership in online communities provides the motivation to learn, and that the ad hoc nature of these activities is fundamental to the generative nature of online networks.

In a later study, Salavuo (2008) argues against the learning management systems currently used within educational institutions. He investigated learning in the music discussion forum of an online music community and found that the learning activities include:

- uploading one's music, and expecting feedback
- listening to music contributed by peers, and providing feedback
- discussing, asking questions, providing answers, and engaging in argument
- recommending music
- connecting to engage in joint projects (p. 7).

He concludes that communities of practice supported by social media provide new opportunities for music learning, and points out that learning management systems in higher education are based on the logic of conventional product-oriented approaches to teaching and learning. Thus, he advocates the integration of popular and familiar social networking platforms within this overall learning environment.

These studies support the use of online social network platforms in new approaches to music education. For conventional studio music education, the master–apprentice model is preferred over reciprocal peer learning. Any shift towards a more ad hoc environment with a focus on peer learning could be challenging for music educators and students alike. Salavuo (2008) explains that, in formal education, students tend to perform for credits or a good grade. The learning design suggested in this current study does not stipulate a particular curriculum, on the understanding that the necessary learning will occur on demand as students navigate the music industry. Following Salavuo, therefore, I am interested in exploring the idea that assessment need not exist in a conventional sense, but rather as an opportunity for students to evaluate and reflect on the authentic music industry projects that they implement and action.

Creative Places and Community

A study that addresses the migration of young workers in the state of Pennsylvania provides an interesting connection between music education in schools and the artistic and cultural wellbeing of the wider community. Between 1995 and 2000, Pennsylvania experienced the fifth largest outward migration of young workers of all US states. The loss of these workers inhibited the state in attracting high paying jobs and promoting entrepreneurialism (Jones, 2005). Florida (2000) suggests that 'knowledge economy workers want to live in vibrant and diverse communities with lively arts scenes' (p. 8), and Jones (2005) points out that such communities are rarely found in Pennsylvania. Florida asserts that while arts and culture are key factors in attracting and retaining the knowledge economy and creative workers, arts and culture, per se, can have positive impacts on a community. Jones (2005), for example, explains that creative workers in Pennsylvania tended to move to Florida to settle because of its vibrant musical life, and cutting-edge music scenes. Jones attributes this situation to the context of music education in Pennsylvania, explaining:

> We have an ingrained paradigm that school music consists of selected "settings" rather than curriculum, that school music equals band, choir, orchestra and elementary general music. The end result is a lack of skills and *modus operandi* of creative workers, limited students in the upper grades and a disconnect between school music and the music in the students' lives outside of schools. The result is little if any impact on the musical life of the community. (p. 9)

In considering how a paradigm shift might occur, Jones reviews various public policy documents and music education traits in Pennsylvania to address two questions:

1. What role can school-based music education play in fostering the types of vibrant communities where creative workers want to live?
2. What role can school-based music educators play in helping their own students develop as creative workers? (p. 6).

Drawing on three different perspectives—public policy, regional economic development, and social work—Jones addresses the first question by recommending that school buildings open after hours and on weekends to serve the community as venues for arts activities. He also suggests that schools employ expert musicians to guide, mentor, and organise musical activities for community members. Jones highlights that music curricula should provide a bridge for students to participate in the musical offerings of the community, and should encourage them to develop their own musical opportunities outside of school. In addressing the second question, Jones reports that schools in the region had no specific guidance on how to develop creative workers.

Jones makes suggestions on how music education might develop creative workers. For example, individuality could be developed through exposure to different styles of music. Creativity could be encouraged through composition, performance and sound engineering.

Technology and innovation could be developed through electronic instruments and digital techniques. Participation could be fostered through making music, designing projects, and making musical decisions. He also suggests that project orientation could be achieved by allowing students to design projects—such as the making of a CD—where they set their own timelines, schedules, rules, and project goals. Eclecticism and authenticity could involve having students play music at open microphone nights at community venues. While Jones' agenda still focuses on musicianship, however, musicians still need to be able to transfer these 'music skills' into broader contexts if they are to become creative workers, capable of building a vibrant music scene and a viable livelihood. Attention to this industry interface is missing in Jones' work.

Carey and Naudin (2006) provide an in-depth qualitative analysis of the plenary sessions, focused discussions and workshops at the 2006 Creative Enterprise Conference held in the UK. At this conference, stakeholders, policymakers, researchers, academics and practitioners were invited to explore relevant issues pertaining to creative enterprise in the UK. They found that the key message emerging from the conference was the need to embed enterprise into existing curricula, with a view to cultivating an enterprising outlook. Some conference attendees argued that this culture is already embedded in the curricula of the creative industries disciplines through the implementation of real-life projects and briefs. Music and arts education in general can develop the skills required to be a creative worker, these skills must be made explicit in a range of contexts, not only in dedicated music institutions, in order to be transferrable into more settings.

Concluding Thoughts on Teaching and Learning for the Music Industry

This chapter reviewed literature regarding the changing nature of the music industry and the skills and personal attributes now required for successful participation therein. Before the explosion of new sound technologies and production possibilities, the music industry simply required musicians to be talented, while the record companies looked after the rest. Today, however, most young musicians, both classical and popular, are vying for a place in the increasingly competitive and uncertain music industry world. Bruenger (2015) argues that a curriculum should reflect the multifaceted and evolving music industry by encouraging students to develop adaptive capacity. The DIY culture especially prominent in the popular music sector requires musicians to develop a broad range of knowledge, skills and attributes in order to manage themselves, promote and organise their own shows, and to develop strategies for building an audience. This broader range of required skills includes effective interpersonal skills, and the ability to establish and maintain networks.

The previous research highlights a growing consensus that musicians need to be able to create their own opportunities, and to develop skills that will enable them to work across the creative industries (Bennett, 2007; Throsby and Zednik, 2011). Operating a business, creating new opportunities, and leveraging networks are recognised as valuable skills for musicians and for the workforce of the modern economies in general. Courses in business and entrepreneurship have been suggested as solutions for addressing these gaps in knowledge (Beckman, 2007; Bennett 2004; Bridgstock, 2013; Carey & Naudin, 2006; Rae, 2004; Sandercock, 2001). However, I would argue that developing these skills out of context only contributes to the perpetuation of the conventional didactic learning 'products' typical of formal education. In order to address this issue, my project focuses on the design of a learning environment that is purposefully entrepreneurial, in this case, a new business venture.

This current research investigates the possibility that, while informal learning cannot be planned for or implemented, it will emerge as students encounter, identify, and solve problems through authentic industry participation. The music industry is reliant on shifting tastes and markets and, therefore, calls for self-directed learners who are enabled by a supporting structure of networks and community ties.

Following on from Carey and Naudin (2006), I build on the principle of industry embeddedness in the design of YMI by co-creating authentic and collaborative music industry projects with students, and 'curating' meaningful and mutual relationships with industry.

This design aligns more generally with Friedman's (2005) flat world concept and Siemen's (2008) network approach to learning, where students, teachers, partners, and stakeholders are all co-creators of value.

References

Apple, M. (2004). Creating difference: Neo-liberalism, neo-conservatism and the politics of educational reform. *Educational Policy, 18*(1), 12–44. https://doi.org/10.1177/0895904803260022.

Baskakova, M., & Soboleva, I. (2019). New dimensions of functional illiteracy in the digital economy. *Voprosy Obrazovaniya/Educational Studies Moscow* (1), 244–263. http://doi.org/10.17323/1814-9545-2019-1-244-263.

Bauman, Z. (2000). *Liquid modernity*. Malden, MA and Cambridge: Polity.

Beckman, G. D. (2007). "Adventuring" arts entrepreneurship curricula in higher education: An examination of present efforts, obstacles, and best practices. *Journal of Arts Management Law and Society, 37*(2), 87–112. https://doi.org/10.3200/JAML.37.2.87-112.

Bennett, D. (2004). Peas in a cultural pod?: A comparison of the skills and personal attributes of artists and musicians. *Australian Journal of Music Education, 1,* 53.

Bennett, D. (2007). Utopia for music performance graduates: Is it achievable, and how should it be defined? *British Journal of Music Education, 24*(2), 179–189. https://doi.org/10.1017/s0265051707007383.

Bennett, D., & Bridgstock, R. (2015). The urgent need for career preview: Student expectations and graduate realities in music and dance. *International Journal of Music Education, 33*(3), 263–277. https://doi.org/10.1177/0255761414558653.

Blackwell, A., & Harvey, L. (1999). *Destinations & reflections: Careers of British art, craft and design graduates*. Centre for Research into Quality, University of Central England in Birmingham.

Bridgstock, R. (2013). Not a dirty word: Arts entrepreneurship and higher education. *Arts and Humanities in Higher Education, 12*(2–3), 122–137. https://doi.org/10.1177/1474022212465725.

Browne, E. (2003). Conversations in cyberspace: A study of online learning. *Open Learning: the Journal of Open, Distance and E-Learning, 18*(3), 245–259.

Bruenger, D. (2015). Complexity, Adaptive Expertise, and Conceptual Models in the Music Business Curriculum. *MEIEA Journal, 15*(1), 99–119. https://doi.org/10.25101/15.5.

Buchanan, K. (2018). *New Zealand: Education bill removes national standards and charter school model.* Retrieved July 2, 2019, from https://www.loc.gov/law/foreign-news/article/new-zealand-education-bill-removes-national-standards-and-charter-school-model-from-law/.

Carey, C., & Naudin, A. (2006). Enterprise curriculum for creative industries students: An exploration of current attitudes and issues. *Education and Training, 48*(7), 518–531.

Chase, D., & Hatschek, K. (2010). Learning that is greater than the sum of its parts: Efforts to build an integrative learning model in music management. *Journal of the Music and Entertainment Industry Educators Association, 10*(1), 125.

Claxton, G. (2004). *Learning is learnable (and we ought to teach it).* Ten Years On, The National Commission for Education Report, 237–250.

Coulson, S. (2012). Collaborating in a competitive world: Musicians' working lives and understandings of entrepreneurship. *Work, Employment & Society, 26*(2), 246–261. https://doi.org/10.1177/0950017011432919.

Cox, S. D., Ninan, A., Hearn, G. N., Roodhouse, S. C., & Cunningham, S. D. (2004). *Queensland music industry basics: People, businesses and markets.* CIRAC, Creative Industries Faculty, QUT.

Creech, A., Papageorgi, I., Duffy, C., Morton, F., Haddon, E., Potter, J., et al. (2008). From music student to professional: The process of transition. *British Journal of Music Education, 25*(3), 315–331. https://doi.org/10.1017/S0265051708008127.

Dalsgaard, C., & Paulsen, M. F. (2009). Transparency in cooperative online education. *International Review of Research in Open and Distance Learning, 10*(3), 15.

D'Andrea, M. (2012). The Ontario curriculum in the arts and the creative economy agenda. *Arts Education Policy Review, 113*(2), 80–88.

Dede, C. (2005). Planning for neomillennial learning styles: Implications for investments in technology and faculty. In *Educating the net generation, 5.* Boulder: EDUCAUSE.

Dewey, J. (1938). *Experience and education.* New York: Simon & Schuster.

Doherty, C., Luke, A., Shield, P., & Hincksman, C. (2012). Choosing your niche: The social ecology of the International Baccalaureate Diploma in Australia. *International Studies in Sociology of Education, 22*(4), 311–332. https://doi.org/10.1080/09620214.2012.745346.

Florida, R. (2000). The creative class. In R. T. LeGates & F. Stout (Eds.), *The city reader*. New York: Routledge.

Folkestad, G. (2006). Formal and informal learning situations or practices vs formal and informal ways of learning. *British Journal of Music Education, 23*(2), 135–145. https://doi.org/10.1017/S0265051706006887.

Forrest, D. (2001). *The odyssey of music industry education*. Paper presented at the ASME XIII Conference, Adelaide.

Freudenberg, B., Brimble, M., & Vyvyan, V. (2010). The penny drops: Can work integrated learning improve students' learning? *e-Journal of Business Education and Scholarship Teaching, 4*(1), 42.

Friedman, T. L. (2005). *The world is flat: A brief history of the twenty-first century*. New York: Farrar, Straus and Giroux.

Goold, L. (2018). *Space, time, creativity, and the changing character of the recording studio: Spaciotemporal attitudes toward "DIY" recording*. Queensland University of Technology.

Green, L. (2002). From the Western classics to the world: Secondary music teachers' changing attitudes in England, 1982 and 1998. *British Journal of Music Education, 19*(1), 5–30.

Green, L. (2005). The music curriculum as lived experience: Children's 'natural' music-learning processes. *Music Educators Journal, 91*(4), 37–42.

Green, L. (2006). Popular music education in and for itself, and for 'other' music: Current research in the classroom. *International Journal of Music Education, 24*(2), 101–118. https://doi.org/10.1177/0255761406065471.

Green, L. (2008). Group cooperation, inclusion and disaffected pupils: Some responses to informal learning in the music classroom. Presented at the RIME Conference 2007, Exeter, UK. *Music Education Research, 10*(2), 177–192.

Gurn, A. M. (2016). Courting corporate philanthropy in public education: Multi-disciplinary literature review of public–private partnerships (PPPs) in urban public schooling. *SAGE Open, 6*(2). https://doi.org/10.1177/2158244016635714.

Hansen, S. L., & Hoag, B. A. (2018). Promoting learning, career readiness, and leadership in student employment. *New Directions for Student Leadership, 2018*(157), 85–99. https://doi.org/10.1002/yd.20281.

Harris, A., & Temmermann, M. (2016). The changing face of creativity in Australian education. *Teaching Education, 27*(1), 103–113. https://doi.org/10.1080/10476210.2015.1077379.

Harvey, L., Moon, S., Geall, V., & Bower, R. (1997). *The graduates' work: Organisational change and students' attributes*. Centre for Research into Quality. Birmingham: University of Central England.

Hearn, G. (2005). *The shift to value ecology thinking and its relevance to the creative industries*. Paper presented at the Open Content Licensing (OCL): Cultivating the Creative Commons Conference, Brisbane.

Homer, M. (2009). Beyond the studio: The impact of home recording technologies on music creation and consumption. *Nebula, 6*(3), 85–100.

Ito, M., Gutiérrez, K., Livingstone, S., Penuel, B., Rhodes, J., Salen, K., … Watkins, S. C. (2013). *Connected learning: An agenda for research and design*. Digital Media and Learning Research Hub.

Jackson, D. (2015). Employability skill development in work-integrated learning: Barriers and best practice. *Studies in Higher Education, 40*(2), 350–367. https://doi.org/10.1080/03075079.2013.842221.

Jaffurs, S. E. (2004). The impact of informal music learning practices in the classroom, or how I learned how to teach from a garage band. *International Journal of Music Education, 22*(3), 189–200.

Jones, P. M. (2005). Music education and the knowledge economy: Developing creativity, strengthening communities. *Arts Education Policy Review, 106*(4), 5–12.

Kazis, R. (1993). *Improving the transition from school to work in the United States*. Cambridge, MA: Jobs for the Future.

Kisiel, J. F. (2010). Exploring a school-aquarium collaboration: An intersection of communities of practice. *Science Education, 94*(1), 95–121. https://doi.org/10.1002/sce.20350.

Lamont, A., Hargreaves, D. J., Marshall, N. A., & Tarrant, M. (2003). Young people's music in and out of school. *British Journal of Music Education, 20*(3), 229–241.

Leadbeater, C. (2000a). *Living on thin air: The new economy*. London: Penguin.

Leadbeater, C. (2000b). *The weightless society: Living in the new economy bubble*. New York: Texere Publishing.

Lindgren, M., & Ericsson, C. (2010). The rock band context as discursive governance in music education in Swedish schools. *Action, Criticism, and Theory for Music Education, 9*(3): 35–54. Retrieved from http://act.maydaygroup.org/articles/Lindgren9_3.pdf.

Mann, C., & Stewart, F. (2000). *Internet communication and qualitative research: A handbook for researching online*. London: Sage.

McWilliam, E. (2005). Unlearning pedagogy. *Journal of Learning Design, 1*(1), 1–11.

McWilliam, E. (2008). *The creative workforce: How to launch young people into high-flying futures*. Sydney: University of NSW Press.

Mitra, S. (2005). Self organising systems for mass computer literacy: Findings from the 'Hole in the Wall' experiments. *International Journal of Development Issues, 4*(1), 71–81. https://doi.org/10.1108/eb045849.

Moenk, T. (2007). The metaverse: Virtual worlds and lifelogging. *Listen, Connect, Influence*. Retrieved June 14, 2013, from http://bit.ly/1uluVCm.

Moyon, E., & Lecocq, X. (2013, June 10–12). *Adopting a business model view to study industry change: The case of the French record industry*. Paper presented at the XXII Conférence Internationale de Management Stratégique, Clermont-Ferrand.

Ninan, A., Hearn, G., & Oakley, K. (2004). *Queensland music industry trends: Independence day?* (CIRAC, Trans.). Kelvin Grove, QLD: Queensland University of Technology.

Oakley, K. (2007). *Educating for the creative workforce: Rethinking arts and education*. Australia Council for the Arts. Retrieved from http://bit.ly/1xLDDB1.

Pras, A., Guastavino, C., & Lavoie, M. (2013). The impact of technological advances on recording studio practices. *Journal of the American Society for Information Science and Technology, 3*(64), 80–90. https://doi.org/10.1002/asi.22840.

Radinsky, J., Bouillion, L., Lento, E. M., & Gomez, L. M. (2001). Mutual benefit partnership: A curricular design for authenticity. *Journal of Curriculum Studies, 33*(4), 405–430.

Rae, D. (2004). Entrepreneurial learning: A practical model from the creative industries. *Education + Training, 46*(8/9), 492–500. https://doi.org/10.1108/00400910410569614.

Reeves, T. C., Herrington, J., & Oliver, R. (2002, July 7–10). *Authentic activities and online learning*. Paper presented at the HERDSA 2002 Quality Conversations, Perth, Western Australia, pp. 562–567.

Regan, P. M., & Steeves, V. (2010). Kids r us: Online social networking and the potential for empowerment. *Surveillance & Society, 8*(2), 151–165.

Rogers, I. K., Ninan, A., Hearn, G. N., Cunningham, S. D., & Luckman, S. H. (2004). *Queensland music industry value web: From the margins to the mainstream* (CIRAC, Trans.). Kelvin Grove, QLD: Queensland University of Technology.

Salavuo, M. (2006). Open and informal online communities as forums of collaborative musical activities and learning. *British Journal of Music Education, 23*(3), 253–271. https://doi.org/10.1017/S0265051706007042.

Salavuo, M. (2008). Social media as an opportunity for pedagogical change in music education. *Journal of Music, Technology and Education, 1*(2–3), 2–3.

Sandercock, P. (2001). *Innovations in entrepreneurship education.* Chicago: Depaul University, Department of Management.

Sefton-Green, J. (2006). *New spaces for learning: Developing the ecology of out-of-school education.* McGill, South Australia: Hawke Research Institute for Sustainable Societies.

Siemens, G. (2008). *Learning and knowing in networks: Changing roles for educators and designers.* Retrieved May 4, 2011, from http://itforum.coe.uga.edu/Paper105/Siemens.pdf.

Sloboda, J. (2001). Emotion, functionality and the everyday experience of music: Where does music education fit? *Music Education Research, 3*(2), 243–253.

Suarta, I. M., Suwintana, I. K., Sudhana, I. F. P., & Hariyanti, N. K. D. (2017). Employability skills required by the 21st century workplace: A literature review of labor market demand. *Advances in Social Science, Education and Humanities Research, 102,* 337–342. https://doi.org/10.2991/ictvt-17.2017.58.

Stewart, C. (2016). Mixed signals: Do college graduates have the soft skills that employers want? *Competition Forum, 14*(2), 276–281.

Throsby, D., & Zednik, A. (2011). Multiple job-holding and artistic careers: Some empirical evidence. *Cultural Trends, 20*(1), 9–24. https://doi.org/10.1080/09548963.2011.540809.

Tinto, V. (2000). What have we learned about the impact of learning communities on students. *Assessment Update, 12*(2), 1–2.

Westerlund, H. (2006). Garage rock bands: A future model for developing musical expertise? *International Journal of Music Education, 24*(2), 119–125.

Williamson, B. (2013). *The future of the curriculum: School knowledge in the digital age.* Cambridge: The MIT Press.

4

Building the Emerging Professional Learning Model

In Chapter 3, I explored a diverse range of literature investigating innovative approaches to education. In particular, this literature supported the argument that high school students are not being educated for the environment that they will eventually inhabit. While researchers are making recommendations for building new contexts that will allow students to develop broader skillsets, there are few design-based studies of high school students' learning in authentic entrepreneurial/industry situations. The core values of entrepreneurship identified by Carey and Naudin (2006) and Rae (2005), (innovation, creativity, collaboration, teamwork, interdisciplinarity, and opportunity recognition) are consistently aligned with social learning theory across the literature. This led me to consider Wenger's work on communities of practice (CoP), and different treatments of social capital.

Communities of Practice

Scholarly interest in community learning environments grew out of earlier studies of reciprocal learning (Palincsar & Brown, 1988; Resnick, 1987). Resnick (1987) articulates the differences between in-school

© The Author(s) 2020
K. Kelman, *Entrepreneurial Music Education*,
https://doi.org/10.1007/978-3-030-37129-6_4

learning and out-of-school learning. Her study of various school pro-grammes that claim to help students attain higher order cognitive abil-ities, lay the foundation for later theories of community of practice. She identifies the common elements of 'successful programs that could point cumulatively toward a theory of how learning and thinking skills are acquired' (p. 19). These include:

> ... out-of-school cognitive performances that involve socially shared intel-lectual work ... organised around joint accomplishment of tasks, so that elements of the skill take on meaning in the context of the whole... they make usually hidden processes overt ...They also allow skill to build up bit by bit, yet permit participation even for the relatively unskilled, often as a result of the social sharing of tasks...The treatment of the subject matter is tailored to engage students in processes of meaning construction and interpretation. (Resnick, 1987, p. 19)

More recently, theorists expanded on these ideas and crystallised them into the theory of CoP (Barab & Duffy, 2000; Lave, 1993; Wenger, 1998).

CoPs are groups of individuals with shared interests who, through personal interaction, learn how to do what it is they do in a better and more meaningful way (1998). An examination of CoPs explains how people learn from one another communally. Wenger's (1998) CoP social learning theory provides a framework to support the idea that 'learning is essentially a fundamentally social phenomenon, reflecting our own deeply social nature as human beings capable of knowing' (p. 5). The primary focus is on 'learning as social participa-tion', conceptualised through four components:

- Meaning: A way of talking about our ability—individually and col-lectively—to experience our life and world as meaningful
- Practice: A way of talking about the shared historical and social resources, frameworks, and perspectives that can sustain mutual engagement in action

- Community: A way of talking about the social configurations in which our enterprises are defined as worth pursuing and our participation is recognisable as competence
- Identity: A way of talking about how learning changes who we are and creates personal histories of becoming in the context of our communities (Wenger, 1998, p. 5).

Lave and Wenger (1991) consider learning to be a function of activity, context, and culture in which learning is 'situated'. Situated learning theory often refers to the idea of a 'community of practice' as an informal and pervasive part of our daily lives. Knowledge and skills are obtained by participating in activities that expert members of the community would perform.

Communities of Practice: Possibilities for Learning

CoP theory understands that learning takes place when individuals within communities negotiate and renegotiate meaning. In this way, CoPs have the potential to expand and extend learning experiences and outcomes for both the individual and the community. Learning in CoPs evolves over three broad stages. CoPs begin as places where people share interests and develop their competence together (engaging); they then move towards connecting to the broader social systems (imagining); and, they coordinate or align their achievements to apply their learning in a way that demonstrates its impacts or effects (aligning).

Engaging in CoPs

A CoP is a group of individuals who engage in a social network based on shared core values and knowledge, to pursue a joint enterprise. The collective learning that takes place over time results in shared practice that reflects these CoP interactions. They are built on the experiences of members who are constantly changing and evolving as they interact with the world dynamically.

Within any theory of situated learning, the meaning is created as members negotiate and renegotiate with each other. Indeed, Wenger refers to meaning as a process of negotiation, having two constituent elements—participation and reification (Wenger, 1998). Participation is the way members interact in conversations, activities and reflections, and reification consists of the artefacts—such as tools, concepts, stories, documents, and resources—that are produced to reflect the community experience. Wenger explains that in order to make sense of experience or to create meaning, both participation and reification are necessary. Duguid (2005) also supports this notion that community is the social locus in which a community is sustained and reproduced over time. Such practice is founded on three elements: mutual engagement, joint enterprise and shared repertoire.

Mutual Engagement

Mutual engagement is the interaction of members as they establish norms and relationships. This engagement is what defines a community. Mutual engagement involves not only a participant's competence, but also the competence of others. It draws on what participants do and what participants know, as well as on their ability to connect meaningfully with what they do not know and do not do; that is, to the contributions and knowledge of others (Wenger, 1998, p. 75).

Shared practice is about discovering how to engage, what hinders engagement, defining identities, establishing who is who, who is good at what, who knows what, who is easy, or hard to get along with. In this sense, shared practice is about organising the distribution of expertise and experience. In this stage of engagement, it is more important to know how to give and receive help than to try to know everything yourself. The ability to engage purposefully or to recognise and agree on what matters in the context of the community, is what gives rise to joint enterprise.

Enterprise

Wenger (1998) describes enterprise as the result of a collective process of negotiation that reflects the full complexity of mutual engagement. While not everyone agrees with everything, some consensus is communally negotiated. Participants must find a way to do this by holding each other accountable to their collectively shared understandings of what the community is about. For an enterprise to be successful, the community must remain open to emergent directions, address gaps in knowledge, and put their energy into learning. Joint enterprise is the energy of a community; it drives the practice forward and gives the members a focus. Wenger (1998) states that, 'enterprise makes sense out of mutual engagement' (p. 82). Over time, the enterprise creates resources, and these are referred to as *shared repertoire*.

Repertoire

Wenger (1998) refers to 'shared repertoire' as communal resources, which can include routines, words, tools, ways of doing things, stories, gestures, symbols, genres, actions, concepts, and documents. This repertoire allows a community to reflect on itself, which is an important aspect in the ability of a CoP to avoid stagnation. Being able to reflect means that patterns can be discovered and hidden possibilities uncovered; that elements can be renegotiated by inventing new terms and redefining old ones; that stories can be retold, routines broken, and new tools produced and adopted.

Concluding Thoughts on Engaging in CoPs

These three dimensions—mutual engagement, joint enterprise and shared repertoire—must work together. Without joint enterprise, the community becomes stagnant; without mutual engagement, it lacks cohesion; and without shared repertoire there is nothing for the group to reflect on, and it becomes 'hostage to its own history' (Wenger, 2000, p. 230).

These three elements distinguish the support structures of learning CoP such as YMI, that enable self-directed learners to engage in informal and peer learning processes.

Imagining in CoPs

Practice is a shared history of learning that requires some initiation for new members. It is not simply an object passed down from one generation to the next. It is an ongoing, social, interactive process. In this way, CoPs are 'emergent structures' (Wenger, 1998, p. 96) because their members produce their practice through their negotiation of meaning. As members interact, they negotiate new meanings and learn from one. They share their competence with new members through a version of the same process by which they developed their own competence. The newcomer is supported by the competence of the older expert members, until the experience of the newcomer resembles the competence of the community.

CoPs have cycles that reflect their emergent nature. They come together, they evolve, they disperse, and it might not be clear where they begin and end. In this way, the existence of a CoP does not depend on fixed membership. The fact that people move in and out is essential to any long-lived cultural practice, as long as membership changes progressively to allow newcomers to be integrated into the community, engage in its practice, and then contribute to its perpetuation. These 'inter-generational' encounters are the aspects of practice that manifest as learning (Wenger, 1998, p. 98). New membership is pivotal to a CoP's sustainability and its source of new ideas and innovations (Hildreth & Kimble, 2005).

Imagination functions as the way in which CoPs extend their learning opportunities through multi-membership and boundary work. First, however, it is important to understand the basic premise and process of membership in CoPs—Legitimate Peripheral Participation.

Legitimate Peripheral Participation

Legitimate Peripheral Participation (LPP) is defined as an inbound trajectory, whereby newcomers must be granted legitimacy; that is, they need to be treated as potential members. Legitimacy can take many forms—being useful, being sponsored, or being considered the right kind of candidate. Only with enough legitimacy, can their 'errors, falls, evitable stumblings and violations become opportunities for learning rather than cause of dismissal neglect or exclusion' (Wenger, 1998, p. 100). Peripherality provides some access to participation and exposure to actual practice, but with less risk. Peripheral participation lies in access to 'mutual engagement with members, to their actions and negotiation of enterprise, and to the repertoire in use' (Wenger, 1998, p. 100).

Newcomers need a sense of how the community operates. While members ultimately strive to be competent, and aligned with more experienced community members, it is essential to also 'imagine ourselves and our communities by reflecting on our situation and exploring possibilities' (Wenger, 2000, p. 227). Imagination provides members with the opportunity to establish some distance from their situation.

New members can also create a ripple of new opportunities for mutual engagement. New relationships can awaken new interests that can spark a renegotiation of enterprise, and the whole process can produce new elements in the community repertoire. For example, when we have an experience that opens our eyes to a new way of looking at the world—insights from a conference or a meeting with a stranger with a different perspective—we bring that experience back into our communities. In this sense, we are trying to change the way in which our community defines competence, while at the same time deepening our own experience. We are using our individual experience to further our community's competence (Wenger, 2000). The LPP process operates in reverse, where the community's competence furthers the novice's experience. Consideration of this fundamental difference is a useful way to consider the value of new CoP members.

Boundary

Wenger's (2000) concept of 'landscapes of practice' acknowledges that CoPs are situated within a wider social system. All members simultaneously participate in multiple communities and bring a little of each community with them as they come and go between these different communities. Wenger refers to this as 'multi-membership', and considers it an inherent aspect of identity. Identities are crucial to our understanding of social learning because they combine competence and experience into a way of knowing, and assist in 'boundary crossing', which causes people to look afresh at their own assumptions (Wenger, 2000).

Boundary should not be considered a limiting or negative aspect of CoPs. While a boundary defines a group of people who are affiliated and share their own language and resources, CoPs are self-organising, emergent structures, with multiple and diverse relationships, and fluid boundaries that can foster collaboration and multidisciplinary approaches (Iaquinto, Ison, & Faggian, 2011). Multi-membership means that we can identify with the boundaries or the riskier peripheries. Wenger (2000) describes the possibilities of being at the boundary as flirting with the mystery of 'otherness' where we can explore the edge of our competence. Boundaries are sources of opportunities, as well as potential difficulties.

CoPs can steward a critical competence; however, they can also become hostage to their history by becoming insular, defensive, closed in and oriented only to their own focus. Wenger argues that CoPs need to be open to new possibilities and new insights. Deep expertise is the convergence of the members' competence at the core, whereas innovative learning comes via divergence of competence at the boundaries (2000, p. 127).

CoPs are at their best when their core and boundaries evolve in complementary ways. Wenger, MacDermott, and Snyder (2002) explains that it is a constant balancing act between developing deep expertise at the core and constant renewal at the boundary. This balancing act is crucial for boundary crossing to occur. If the competencies of the core (old) and the boundary (unknown) are too close, there can be a lack of learning as there are no challenges. If the distance between core and boundary practices is too great, learning is also unlikely to occur. In other words, there needs to be a productive tension between the two.

In the YMI design, learning at the boundary involves developing competency by being at the periphery of another community of practice, such as a professional music organisation. Bringing new knowledge and perspectives back into YMI gave the group a purpose for interaction, inspiration, a point of departure, activity, and further access to engagement.

For differing perspectives to be coordinated, Wenger (1998, p. 105) argues that there needs to be 'boundary objects' through which people can connect. Boundary objects include the language and terms used to describe joint perspectives, as well as concrete artefacts, such as documents, that recruit different communities to a common cause and purpose for interaction. For example, the Little BIGSOUND Conference served as a boundary object that enabled an ongoing partnership between YMI students and QMIA. The 'Broker' is another term used by Wenger (1998, p. 105) to describe individuals who can introduce elements of one practice into another. This capacity to absorb and coordinate multiple perspectives, innovation, creativity, or new ideas is imperative if a CoP is to make an impact on the world in which it lives. Wenger refers to this coordination as 'alignment' (1998, p. 178).

Alignment in CoPs

If Imagination allows us to reach beyond our community boundaries, then alignment grounds this imagination to make sure that the learning is effective. It also ensures that our local activities are sufficiently aligned with other processes so that they can be 'effective beyond our own engagement' (2000, p. 228). The challenge is for a community to connect their local efforts with the industry that operates in a broader social system. Alignment expands the scope of the community's effects on the world and provides focus and direction. A CoP can exploit this focus and direction to create unique artefacts, and to give the community a sense of what is possible and how it might realise higher goals.

Wenger explains that it is not about submitting to external authority and mere compliance; rather, it is about having the resources to interpret, challenge and negotiate with, and appropriate from, the broader system.

Alignment also builds community allegiance—a set of commitments that unite parties. Investing energy and coordinating this energy is about negotiating perspectives; finding common ground; convincing, inspiring, and uniting; defining broader visions and aspirations; and about setting up procedures and control measures. This work requires multi-membership and boundary crossing so that members can do the work of translation or 'brokering' in aligning with a broader system and its opportunities.

CoP Summary

CoP theory offers a framework to design and conceptualise learning and to investigate learning. CoP theory recognises that relationships, participation, reciprocity, membership and collaboration must play a part in any theory of human learning through an individual's experience of living in the world. CoPs have been embraced as an effective means of fostering knowledge in the twenty-first century, in a variety of settings. Their competitive advantage is that tacit knowledge is embedded in their members, and their competencies exist because their members develop them (Ardichvili, Page, & Wentling, 2003; du Plessis, 2008).

Blackmore (2010) argues that while CoPs cannot be engineered, the circumstances for their emergence and continuance can be understood and managed. This argument aligns with Wenger's (1998) belief that 'learning cannot be designed', (p. 225) and that it belongs to the realm of experience and practice. Typical school structures such as timetables, fixed subject times, segregation into year levels, or fixed classrooms within a building, do not allow the flexibility needed to deal with the realm of experience and practice.

In this regard, online social network platforms could play a significant role. However, members move in and out of various online communities, and this has implications for CoP sustainability.

Wenger's theory, however, is not dependent on a fixed membership. He acknowledges that people move in and out of CoPs. He asserts that an essential aspect of any long-lived practice is the arrival of new generations of members. As long as membership changes at a pace that allows for sustained inter-generational encounters, newcomers can be integrated into the community, engage in its practice, and then—in their own way—perpetuate it. Table 4.1 provides a summary of the evolution of CoPs and their various elements.

While learning in CoPs cannot be guaranteed, the conditions and environment for learning can be fostered. These conditions are the elements of CoPs at their varying stages, as summarised in Table 4.1. In this study, providing the enabling conditions for students to connect with industry through partnerships, exposes both groups to each other's practices and overlaps their boundaries. This allows student CoPs to 'imagine' and to develop new competencies, but also to align themselves with the broader music industry. The result is the creation of learning that has direct impacts and effects on the wider community.

CoPs are horizontally organised contexts for learning where the competency and experience of members is valued, regardless of whether they are participating in the centre or the periphery of the group. Learning occurs through engagement and imagination in CoPs. In this sense, students develop competency through LPP, either learning from more expert, or as peripheral members learning from professional industry partners. Students work together, bringing their diverse range of expertise, perspectives, skills and knowledge to solve complex problems. They also develop competence as they collaborate with industry professionals through boundary crossing. In this sense, young people can offer new perspectives, knowledge and skills to the partnership to progress projects.

Table 4.1 The evolution of CoPs—stages and elements

Stages of CoP development and learning	Elements
Engaging in CoPs	Mutuality, Enterprise and Repertoire
Imagining in CoPs	Boundary, Diversity, Multi-membership
Aligning in CoPs	Convergence, Coordination

Social Capital: An Introduction

While social capital has the ability to be applied in various contexts, the exact meaning of the term has been 'hotly disputed and its utility in the scientific discourse remains contested' (Castiglione, Van Deth, & Wolleb, 2008, p. 1). Quite commonly, social capital is explained in terms of 'it's not what you know, but who you know' (Woolcock, 2001, p. 2), and this would suggest that it simply refers to social networks that create positive outcomes. Warren (2008) contends that if social capital is simply about participating in social groups and networks that have positive consequences for both individuals and society, then 'there is nothing very new about the idea' (p. 124).

While there have been many contributions to the theory of social capital, its underlying elements are its dependence on social networks, the reciprocities that arise within them, and the mutual benefits derived for both individuals and the groups. The varying treatment of these elements by scholars informs a social capital framework pertinent to a study that examines community learning.

Pierre Bourdieu on Social Capital

In the following section, I briefly acknowledge Bourdieu's social capital theory due to its intersection with CoP work. However, Coleman and Putnam's, theory of social capital are explored in more depth due to their relevance to the study of youth communities. Bourdieu defines social capital as 'the aggregate of the actual or potential resources which are linked to possession of a durable network of more or less institutionalised relationships of mutual acquaintance and recognition' (Bourdieu & Wacquant, 1992). Membership in certain groups allows each member the backing of collectively owned capital, a credential that entitles the member to forms of credit to which other people do not have access. These connections or social relationships can mobilise the economic and cultural capital of individuals within these networks, to secure positional advantage, which Bourdieu would relate to the reproduction of social inequality (Fram, 2004). However, France (2009) argues that we need to look more widely beyond seeing social capital as the product of the privileged, and look at the more open and loose social relationships of late modernity, especially among youth.

Field (2005) employs relevant concepts in Bourdieu's work in his study of youth; in particular, the idea that social capital is the property of groups, and, more particularly, a product of collective interaction. The field also acknowledges that we do not always join groups with underlying motives, and that most people tend to cooperate with people whom they like, and whose company they enjoy. This aspect of social capital is particularly pertinent to this research where, in the first instance, students have come together with people with whom they share a friendship, in the interests of a potentially dynamic and enjoyable learning experience.

Many would argue that Bourdieu's theory of social capital does not apply to, or account for young people and children. Bohman (1999) expresses his views that Bourdieu's work does not capture social change or transformation, and that agents need to reflect upon their social conditions, critique them, and articulate new interpretations of them. It is critical that any adaptation of social capital theory recognises young people as agents in transforming their own education and lives, not simply as inheritors of their parents' status. Jenkins (1992) argues that Bourdieu hands so much power to the social context that 'things happen to people rather than a world in which they can convene in their individual and collective destinies' (p. 91). Finally, Bourdieu's emphasis on the work or 'investment' required to build, then maintain, social capital has significant implications for young people as it draws attention to the social and communicative skills involved in the processes of 'mutual cognition and recognition' (Field, 2005, p. 23). Given the very social nature of the learning, the CoP framework, aligns better with this application of social capital.

James Coleman on Social Capital

In contrast to Bourdieu's view, in his studies of education, Coleman found that social capital is not limited to the powerful, but also has benefits for the poor and marginalised.

Social capital, according to Coleman represents a resource because it involves the expectation of reciprocity, and goes beyond any given individual to involve wider networks whose relationships are governed by a high degree of trust and shared values. (Field, 2005, p. 23)

Coleman's interest in social capital is concerned with the issue of children's educational attainment. The most significant and most criticised aspect of Coleman's work, of particular relevance to this study, is his focus on the role of close or dense ties (closed networks). He considers that the creation of social capital is assisted by the closure of networks. This closure offers stability, a common shared ideology, and the capacity to improve sanctions (Coleman, 1994, pp. 104–108). The role of closed networks as a source of social capital is of interest to this current study, and the notion articulates with the establishment of a community of practice, where shared norms of trust and reciprocity enable a culture of learning, and where skills (human capital) can be shared and acquired.

Coleman considers that the 'patriarchal family' is in decline, and that social organisations such as churches and schools are taking greater responsibility for the socialising of children (Coleman, 1988, p. 9). For example, social capital can contribute to learning by creating pressure from peers and others in close-knit communities with strongly shared norms, forming a powerful consensus around the value of skills, knowledge and qualifications, as well as placing negative sanctions on those who deviate from the social consensus (Coleman, 1988).

Portes (1998) criticises Coleman for overplaying the role of close or dense ties, and underplaying the significance of weak or loose ties. While I see value in Coleman's argument, especially in the early stages of a community of practice, strong norms and shared values might eventually restrict individual freedom, autonomy, creativity and the expression of a unique identity (Portes, 1998). It is also possible that if learning aspirations are affected by the norms of those with whom they connect, then a low aspiration culture can have adverse effects (Field, 2005, p. 30). Thus, a dense, closed network should be understood to have both potential strengths and potential weaknesses.

For the purposes of this research, I build on the premise that young people can be active in the formation of social capital, independent of their parents. While Coleman offers an optimistic view of social capital, whereby individuals participate in social structures based upon strong norms, this view does not really account for the modern refracted world of young people who engage in multiple CoPs. Robert Putnam's theory, on the other hand, is more concerned with understanding variety within social networks, and with their capacity to build social capital.

Robert Putnam on Social Capital

In his article *Bowling Alone: America's Declining Social Capital*, Robert Putnam defines social capital as the 'Connections among individuals – social networks and the norms of reciprocity and trustworthiness that arise from them' (Putnam, 2000b, p. 19). As a political scientist, Putnam was concerned with the loss of civic engagement and social interaction and saw this as troublesome, particularly because of his belief that social capital explains a society's efficiency and cohesion. In particular, Putnam considers the state of democracy and community, and the relationships between government and civil society, and emphasises the importance of fostering norms of reciprocity and trust. In *Making Democracy Work: Civic Traditions in Italy* (Putnam, Leonardi, & Nanetti, 1993), he uses the concept of social capital to show the differences between the more affluent and civic-minded North and the poor, ill-governed South (Field, 2005).

Later, came the pivotal book *Bowling Alone: The Collapse and Revival of American Community* (Putnam, 2000a), where Putnam comments on the decline of associational life in America since the 1960s. He notes five possible explanations for the decline in civic engagement: 'generational change; television; suburbanisation; commuting and urban sprawl; and everyday pressures' (Putnam, 2000b, p. 215). For Putnam, social capital refers to 'features of a social organisation, such as trust, norms and networks that can improve efficiency of society by facilitating coordinated actions' (Putnam et al., 1993, p. 167), and these networks contribute to collective action. Of relevance to my study of young musicians in CoP, is Putnam's theoretical proposition that when people come together in shared interest to build trust and reciprocity, these connections enhance their productivity (or learning) as individuals and groups.

Putnam makes a distinction between two forms of social capital: bonding and bridging. Putnam refers to *bonding* social capital as the capital cultivated in dense networks such as families and friendship groups, which 'bolster our narrower selves and is good for getting by', whereas *bridging* social capital is seen as links to external networks or relationships with people outside of immediate family and friendship circles. This type of capital is recognised as 'broadening people's opportunities, generating broader identities and reciprocities, and is good for getting ahead' (2000b, p. 23). This distinction reflects what network analysts would describe as 'strong and weak ties'. Granovetter (1983) explains:

> Individuals with few weak ties will be deprived of information from distant parts of the social system and will be confined to the provincial news and views of their close friends. This deprivation will not only insulate them from the latest ideas and fashions but may put them in a disadvantaged position in the labour market. (p. 202)

While close bonding facilitates the sharing of information in more informal learning scenarios, it also limits access to skills and knowledge that are not available within the group (Field, 2005). Drawing from Putnam's work, Woolcock (1998) summarises three different types of social capital connections. The first two of these types are defined as:

- Bonding social capital: dense, bounded networks, homogeneity of membership, high levels of reciprocity and trust, exclusion of outsiders
- Bridging social capital: loose and open-ended networks, heterogeneity of membership, shared norms and common goals, where levels of trust and reciprocity might be more limited.

Later, Woolcock (2001) describes *linking* social capital, a category that emphasises a vertical shift that allows individuals or communities to access formal networks of information or resources through their informal connections.

- Linking social capital: loose and open-ended networks, variety of membership, shared norms and common goals, levels of trust and reciprocity might be circumscribed by competing demands.

The benefit of linking social capital is that it reaches out to different communities in different situations; that is, to those who are entirely outside the community, thus enabling members to leverage a far wider range of resources than are available within their 'bonded' community of practice (Woolcock, 1998, pp. 13–14). While closed networks could have limited social capital, some would also argue that the closed networks Coleman talks about allow a community to develop stronger bonds by building a higher level of trust. This trust could potentially serve as an effective starting point from which to later bridge into wider networks. In this way, the YMI design aimed to harness the valuable potential of both bonding and bridging social capital. For entrepreneurial innovation such as the YMI project, bonding capital establishes the community's practice, and bridging capital can keep members in touch with new ideas and practices.

Concluding Thoughts on Social Capital

This exploration of the three major theories of social capital demonstrates how the concept of social capital is not simply about participating in social groups and networks with positive consequences: as Warren (2008) stated, 'there is nothing very new about the idea' (p. 124). We have seen the dependence of social capital on social networks, the reciprocities that arise from these networks and their mutual benefits for both individuals and groups. However, it is the varying dimensions and architecture of these networks that are of interest to my project.

Social capital is seen by Coleman and Bourdieu as a resource for individuals. Field (2005) suggests that they are more focussed on bonding capital, while Putnam's work focuses on social capital as belonging to groups. Coleman and Putnam's approaches contrast with Bourdieu's, in that they see social capital in a more integrated way—as being the collective good of reciprocity, trust and cooperation. Putnam's social capital is evidenced in civic engagement, while Coleman's social capital is a resource that focuses on family and community cohesion. For Coleman and Putnam, social capital is inherently a good thing, while Bourdieu sees it in a less positive light, as reproducing social inequality and cronyism. This current research is interested in the different forms of social capital as having both potential strengths and weaknesses.

While bonding capital can develop a strong community culture, it can also be restrictive, insular and exclusionary, and this can have negative impacts on a group's ability to be creative, innovative and sustainable. In this vein, Schaefer-McDaniel (2004) argues that not all community outcomes are positive, and that there are other groups, such as gangs or the mafia, who have an abundance of bonding social capital, but are associated with negative consequences. Bridging capital is understood in my research as offering a broader set of opportunities to connect with, and access, new ideas and knowledge, and to participate in networks that could be advantageous for 'getting ahead' in the music industry.

Linking capital, or 'synergy', as expressed by Schaefer-McDaniel (2004, p. 157), is realised in the possibility of students interacting with other institutions to work towards common goals. These types of connections allow the students to access a multiplicity of information, which Field (2005) suggests might promote ambition and effort. In particular, linking connections would allow the students to demonstrate the outcomes of their learning as community assets (Putnam, Leonardi and Nanetti, 1993). For the purposes of this research, I see bonding, bridging, and linking capital as potentially contributing to learning in important and complementary ways.

A major consideration for the application of social capital theory to my study is Bourdieu, Coleman and Putman's failure to recognise or account for youth agency. It has been useful to explore empirical studies of social capital among youth to try to understand how others have drawn on the theory and its contrasting elements. Leonard (2008) explains that, 'young people's ability to develop stocks of social capital is under-played' in the theory. What these approaches have in common is a tendency to see young people as 'human becomings rather than human beings' (p. 226).

Empirical studies evidence the way in which young people generate social capital that is having an impact on social change. Bedell (2003), for example, describes how young children and teenagers joined in solidarity with their counterparts across the world to protest against the war in Iraq in 2003 and recently during the 2018 climate change protests. These events contradicted the widespread concern with teenage apathy, and showed young people as active citizens who were using their social networks (via text messages and the internet) to organise demonstrations and to rally support. This study also contradicts the criticism that Putnam (2000b) has of the internet, which he believes is a mere 'simulacra' of most classic forms of social connectedness and civic engagement (p. 170). Putnam argues that while Americans were joining organisations such as Greenpeace and making donations, it was simply 'mail-order membership' due to the lack of action or face-to-face meeting. In contrast, Bedell's study shows how the internet can enhance and mobilise young people's social capital, and has become a mainstream way of connecting people.

The role of social online networking similarly plays a major role in my research, as it is the predominant vehicle for the students in not only organising themselves, but in their reaching out to the wider community. Weller (2006) in her study *Skateboarding alone* shows how teenagers in a low-socio economic suburb in the UK deployed social capital at the local level in order to save a space they valued. The study highlights how the positive relationships of linking capital were built between the youth and the local council to renegotiate previous conflicts and to build new relationships of trust and reciprocity. The students' ability to build trust and reciprocity with government and other institutions is also a key factor in my project.

Studies that focus on youth address an aspect of Bourdieu's theory that has been overlooked in the literature; that is, sociability

(Schaefer-McDaniel, 2004). Young people need to learn the 'skills of exchange' (sociability) that enable and sustain these relationships, but also the skills that enable them to create social and cultural capital of their own (Allat, 1993, p. 154). Schaefer-McDaniel (2004) views inter-action as the cornerstone of social capital, and holds that these inter-actions will develop young people's sociability. Further, Morrow (2001) argues that community members need to be able to recognise their net-works as a resource in order for these networks to constitute social capi-tal (p. 56).

When exploring social capital in youth, Schaefer-McDaniel (2004) extends Putnam's work to include a 'sense of belonging'. In the same way, the concept of LPP stresses the importance of members feeling that their participation in the community, whether as a novice or a more competent member, is valued and legitimised in the overall community. This 'sense of belonging', according to McMillan and Chavis (1986), requires membership (the sense of feeling part of a group or environ-ment) and influence (the sense that the individual matters to the group; that the group is cohesive, and is complete only with the individual).

Summary of Social Capital

Theories of social capital inform this research and its design of entrepre-neurial learning. As such, the learning environment did not operate in the conventional sense of formal education but, rather, adopted a net-worked, 'flat world' approach to learning. In this sense, there was no curriculum or formal instruction, and the students largely determined the direction and activities of their community; that is, they developed their own community of practice. Through mutual engagement, they mobilised bonding social capital, which established community norms of trust and reciprocity, a shared repertoire, and a sense of purpose or joint enterprise.

The students were not told what to learn; rather, they were respon-sible for identifying the gaps in their knowledge, and where this knowledge might be accessed within their networks. The pro-cess of imagination and alignment in CoPs, enabled them to build

Table 4.2 Social capital mobilised through CoP development and learning

Stages of CoP development and learning	Elements	Type of social capital most likely developed
Engaging in CoPs	Mutuality, Enterprise and Repertoire	Bonding
Imagining in CoPs	Boundary, Diversity, Multi-membership	Bridging
Aligning in CoPs	Convergence, Coordination	Linking

bridging and linking social capital. Mobilisation of bridging and linking capital had the potential to build new knowledge and new perspectives, to reinvigorate the community's enterprise, and to develop new repertoire. Social learning theory provides a way of explaining how and what the students learn in such an enterprise.

Table 4.2 summarises the types of social capital targeted and mobilised in the YMI design through the various phases of CoP learning.

Entrepreneurial Learning

There is ongoing debate about whether entrepreneurship is disciplinary knowledge that can be learned, or whether it is something driven by desire and passion that cannot be taught (Drucker, 1985). Riese (2011), in her discussion of education policies in Norway, describes entrepreneurship education as a combination of general virtues (the promotion of activities that encourage the use of initiative, creativity and problem-solving) and business (encouraging students to start new businesses). Beckman (2007) proposes a context-based curriculum, where students develop their own innovative and authentic industry outcomes to transition from student to professional.

In a project aimed at developing entrepreneurial characteristics in youth, Rasheed (2000) proposes that learning designs, which include active experimentation balanced with concrete experience, enhance entrepreneurial competence. His experiments in high schools established simulated business situations as a context for learning. He cites a number of attributes that act as predictors of entrepreneurial behaviour:

the need for achievement, creativity, initiative, risk-taking, setting objectives, independence, autonomy, motivation, energy, and commitment. Some studies show that entrepreneurial characteristics in students actually decrease over time as they advance through the school grades (Moser, 2005). Rasheed and Rasheed (2004) found that 25% of kindergarten students, compared with 3% of high school students, demonstrate important entrepreneurial characteristics. They also found that students who had training in enterprise experience developed characteristics commonly associated with entrepreneurial attributes, and that effective training prepares young people to be entrepreneurs and to contribute to sustainable communities. Rasheed and Rasheed's study shows that students who received entrepreneurial training gained a higher motivation to achieve and were likely to be innovative.

Rae (2005) explains the development of an entrepreneurial identity through personal and social emergence. Rae argues this is achieved through interaction with others, where participants learn how to apply their abilities within networks. He describes this as 'translating possibilities of "what could be" into enacted reality and self-belief and confidence that they are able to make that happen' (p. 328).

This project adopts an environment of entrepreneurial learning that is similar to Beckman's (2007) understanding: that it is an authentic, embedded activity that develops entrepreneurial behaviour leading to the emergence of an entrepreneurial mindset, rather than a stand-alone subject suited to a didactic content-led curriculum. Empirical research suggests that experience and social skills are more crucial to success than formal education (Johannisson, 1991, p. 67), and that entrepreneurial training calls for a contextualised approach. Johannisson (1991) argues that an action perspective on entrepreneurship learning is needed, and suggests a framework for identifying the competencies needed for an entrepreneurial career. His suggested action theory of entrepreneurship stresses that entrepreneurial learning does not take place in a social vacuum; a context for entrepreneurial action must be included. He defines five entrepreneurial competencies: Know-Why (attitudes, values, motives), Know-How (skills), Know-Who (social skills), Know-When (insight), and Know-What (knowledge). These five competencies inform the learning design in this research. They also inform its analysis

Table 4.3 Entrepreneurial competencies

Term	Description	Definition
Know-Why	Attitudes, values, motives	Defined as self-confidence, drive, ability to take risks, entrepreneurial enthusiasm and availability of mentors and role models
Know-How	Skills	Defined as imitating and/or acquiring skills that can be used in action
Know-Who	Social skills	Defined as networking capability in production and social networks, embedded in personality characteristics and developed through practice in context
Know-When	Insight	Defined as experience and intuition to know when, opportunity, timing management
Know-What	Knowledge	Defined as encyclopedic knowledge and institutional facts

Source Adapted from Johannisson (1991)

to identify what the YMI community learns about entrepreneurialism. Table 4.3 offers a description and definition of each competency, as adapted from Johannisson (1991, p. 71).

Putting It Altogether: The Emerging Professional Learning Model

This section draws together a range of theories into a coherent model to develop a learning design for the YMI project. The emerging professional learning model (EPLM) responds to studies that signal the crucial importance of social capital in entrepreneurialism.

Corbett (2007) explains that entrepreneurship is socially situated, whereby the social environment is in constant interplay with individuals and organisations to drive the discovery, evaluation, and exploitation of opportunity. More particularly, Gedajlovic, Honig, Moore, Payne, and Wright (2013) note that there is an increased interest in, and appreciation of the importance of social relationships in entrepreneurship, and suggests that integrative theories will advance research in the area. In this vein,

Nahapiet and Ghoshal (1998) explain that the acquisition and management of social capital plays an essential role in the entrepreneurial success of both individuals and collectives. Kim and Aldrich (2005) suggest that knowing how to use social ties skilfully can reap financial rewards and commercial success. They claim that individuals have only a few strong, regular ties, and many weak ties. While the latter are much more difficult to maintain and manage, they are essential for entrepreneurialism.

In this research, social capital theory provides a compatible and productive way of understanding the processes and social interactions that YMI learners engaged in across a diverse set of entrepreneurial situations and contexts. Figure 4.1 offers a visual representation of the integrated theoretical framework, presented here as the EPLM.

This project places social capital and CoP at the heart of this theoretical framework as a means of understanding the processes and resources—such as knowledge, skills, dispositions and contacts—that were acquired within the students' own CoP, and through their participation within industry CoPs. Entrepreneurial initiatives and the social capital in CoP are understood to be mutually dependent, requiring the cultivation and maintenance of all three types of social capital—bonding, bridging, and linking.

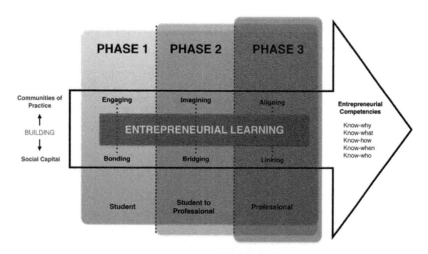

Fig. 4.1   The emerging professional learning model

Bonding capital can **engage** and help to maintain a CoP, and build entrepreneurial spirit and shared purposes. However, relying solely on these close ties can limit access to potential resources and opportunities, as strong boundaries can deflect social relationships back on themselves, thus fostering a dense but limited social network of close ties. **Bridging** capital can help bring about CoP **imagination** and innovation through being exposed to new ideas and perspectives outside the CoP. **Linking** capital is advantageous for accessing greater financial support for entrepreneurial activities, and requires participating CoPs to **align** processes and procedures with external institutional practices. Bridging and linking capital are desirable but more challenging because they require community members to cross boundaries. This presents risks around building trust, as individuals and collectives do not know what lies beyond their boundaries, or within indirect or weak ties.

The aim of this research is to understand **how** the students participating in YMI as a CoP engaged with entrepreneurial competencies through mobilising different levels of social capital. The research also asks what YMI as a CoP learned across the phases of engaging, imagining and aligning their community's venture. By examining the YMI CoP through the lenses of social capital and social learning theory, this project comes to an understanding of the students' growing entrepreneurial maturity by identifying evidence of Johannisson's entrepreneurial competencies. The model accounts for students expanding into different phases of learning by imposing them as new layers but not discarding previous phases. For example, moving into Phase 2 still requires the bonding capital work that occurs in Phase 1.

The EPLM, as seen in Fig. 4.1, responds to a field void of any design-based studies that aim to test how high school students might learn about the music industry though environments engineered to foster entrepreneurial capacity. It also shows how student status transitions to professional status through the students' participation in the cumulative phases of extended CoPs within an entrepreneurial context. Finally, the model shows how these expanding phases of participation build different types of social capital, and lead to greater opportunities to develop entrepreneurial competencies.

References

Allat, P. (1993). Becoming privileged: The role of family process. In I. Bates & G. Riseborough (Eds.), *Youth and inequality*. Philadelphia, PA: Open University Press.

Ardichvili, A., Page, V., & Wentling, T. (2003). Motivation and barriers to participation in virtual knowledge-sharing communities of practice. *Journal of Knowledge Management, 7*(1), 64–77. https://doi.org/10.1108/13673270310463626.

Barab, S. A., & Duffy, T. (2000). From practice fields to communities of practice. *Theoretical Foundations of Learning Environments, 1*(1), 25–55.

Beckman, G. D. (2007). "Adventuring" arts entrepreneurship curricula in higher education: An examination of present efforts, obstacles, and best practices. *Journal of Arts Management Law and Society, 37*(2), 87–112. https://doi.org/10.3200/JAML.37.2.87-112.

Bedell, G. (2003). Voices of tomorrow don't wait to protest: Children and theater. *The Observer (1901–2003)*, p. 12.

Blackmore, C. (Ed.). (2010). *Social learning systems and communities of practice*. London: Springer.

Bohman, J. (1999). Practical reason and cultural constraint: Agency in Bourdieu's theory of practice. In R. Shusterman (Ed.), *Bourdieu: A critical reader* (pp. 129–152). Malden, MA: Blackwell Publishers.

Bourdieu, P., & Wacquant, L. J. D. (1992). *An invitation to reflexive sociology*. Chicago: University of Chicago Press.

Carey, C., & Naudin, A. (2006). Enterprise curriculum for creative industries students: An exploration of current attitudes and issues. *Education and Training, 48*(7), 518–531.

Castiglione, D., Van Deth, J. W., & Wolleb, G. (2008). *The handbook of social capital*. Oxford: Oxford University Press.

Coleman, J. (1988). Social capital in the creation of human capital. *American Journal of Sociology, 94*(S1), S95–S120. https://doi.org/10.1086/228943.

Coleman, J. (1994). *Foundations of social theory*. Cambridge, MA: Harvard University Press.

Corbett, A. C. (2007). Learning asymmetries and the discovery of entrepreneurial opportunities. *Journal of Business Venturing, 22*(1), 97–118. https://doi.org/10.1016/j.jbusvent.2005.10.001.

Drucker, P. (1985). *Innovation and entrepreneurship: Practice and principles*. London: Heinemann.

Duguid, P. (2005). "The art of knowing": Social and tacit dimensions of knowledge and the limits of the community of practice. *Information Society, 21*(2), 109–118. https://doi.org/10.1080/01972240590925311.

du Plessis, M. (2008). The strategic drivers and objectives of communities of practice as vehicles for knowledge management in small and medium enterprises. *International Journal of Information Management, 28*(1), 61–67. https://doi.org/10.1016/j.ijinfomgt.2007.05.002.

Field, J. (2005). *Social capital and lifelong learning.* Bristol: Policy Press.

Fram, M. S. (2004). Research for progressive change: Bourdieu and social work. *Social Service Review, 78*(4), 553–576. https://doi.org/10.1086/424544.

France, A. (2009). Changing conceptions of youth in late modernity. In J. Wood & J. Hine (Eds.), *Work with young people: Theory and policy for practice* (pp. 15–26). Los Angeles: Sage.

Gedajlovic, E., Honig, B., Moore, C. B., Payne, G. T., & Wright, M. (2013). Social capital and entrepreneurship: A schema and research agenda. *Entrepreneurship Theory and Practice, 37*(3), 455–478. https://doi.org/10.1111/etap.12042.

Granovetter, M. (1983). The strength of weak ties: A network theory revisited. *Sociological Theory, 1,* 201–233.

Hildreth, P., & Kimble, C. (2005). Knowledge networks: Innovation through communities of practice. *Information Management, 18*(1/2), 24.

Iaquinto, B., Ison, R., & Faggian, R. (2011). Creating communities of practice: Scoping purposeful design. *Journal of Knowledge Management, 15*(1), 4–21. https://doi.org/10.1108/13673271111108666.

Jenkins, R. (1992). *Pierre Bourdieu.* New York: Routledge.

Johannisson, B. (1991). University training for entrepreneurship: Swedish approaches. *Entrepreneurship & Regional Development, 3*(1), 67–82. https://doi.org/10.1080/08985629100000005.

Kim, P. H., & Aldrich, H. E. (2005). *Social capital and entrepreneurship.* Delft: Now Publishers Inc.

Lave, J. (1993). Situating learning in communities of practice. In L. B. Resnick, J. M. Levine, & S. D. Teasley (Eds.), *Perspectives on socially shared cognition* (pp. 17–36). Washington, DC: American Psychological Association.

Lave, J., & Wenger, E. (1991). *Situated learning: Legitimate peripheral participation.* New York: Cambridge University Press.

Leonard, M. (2008). Social and subcultural capital among teenagers in Northern Ireland. *Youth & Society, 40*(2), 224–244. https://doi.org/10.1177/0044118X08314243.

McMillan, D. W., & Chavis, D. M. (1986). Sense of community: A definition and theory. *Journal of Community Psychology, 14*(1), 6–23.

Morrow, V. (2001). *Networks and neighbourhoods: Children's and young people's perspectives.* London: NHS Health Development Agency.

Moser, S. (2005). *The impact of internships on entrepreneurial aspirations.* Paper presented at the Midwest Academy of Management Annual Conference, Chicago, IL.

Nahapiet, J., & Ghoshal, S. (1998). Social capital, intellectual capital, and the organisational advantage. *Academy of Management Review, 23*(2), 242–266.

Palincsar, A. S., & Brown, A. L. (1988). Teaching and practicing thinking skills to promote comprehension in the context of group problem solving. *Remedial and Special Education, 9*(1), 53–59.

Portes, A. (1998). Social capital: Its origins and applications in modern sociology. *Annual Review of Sociology, 24*(1), 1–24. https://doi.org/10.1146/annurev.soc.24.1.1.

Putnam, R. D. (2000a). Bowling alone. In R. T. LeGates & F. Stout (Eds.), *The city reader.* New York: Routledge.

Putnam, R. D. (2000b). *Bowling alone: The collapse and revival of American community.* New York: Simon & Schuster.

Putnam, R. D., Leonardi, R., & Nanetti, R. (1993). *Making democracy work: Civic traditions in modern Italy.* Princeton, NJ: Princeton University Press.

Rae, D. (2005). Entrepreneurial learning: A narrative-based conceptual model. *Journal of Small Business and Enterprise Development, 12*(3), 323–335. https://doi.org/10.1108/14626000510612259.

Rasheed, H. (2000). *Developing entrepreneurial potential in youth: The effects of entrepreneurial education and venture creation.* Florida: University of South Florida.

Rasheed, H., & Rasheed, B. (2004). Developing entrepreneurial characteristics in minority youth: The effects of education and enterprise experience. *Ethnic Entrepreneurship: Structure and Process, 4,* 261–277.

Resnick, L. B. (1987). The presidential address: Learning in school and out. *Educational Researcher, 16*(9), 13–54.

Riese, H. (2011). Enacting entrepreneurship education: The interaction of personal and professional interests in mini-enterprises. *Cambridge Journal of Education, 41*(4), 445–460. https://doi.org/10.1080/0305764X.2011.624998.

Schaefer-McDaniel, N. J. (2004). Conceptualising social capital among young people: Towards a new theory. *Children Youth and Environments, 14*(1), 153–172.

Warren, M. E. (2008). The nature and logic of bad social capital. In D. Castiglione, J. W. V. Deth, & G. Wolleg (Eds.), *The handbook of social capital* (pp. 122–149). Oxford: Oxford University Press.

Weller, S. (2006). Skateboarding alone? Making social capital discourse relevant to teenagers' lives. *Journal of Youth Studies, 9*(5), 557–574. https://doi.org/10.1080/13676260600805705.

Wenger, E. (1998). *Communities of practice: Learning, meaning, and identity.* Cambridge, UK: Cambridge University Press.

Wenger, E. (2000). Communities of practice and social learning systems. *Organisation, 7*(2), 225–246.

Wenger, E., MacDermott, R. A., & Snyder, W. M. (2002). *Cultivating communities of practice: A guide to managing knowledge.* Boston: Harvard Business School Press.

Woolcock, M. (1998). Social capital and economic development: Toward a theoretical synthesis and policy framework. *Theory and Society, 27*(2), 151–208. https://doi.org/10.1023/A:1006884930135.

Woolcock, M. (2001). The place of social capital in understanding social and economic outcomes. *Canadian Journal of Policy Research, 2*(1), 11–17.

5

Designing an Entrepreneurial Learning Project

This chapter investigates how the research design influences the learning design for the students. As such, there is no way to discuss the findings without understanding how the project was designed and how the research methodology influenced the creation of the YMI project. I begin with a discussion of the qualitative nature of the research surrounding the YMI project. The chapter then introduces the participants and the research site, followed by a descriptive narrative of the design phases and methods used. I also make explicit ethical considerations and discuss my approach to data analysis, and how the iterative nature of the data analysis influenced my evolving research design. The chapter concludes with an exploration of the issues of research quality—with specific respect to how I ensured my research was trustworthy.

The Qualitative Paradigm

This research aims to the capture of entrepreneurial learning in real-world contexts; thus, the usefulness of a qualitative approach is obvious, as it allows phenomena to be studied in natural settings (Anderson, 1998).

© The Author(s) 2020
K. Kelman, *Entrepreneurial Music Education*,
https://doi.org/10.1007/978-3-030-37129-6_5

Qualitative research also enables a researcher to simultaneously reflect on, and conduct research in a context-dependent environment. In this way, the context of the activities being studied, and the meanings of these activities for participants are given equal importance (Becker, 1998; Bresler & Stake, 2002).

In the 1990s, there was an emergence of participatory and advocacy practices in qualitative educational research, a recognition that research has a role in creating change and bettering the lives of individuals (Denzin & Lincoln, 2003). More recently US governmental involvement in educational research has led to a resurgence of positivist methods, which marginalised the work of critical researchers as idealists at the other end (Lather, 2006). I find Lather's (2006) advice to researchers helpful in that we need to move beyond mere application of technical methods and procedures, and engage in 'paradigm talk as a good thing to think with' (p. 35). Lather also asserts that the goal is to move educational research in many different directions in the hope that more interesting and useful ways of knowing will emerge. My position subscribes to the approach that 'knowing' involves intervening to effect change, and it is from this position that I have chosen a design-based research methodology, which is informed by pragmatic theory.

Design-Based Research

Improving educational practice, designing a learning environment, and building and developing theories in the real world of the music industry were central to this project, and justified a design-based research approach (DBRC, 2003). This evolving approach was conceived by Brown (1992), who describes it as a process of building a methodology that involves the implementation of intervention designs in situ to develop theories of learning and teaching that account for the numerous interactions of people acting in a complex social setting. Design-based research methodology uses iterative cycles of development, implementation and study; this allows the designer to gather more information that might lead to a better design: 'Models of successful innovation can be generated through such work — models, rather than particular artefacts or programs, are the goal' (DBRC, 2003, p. 7).

The purpose of using design-based research methodology for this project was to develop educational principles based on empirical evidence of the way in which students learn music industry skills in a real-world music industry organisation. In this case, the project utilised an integrated framework based on sociocultural theories such as communities of practice and social capital. These theories informed the design of YMI. This design, in turn, encouraged self-directed learning from social interaction with each other and the wider community, and the development of learners who would become professionals (producers, managers, and entrepreneurs) who love what they do, and know how to seek knowledge for themselves.

Research Design

Design-based research uses interventions to provide insight into learning in real-world contexts (Joseph, 2004). There is no one approach, but a series of approaches, with the intent always to produce new theories, artefacts and practices that potentially impact learning and teaching in naturalistic settings. Cobb, Confrey, diSessa, Lehrer, and Schauble (2003) state that:

> design experiments entail both 'engineering' particular forms of learning and systematically studying those forms of learning within the context defined by the means of supporting them. This designed context is subject to test and revision, and the successive iterations that result play a role similar to that of systematic variation in experiment. (p. 9)

For the YMI project, the work of Gravemeijer and Cobb (2006), and Reeves (2000) was most useful. They both provide approaches to design-based research that are pragmatic and acknowledge the theory developed through collaborative processes with researchers, teachers, students, and industry partners. Both approaches also see the methodology as solving real problems, while also constructing design principles

Design-Based Research

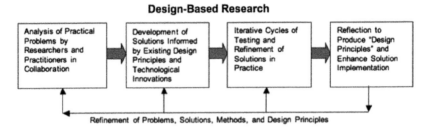

Refinement of Problems, Solutions, Methods, and Design Principles

Fig. 5.1 Development approach to IT research (Reeves, 2000, p. 9)

that can inform future decisions. In their approach, Gravemeijer and Cobb (2006), Reeves (2000) include a preparation phase, a development and implementation of interventions phase, and a reflection phase that leads to the production of design principles.

Reeves (2000) provides a visual representation of the steps to be carried out in design-based research (Fig. 5.1), and these steps were closely followed in this research. These involved a literature review; discussions with my students to gain an understanding of the gaps in the literature in a music education sense; the development of interventions, which were underpinned by communities of practice research, and theories of social capital; the testing of these interventions in real-world situations; retrospective analysis; and the implementation of new interventions to improve the effectiveness of the learning environment.

Participants and Research Site

As discussed in Chapter 2, the research took place in an arts-based selective government school in Queensland, Australia. The site, now in its twelfth year, was chosen because I was the music teacher at this school, and I was responsible for the design and implementation of the music programme. It was not necessary to use deliberate sampling strategies to choose participants for this research, as students were regularly questioning the music curriculum and its link to career pathways in the music industry. The students were dissatisfied with the weight assigned to older classical forms of music in the school curriculum, and they wanted to balance their learning with more modern approaches to music education.

Over time, these student conversations sparked my desire to introduce an intervention. I challenged my students with a newspaper article, where a 16-year-old Brisbane girl discussed the lack of venues and opportunities for young musicians to play their music. I invited my students to provide a solution, not only to this problem, but also to the problems that they themselves faced as musicians in the present who were worried about their future. All my students, from Years 10 to 12, were invited to participate in the conversations and, eventually, a group of nine students emerged as regular participants who became committed to the development and implementation of YMI. At the beginning of year 1, these students were between 15 and 16 years of age and, in most cases, were contemporary musicians who showed a strong interest in a career in the music industry. One of the students dropped out of the formal music curriculum to study Visual Arts, and used YMI as a vehicle for gaining music industry experience, which she felt was more relevant to her future aspirations. Two other members of the YMI team were not studying the formal music curriculum but also saw YMI as a vehicle for applying their artistic skills (visual arts, graphic design, and film) within the music industry. In the first two years, the core team of nine students also engaged many volunteers to work on YMI projects. In year 3, some of these volunteers became peripheral members of the YMI team.

An overview of the core members is provided below. In order to protect the identities of the students in this research, I use pseudonyms.

Ivan

At the commencement of the project, Ivan was 16. He is a passionate singer and aims for a career in the music industry. He would love to be both a performer in musical theatre and to work in event management. He is a confident performer and speaker, and quite often takes the lead in activities. Ivan performs in amateur musical theatre.

He did study classroom music, but was not present during year 3 due to moving interstate. Ivan took on a leadership role in YMI—in strategic direction, in coordinating events, and as the public face of YMI who pitched ideas to the school and to the wider community.

Hayden

At the commencement of the project, Hayden was 16. He migrated to Australia when very young. He is a competent guitarist in the finger-picking style, and enjoys both latin, jazz, and rockabilly music. Hayden writes original music with his rockabilly band and has a charismatic personality on stage. He is very sociable and confident and quite often takes the lead in activities. Hayden studied classroom music and is very much interested in the business side of music. He also took a leadership role in YMI's strategic direction, event coordination, and partnership building. This role increased significantly in year 3 after Ivan left YMI.

Tom

At the commencement of the project, Tom was 17. He is a talented singer-songwriter and works hard to develop his craft, and to acquire gigs and opportunities for himself and his band. He is confident and sociable, and has a strong desire to make connections within the music industry. Tom's main ambition is to be a successful singer-songwriter on the Australian music scene. He studied classroom music and is a talented visual artist. He took on several roles in YMI; in particular, he coordinated artists, and worked on the technical side of events. In year 3, he became more interested in the strategic direction of YMI and event management.

Tristan

At the commencement of the project, Tristan was 16. He is a talented guitarist, and plays and sings in a number of bands. These bands varied from connections he made within his church, and at his previous and current schools. Tristan also writes original music and performs this with his bands. He displays a strong sense of social justice, presents confidently, and has a strong desire to work within the music industry, not only as a performer but also in event management. Tristan studied classroom music and is a talented visual artist. He worked hard behind the scenes, in particular, liaising with and coordinating artists; programming events; and working on the technical, marketing, and promotion sides of events. While not always looking for a leadership role, he was an effective team player, always encouraging others.

Faith

At the commencement of the project, Faith was 16. Faith is a talented contemporary singer but does not desire to be a performer. She is an avid music lover and is extremely knowledgeable on the local and Australian music scene. Her father is a music industry CEO, and this has exposed her to the workings of the industry and, in particular, given her access to many festivals and events. She is a quiet and reserved person and works hard behind the scenes. Faith is passionate about the music industry and the wider creative industries, and is a talented visual artist with an interest in fashion. Faith studied classroom music, though did not always feel confident in her abilities; preparing for performance was nerve-racking for her at times. She worked behind the scenes in YMI and took some time to find her place within the organisation. She eventually realised her strengths were in administration, where she coordinated meetings and dealt with logistical aspects such as merchandise, ticket sales, and food vendors.

Matt

At the commencement of the project, Matt was 16. Matt is a talented guitarist and singer and plays in a number of bands; he particularly enjoys hard rock. He plays gigs and is very proactive in making connections with other musicians. He is also a talented songwriter and composer, and plays his original music with his bands. Matt studied classroom music.

He mostly worked behind the scenes in YMI, coordinating and liaising with artists and working on the technical side of events.

Indigo

At the commencement of the project, Indigo was 16. Indigo sings and plays guitar. She has dabbled in songwriting and has put small 'folk-type' groups together at times for performances; however, she does not see herself as a performer. She dropped out of classroom music at the end of year 1 to concentrate on visual art but was still very involved in the choirs. She saw YMI as a more relevant platform on which to engage with her interests in photography and event management. She is confident and sociable, and worked hard behind the scenes, coordinating the media team and marketing strategies.

Brandon

At the commencement of the project, Brandon was 16. Brandon does not study music and is not a musician. He is an avid music lover and saw YMI as the only platform on which he could utilise his skills in design and film in a music industry context. His contributions to the group included anything to do with online technical set up, including the design of the website. He also made all the promotional videos for YMI and its events, worked behind the scenes in regards to the technical side of events, and played a role in the media team, filming, and photographing. He was very supportive of the YMI team and worked hard behind the scenes. He sees a future for himself within the creative industries.

Chris

At the commencement of the project, Chris was 15. Chris does not study classroom music but has dabbled in music over the years. He does not aspire to be a musician; rather, he wishes to apply his interest in business to the music industry. His role was to monitor the budget, and to draw up the agreements between YMI and other parties, including bands and food vendors. He also saw his contribution to YMI in terms of organisational and strategic development.

The Research Phases

In the following section, I unpack the research phases (learning design) to show the goals of each phase, the interventions implemented, and the research instruments I used to collect data. I also provide descriptions of the events that the students curated, which give context to the scenarios in which the students learning takes place. Following the steps of design-based research according to Reeves (2000), the student events were staged several times with opportunities for reflection and intervention.

Research Phase

In Phase 1, one of my Year 10 music students was successful in achieving a top 5 position in a national online songwriting competition. Hundreds of young musicians across Australia uploaded their original songs to the competition in the hope that the public would vote them into the top ten. The competition website had interactive features that enabled the songwriters to build a fan base, and included blog tools for feedback and dialogue with fans. I was intrigued at the amount of interaction young people were having on the site, and found the feedback from fans and industry professionals was highly constructive. The competition website struck me as a powerful learning environment. It was at this stage that I decided to write an article for the Music Council of Australia's (MCA) quarterly journal, *Music Forum*.

In this article, *Too cool for school* (Kelman, 2010), I explored the potential of creative partnerships and networks for nurturing creativity and learning in both music practice and pedagogy. My students revealed how motivated they were to improve their own practice through being exposed to other young musicians. They also valued the ownership they felt in the online community, and appreciated the feedback they received from their peers. These early conversations with my students provided the impetus to imagine a new kind of learning environment for music education. During this research phase, I conducted a thorough review of the relevant literature and theory. Various concepts would eventually merge to become the Emerging Professional Learning Model. These concepts included

- Engaging students directly with the music industry
- Learning in networks and through partnerships
- Learning based on student-interest and needs
- Opportunities for peer-learning and self-directed learning
- Authentic problems and challenges.

Serendipitously, around the same time, I found the newspaper article (previously mentioned) and used this as a catalyst for starting YMI. Interested students and I met over a series of lunchtimes to brainstorm how we could address the problems outlined in the article.

Phase 1: Music Industry Learning Goals with Teacher Guidance

This group eventually settled into a consistent group of students who formed the idea of starting an organisation that would create opportunities for young musicians to play live concerts, to expand their fan base, and to network with other young musicians. Two months into this phase, the students were ready to pitch their idea to the principal of the school and their classmates. Their original pitch introduces the concept of YMI and the initiatives they hoped to implement.

This phase was informed by Community of Practice theory (Wenger, 1998), in particular, the notion of engaging in CoPs to build bonding social capital (Putnam, 2000; Coleman, 1994). Students worked for many hours a week, building their vision and planning their initiatives. Through this process, their CoP was established.

The students negotiated and designed two key events that became the major outputs of their new venture—*Emerge*, and the *Four Walls Festival* (At the end of this section I provide a detailed description of these events and their progression over the life of this project).

These events were clearly researched and carefully pitched before they were implemented. Throughout these planning meetings, I created the space and time for the students to develop their ideas, while providing them with guidance and advice. I also brokered the working relationship between the students and the principal, and negotiated many of the larger deals with managers of high-profile musicians whom we were booking for our festival.

Throughout this phase, I observed the students working at their events and interacting in face-to-face meetings. I audio-recorded and transcribed these meetings in order to gauge what the students needed, and were learning. These observations largely informed the next phase of YMI, which was directed at giving students more responsibility and space to further refine and build their CoP.

Phase 2: Music Industry Learning Goals with Minimal Teacher Guidance

This phase was informed by Wenger's (1998) concept of *imagining* in CoPs. Imagining is a way of extending CoP learning opportunities through multi-membership and boundary work. I created these new learning opportunities (interventions) through the introduction of new younger members, and by brokering partnerships between the students and professional music industry organisations. I also purposefully handed ownership to the students in this phase, giving them greater responsibility to design and implement their initiatives, to negotiate with the industry, and to manage their finances.

With the addition of grant funding, *Emerge* now became a frequent event, and the *Four Walls Festival* was able to expand and attract bigger headline acts. I encouraged the students to find ways to bring younger members on board, with the idea that new members would not only provide infrastructural support, but would also create new opportunities for learning and innovation.

The experience that the students had gained in Phase 1 provided them with credibility in the eyes of industry peak bodies. QMIA is Queensland's peak body whose mission is to support a healthy music industry. They are also responsible for the largest music industry conference and showcase in the southern hemisphere, *BIGSOUND*.

The students pitched their idea of staging a one-day spin-off to the conference, which they called *Little BIGSOUND*, to provide industry education and networking to young people aged between 14 and 25. They also pitched that this event would be run by YMI, with mentoring and support from QMIA. Opportunities to collaborate with industry professionals were deliberately engineered (intervention) to extend students' learning and expand their networks to build bridging social capital (Putnam, 2000). At the same time, they were enhancing their own community engagement and bonding social capital (A detailed description of *Little BIGSOUND* is also provided at the end of this section).

In this phase, the students also set up a private Facebook meeting group where they would continue their YMI work outside of school hours. My observations in this phase consisted of both face-to-face and online Facebook meetings. I interviewed students individually towards the end of Phase 2, in order to capture their thoughts on what and how they were learning in YMI, and on what they felt needed improvement. Interview data provided insight into the themes that were emerging from the Facebook threads, and informed the interventions for Phase 3 of the design. The data and outcomes of Phase 2 provided the evidence and rigour for another successful award of $30,000, which supported the YMI/QMIA partnership in continuing *Little BIGSOUND* but also initiate collaborative initiatives in regional Queensland.

Phase 3: Music Industry Learning Goals with Teacher as Equal Participant

This phase was informed by Wenger's (1998) concept of aligning in CoPs. In this context, this concept involved taking all that was learned and grounding it in processes that aligned with the broader industry practice. Opportunities to learn through alignment work towards building linking social capital (Woolcock, 2001) by providing access to a wider range of resources and information. The students reflected on the desire to operate like their professional partner organisations, evident in both Facebook interactions, face-to-face meetings and interviews conducted at the end of Phase 2. As intervention for this phase I engaged a creative industries facilitator to work with the students, industry partners and myself in developing a business plan and governance model that would assist in realising their vision for this next 'professional' phase. I audio-recorded and transcribed the entire facilitated workshop, which provided further insight into the students' development.

Emerge, *Four Walls Festival* and *Little BIGSOUND* continued, with the students now operating the events under their new governance model. As part of the successful funding we received in recognition of our industry partnerships, we developed a partnership with the Cairns Regional Council. Together, YMI and QMIA travelled to Cairns to work with young musicians. The event included an *Emerge* night at the prestigious TANKS Arts Centre, with a music industry workshop delivered by YMI students and QMIA staff.

I observed the one-day facilitated workshop and continued to observe the face-to-face and Facebook meetings, transcribing audio recordings and note taking on a regular basis. At the conclusion of Phase 3, I began the task of making sense of the variety of data collected and generated over three years in order to produce the design principles outlined in the final chapter. Table 5.1 presents a visual overview of each of the phases and a succinct description of the interventions that were designed in response to the previous phase.

Detail of Student-Curated Events Over the Life of the Project

Emerge events were 'all ages' shows and provided opportunities for up-and-coming bands from the local area to perform on a professional stage in front of a live audience. YMI offered these events as creative

Table 5.1 Summary of design-based research design phases and interventions used in this study

Phase and Interventions	Aims
Research Phase (Analysis of practical problems)	Address discontent among students in regards to the formal music curriculum
Review of literature related to music education and the music industry	Ascertain students' perceptions of what music education should look like in the present age
	Address the needs of young musicians
Conversations with students	Analyse practical problems and develop solutions
Phase 1: Music industry learning goals with teacher guidance (Solutions, Methods, Reflection)	Engage students in the entrepreneurial process of venture creation, discovery, and exploitation
	Prepare the environment to nurture a CoP
Organisation, strategic planning, implementation of trial events (*Emerge*, *Four Walls Festival*)	Encourage a heuristic approach to project management and event management
Reflection on, and documentation of the design in collaboration with students	Refine the design and solutions for the next phase
Establishment of a theoretical framework based on social capital and social learning theories	
Phase 2: Music industry learning goals with minimal teacher guidance (Solutions, Methods, Reflection)	Enable students with a sense of ownership to encourage community learning and problem-solving
	Develop entrepreneurial behaviour through development of related skills and qualities such as risk-taking, problem-solving, initiative, independence, recognition of the need for achievement, networking, teamwork, communication
Establishment and refinement of key events of the previous year through regular staging of *Emerge*, and larger scale implementation of *Four Walls Festival* (after receiving funding)	
Expansion of YMI by facilitating partnerships between YMI and the music industry with the addition of the youth music conference *Little BIGSOUND*	Develop industry knowledge and skills such as project/event management skills, and marketing and publicity skills
	Enable learning through working with industry professionals
Recruitment of new, younger students to the YMI team	Develop professionalism (reliability, punctuality, communication, and collaboration) and further develop music industry knowledge and skills
Reflection on, and documentation of the design in collaboration with students	Enable CoP multi-membership and boundary-crossing to include industry organisations, thus allowing for exposure to new perspectives and knowledge
	Build networking capabilities and expand networks
	Understand how to leverage networks as resources
	Refine solutions for the next phase

(continued)

Table 5.1 (continued)

Phase and Interventions	Aims
Phase 3: Music industry learning goals with teacher as equal participant (Solutions, Methods, Reflection)	Fulfil the students' desire to clearly identify roles within the group
	Empower students to take ownership of their role and to lead and teach others
Establishment of a structure or governance model and refinement of member roles	Continue to develop entrepreneurial competencies, including music industry knowledge
Continuation of key YMI events (*Emerge, Four Walls* and *Little BIGSOUND*)	Build on the networks they have created through new partnerships
	Build creative capacity and innovation by reinvigorating old forms
Establishment of new partnerships to secure new venues for *Emerge*	Expand networks beyond the Brisbane region by expanding the CoP to encourage new partnerships, new learning and new possibilities for future collaboration
Regional YMI tour to North Queensland for workshops with other young musicians to share 'lessons learned' so they could develop their own youth music scene; tour includes production of *Emerge* at a leading regional entertainment venue	Apply music industry skills learned (project and event management, marketing, publicity, and technical production) in a high stakes environment
	Apply learned entrepreneurial competencies, including risk-taking, networking, communication, opportunity recognition, and the need for achievement
Final analysis of completed data and emergence of design principles	To reflect on processes; to determine research limitations; to recommend avenues of future research
	To establish design principles

and innovative approaches to developing a fan base for the twenty-first century. *Emerge* was staged 5–8 times a year, 16 times in total over the life of this project. The *Emerge* nights were the first events attempted by the YMI team and were held in the school theatre. *Emerge* nights eventually moved into professional venues across Queensland, including the Tanks Arts Centre in Cairns, Kirra Hill on the Gold Coast, and the Edge—a public youth space in Brisbane City.

Emerge provided a training ground for YMI students to learn about event and project management, audience development, programming, and talent searching. When *Emerge* evolved to be staged off the school grounds, the students had the opportunity to work with industry professionals. These events increased in size, complexity, and frequency throughout the life of this project.

The *Four Walls Festival* began in 2010, was planned on a much larger scale than *Emerge* and became an annual event. The festival required the YMI students to manage performances on three school stages over a 10-hour programme; to provide for a capacity audience of 600 people on four floors of the school building; and to coordinate over 100 musicians throughout the day.

YMI's vision for the festival was for young emerging musicians to feature alongside well-known Australian bands. In running the event, YMI students gained experience in all aspects of the music industry: event management and budgeting, marketing and communications, journalism and photography, sound and lighting, programming and research, and networking and negotiating with managers and booking agents. The festival also offered an affordable, alcohol-free event that young people could attend with a large foodcourt featuring DJ entertainment. Each year, this event increased in size of audience, complexity, number of musicians playing, and financial viability.

Programmed by youth for youth, the annual *Little BIGSOUND* conference started in 2011. It was planned as a collaboration between YMI and Queensland's premier music industry organisation, QMIA. The event was a one-day conference for young people aged 14–25 who aspired to a career in the music industry.

Little BIGSOUND was conceived as a youth version of *BIGSOUND*, the Southern Hemisphere's largest music industry gathering. YMI worked with QMIA industry professionals to programme and run the event. YMI students were responsible for every aspect of the day, including researching and contacting speakers from around Australia; marketing; logistics; music showcasing; content programming; catering organisation; and responsibility for the administration of the event, including ticketing, registrations, enquiries, website, and emails. QMIA staff guided students through regular meetings and provided access to a wide network of music industry professionals. Two iterations of this annual event occurred over the life of this project.

Data Analysis

This project created a large data set, which presented a challenge for analysis. Transcript-based analysis is said to be the most rigorous and time-intensive stage of analysing data (Onwuegbuzie, Dickinson, Leech, & Zoran, 2009), and this project confirms this contention. I audio-recorded every interview and meeting over a three-year period, and transcribed these verbatim. I collected 6283 comments in Facebook over a two-year period and imported these directly into an excel spreadsheet. I transcribed interviews and meetings myself as this allowed me to be fully immersed in the data, where I was able to glean emergent insights and themes. This also afforded me the opportunity to obtain a sense of the data set as a whole (Patton, 2002).

Shortly after each interview or meeting was recorded, I transcribed the data and took notes. I conducted preliminary analysis throughout each of the design phases in order to inform interview questions, refine iterations and design interventions. At the end of Phase 3, I read the database as a whole to get a general sense of the information and to reflect on its overall meaning.

Coding is largely an intuitive process, which is informed by the purpose of the research (Merriam, 1998). In this first stage of coding, I asked questions such as 'What is going on here?' to seek out underlying meaning. I highlighted a particular paragraph, sentence or segment and coded it with a short description, sometimes using an actual word or phrase from the text. The coding categories were then constructed through a constant bouncing back and forth across the data, a strategy known as 'constant comparison' (Glaser & Strauss, 1967/2006, p. 102). Using this rigorous process, I was able to decide upon the key categories to address my research questions.

The units of analysis were specifically focused around aspects of students' learning, for example, conflict resolution, negotiation, networking, and specific music industry knowledge such as copyright. It is important to note at this stage, that I designed the interventions in response to what I observed the students' learning and how I could advance that learning along the student to professional continuum.

My objective was not to analyse the events, however as a consequence to the refinement of student learning, the events were improved and expanded on over time.

Researcher Role

In this research I assumed multiple roles—designer, teacher, researcher, and participant. This context created a unique opportunity for observing how design questions, research questions and questions of practice can feed and flow into one another (Brown & Edelson, 2003; Cobb, 2000). This position also afforded me access to observe how the design, as enacted, impacted on learning in YMI. I had already developed a strong rapport and trust with all students involved before the start-up of YMI mainly due to my role as their teacher, but also because I had created the space for many open and honest discussions. As we were all contributing designers and participants in the development of YMI, the power nature of the teacher–student relationship was blurred. This became evident in the data with students feeling comfortable to correct me on various issues, and to make decisions without me.

As previously discussed, I have ensured that students had every opportunity to raise concerns and ask questions. They were also made aware (through an information package and ongoing discussion) that they could withdraw from the research at any time. I placed no pressure on students to participate in interviews given the nature of their academic workload. I was always clear in making it known to the students which role I was in, and students were particularly honest in letting me know when my 'researcher' role was getting in the way of YMI business.

Participant Constraints and Confidentiality

YMI operated outside of the classroom. The school would consider this an extracurricular activity; however, in the eyes of the students, they were operating a music business. Most work-related communication occurred out of school hours, including evenings, weekends, and school holidays. Every effort was made to minimise any negative impact on school life. Key events where possible were timetabled away from exam blocks, and any face-to-face meetings occurred in lunch breaks, after school, and school holidays. The participants were encouraged at all times to be open about what was manageable and what was not, and the flexibility of the design could continuously take this into account.

All participation was entirely voluntary, and all responses were treated in the strictest confidence. All results were presented anonymously with pseudonyms used for the school, participants, and anyone else referred to, for example, participants' friends, musicians, or bands. Ethical research requires an approach that does not simply follow a set of static guidelines. It also displays principles that protect the welfare and rights of participants, facilitates research that will be of benefit to the researcher's community, and informs practice that informs every stage of the research—design, data collection, analysis, and reporting.

Trustworthiness in Qualitative Research

As the researcher, I acknowledge that I am responsible for discovering and interpreting what is observed, and for drawing connections between the observations and the conclusions (Hoepfl, 1997). It is therefore imperative that I have a thorough understanding of the related issues and can demonstrate that the appropriate measures have been taken to ensure that the research is rigorous and ultimately useful.

Given the nature of my various roles within this research project, I acknowledge that I was emotionally and historically invested in YMI. We do not 'control' research, however, as a participant-observer, I did not intend to completely remove myself from the knowledge and experiences that informed me as a person. Rather, it was imperative that I acknowledged the research biases that exist (Miles & Huberman, 1994). Miles and Huberman (1994) also argue that rather than restraining ourselves in the name of objectivity, we should become immersed in the phenomena under observation and should make our personal reactions explicit, rather than trying to manage or restrain them.

In the interests of credibility, Creswell (2013) argues the importance of clarifying any bias that a researcher brings to the research. He suggests that self-reflection creates an open and honest narrative in the form of researchers' comments about how their interpretation of the findings is shaped by their background and investments. He also notes that spending prolonged time in the field is recognised as a way to increase credibility (Creswell, 2013).

On deciding to use YMI as a research site, I resolved that the goal should be to examine what actually occurred, regardless of whether it matched my preconceived ideas of what and how music students should be learning. Thus, the design and its iterations would be informed by my beliefs and values. Then, however, in response to the interventions, it was necessary for me to acknowledge how my personal values and beliefs had changed throughout the process, and how these new beliefs and values would impact on subsequent iterations. In short, I had to allow the research to surprise me.

Dependability, refers to the consistency of results over time and the accurate representation of the population being studied (Lincoln & Guba, 1985). Lincoln and Guba (1985) argue that the very nature of qualitative research acknowledges that situations being studied are unique and constantly evolving. The individuals and environments making up the context can never be identical in any period after the moment in which the data was captured. I have provided reflection boxes (indicated in grey shading) as counter-narratives throughout Chapters 6, 7 and 8 in order to balance out what can easily become a 'celebratory' reporting of learning outcomes. An adherence to these principles establishes the dependability of the investigation.

Chapter Summary

Design-based research has been determined and justified as the appropriate methodology for exploring an authentic and innovative approach to music education that aims to build students' entrepreneurial competency. In this chapter, I considered the important methodological concerns arising in this design-based investigation. It explicitly outlined the research phases, methods and procedures of collecting data, and the data analysis process. Issues of trustworthiness and ethical consideration were explored in order to situate this research as credible and dependable. The design is flexible and theory-driven, and is capable of refining local efforts and making global contributions to the field.

The following three chapters will present the analysis in conversation with the Emerging Professional Learning Model, and the purpose of the research.

References

Anderson, G. (1998). *Fundamentals of educational research* (2nd ed.). London: Falmer.

Becker, H. S. (1998). *Tricks of the trade: How to think about your research while you're doing it*. Chicago, IL: University of Chicago Press.

Bresler, L., & Stake, R. (2002). Qualitative research methodology in music education. In R. Colwell & C. P. Richardson (Eds.), *The new handbook of research on music teaching and learning* (pp. 270–312). New York: Oxford University Press.

Brown, A. (1992). Design experiments: Theoretical and methodological challenges in creating complex interventions in classroom settings. *The Journal of the Learning Sciences, 2*(2), 141–178. https://doi.org/10.1207/s15327809jls0202_2.

Brown, M., & Edelson, D. (2003). *Teaching as design: Can we better understand the ways in which teachers use materials so we can better design materials to support their changes in practice*. Evanston, IL: The Center for Learning Technologies in Urban Schools.

Cobb, P. (2000). Conducting teaching experiments in collaboration with teachers. In A. E. Kelly & R. A. Lesh (Eds.), *Handbook of research design in mathematics and science education*. Mahwah, NJ: Lawrence Erlbaum Associates Inc.

Cobb, P., Confrey, J., diSessa, A., Lehrer, R., & Schauble, L. (2003). Design experiments in educational research. *Educational Researcher, 32*(1), 9–13. https://doi.org/10.2307/3699928.

Coleman, J. (1994). *Foundations of social theory*. Cambridge, MA: Harvard University Press.

Creswell, J. W. (2013). *Research design: Qualitative, quantitative, and mixed method approaches*. Los Angeles, CA: Sage.

DBRC. (2003). Design-based research: An emerging paradigm for educational inquiry. *Educational Researcher, 32*(1), 5–8. https://doi.org/10.2307/3699927.

Denzin, N. K., & Lincoln, Y. S. (2003). *Collecting and interpreting qualitative materials*. Thousand Oaks, CA: Sage.

Glaser, B. G., & Strauss, A. L. (1967). The constant comparative method of qualitative analysis. *The Discovery of Grounded Theory: Strategies for Qualitative Research, 101,* 158.

Gravemeijer, K., & Cobb, P. (2006). Design research from a learning design perspective. In J. V. d. Akker, K. Gravemeijer, S. McKenney, & N. Nieveen (Eds.), *Educational design research* (pp. 17–51). New York: Taylor and Francis.

Hoepfl, M. C. (1997). Choosing qualitative research: A primer for technology education researchers. *Journal of Technology Education, 9*(1), 47–63.

Joseph, D. (2004). The practice of design-based research: Uncovering the interplay between design, research, and the real-world context. *Educational Psychologist, 39*(4), 235–242. https://doi.org/10.1207/s15326985ep3904_5.

Kelman, K. (2010). Too cool for school. *Music Forum: Journal of the Music Council of Australia, 17*(1), 34–36.

Lather, P. (2006). Paradigm proliferation as a good thing to think with: Teaching research in education as a wild profusion. *International Journal of Qualitative Studies in Education, 19*(1), 35–57.

Lincoln, Y. S., & Guba, E. G. (1985). *Naturalistic inquiry*. London: Sage.

Merriam, M. B. (1998). *Qualitative research and case study applications in education*. San Francisco: Jossey-Bass Publishers.

Miles, M. B., & Huberman, A. M. (1994). *An expanded sourcebook: Qualitative*. Thousand Oaks, CA: Sage.

Onwuegbuzie, A. J., Dickinson, W. B., Leech, N. L., & Zoran, A. G. (2009). A qualitative framework for collecting and analyzing data in focus group research. *International Journal of Qualitative Methods, 8*(3), 1–21.

Patton, M. Q. (2002). *Qualitative research and evaluation methods* (3rd ed.). Thousand Oaks, CA: Sage.

Putnam, R. D. (2000). Bowling alone. In R. T. LeGates & F. Stout (Eds.), *The city reader*. New York: Routledge.

Reeves, T. C. (2000). Enhancing the worth of instructional technology research through "design experiments" and other development research strategies. *International Perspectives on Instructional Technology Research for the 21st Century, New Orleans, LA, USA.*

Wenger, E. (1998). *Communities of practice: Learning, meaning, and identity.* Cambridge, UK: Cambridge University Press.

Woolcock, M. (2001). The place of social capital in understanding social and economic outcomes. *Canadian Journal of Policy Research, 2*(1), 11–17.

6

Developing Social Skills for Entrepreneurship in the Music Industry

The following three chapters present the findings of the YMI study. Each chapter investigates a different aspect of entrepreneurialism including, social interaction, project management, and knowledge acquisition. Each of these chapters interrogate three core questions, the following chapter begins with the question, what social skills do students acquire through an education designed to foster entrepreneurial capacity in the music industry, and how did this learning occur? Results from the data will be shown chronologically according to the phases of the research design. However, at times it is necessary to move forwards or backwards to make comparisons between design iterations.

Networking Skills

Skills in networking were essential for the implementation of successful projects and there were various levels of networking that offered benefits to students. First, evidence in the forthcoming data points to strong internal networking, whereby students discovered ways to connect with each other's expertise. When the students assembled as a

© The Author(s) 2020
K. Kelman, *Entrepreneurial Music Education*,
https://doi.org/10.1007/978-3-030-37129-6_6

group, they were developing competence through the competence of others; knowing who was good at what; connecting what they did and did not know; and developing the ability to give and receive help. Second, opportunities for learning and innovation potentially exist at the periphery or boundary beyond the CoP. Entrepreneurial behaviour is evidenced in the data as students recognise and exploit such opportunities in their network building.

Exploring Personal Networks

In Phase 2 of the design, I handed greater responsibility and ownership to the students. Part of my design intervention was to encourage them to start pitching to industry organisations that we had identified as potential partners. The students still considered regular *Emerge* nights and the *Four Walls Festival* (August) as their key events, and *Little BIGSOUND* (September) was conceptualised in dialogue with our new partners, QMIA. In this phase, a more experienced group of students expanded their audience reach, while working alongside industry professionals. It is also important to note that, at this stage, the students had decided to start a YMI Facebook group as a system for managing all communication.

In building on the efforts of Phase 1, the students recognised themselves as a group of 'like-minded' creatives who knew each other's strengths and weaknesses. As a group, all of whom were originally friends, they had developed and benefited from strong internal networking, and had used this to their advantage in establishing the organisation and its activities. In Chris's words: 'I mean it's all about, um, a lot of the group has, well we've benefited off each individual's abilities, they're good at this, and they're good at that' (Interview, September, Phase 2).

Tristan's comments support this idea of leveraging from one's own networks. He explains:

We've got a fair variety of different characters, which is good, because to have a successful team you sort of need to have different areas and thinking. I suppose like, Hayden he's a, well he thinks about things a lot and sort of dwells on them, which is good, because he comes up with other thoughts that might be we should think about as well, and then I suppose someone like me who's creative in thinking of ways to combat that, so like if Hayden thinks there's 'this problem' than I can suggest ways to fix it like that and so like there's that sort of thing going on. (Tristan, Interview, September, Phase 2)

In these two excerpts, both Chris and Tristan identify that the strengths of the team lie in the diversity of thinking and expertise of its members. Chris sees value in working within this type of environment, as he is acquiring skills from his peers. This attitude is reflected in Coleman's theory of social capital, which appreciates the value of strongly bonded networks for the acquisition of learning and skills as a form of cultural capital. Recognising the expertise and diversity that exists within the group became a skill in itself, enabling students to solve problems related to their projects that might not have been solved by one person alone.

Other students also used the expression 'like-minded' (in terms of similar goals and common purpose), recognising that strong internal networking does not only benefit the organisation, but has far-reaching benefits for keeping each other motivated and inspired to reach their potential. For example, Ivan explained: 'It's about like-minded people, um striving for the same thing that I want to do…you can ride off other people's enthusiasm and you won't lose hope' (Interview, Phase 2). Rather than simply considering the network as a means of acquiring new knowledge, he also considers it a motivating force. Over time, through their interactions, students also develop a collective understanding and shared purpose. In other words, they are developing their joint enterprise, which provides the energy of the community (Fig. 6.1).

> *While mutual engagement and strong internal networking helped the students identify a range of expertise and skills amongst the group, along with a general shared desire to be successful, it was inevitable that there would also be a range of levels of commitment. Sometimes students volunteered to take on specific jobs but wouldn't commit to timelines. For example, an event couldn't be advertised and finalised until a poster had been finished or line-up of bands confirmed, and I would sometimes have to intervene and chase up this information. Sometimes this also involved competing for the student's attention with another teacher leading a different activity. These situations took time, and I learned how important it was to plan the calendar of events well in advance.*

Fig. 6.1 Reflection Box 1: timetables and time management

Designing Opportunities to Broaden Networking Capacity

Throughout Phase 2, it became apparent that the students were starting to think more about the potential opportunities that could be accessed and exploited through external networks. In the following example Facebook excerpt, Hayden suggests that the YMI team contact students from their old schools directly, to assist with publicity.

Hayden	EVERYONE
	Write down names of people that you know from other high schools and the school that they attend if you think they will be able to speak at their assembly by Wednesday
Tristan	Elise – [School A] Arts Captain
	Dane – [School B] Arts Captain
Scott	I can check at [School C] if you want?
Christine	Wait, speak about what?
Hayden	Yes, check all your contacts, and send them to me in an email about Little BIGSOUND
Chris	why don't you to the school websites and contact them directly?
Scott	True
Tristan	They don't respond.
Scott	Truer
Hayden	No Chris, we are getting students to speak at their assembly's
	Teachers don't reply
Indigo	Sharnie – school captain? [School D]

This interaction illustrates the students discussing the validity and practicality of the suggestions put forward through a process of negotiation. These are crucial skills in project management. Part of the design of Phase 2 was to encourage the students to make connections with new communities in order to apply their learning in more contexts, and to develop the ability to work collaboratively with different people.

In Phase 3, *Little BIGSOUND* was much more successful in attracting students from many schools across South East Queensland. They realised that the issue was not the lack of teacher interest, but the nature of schools and teachers' busy and hectic lives. In phase 3, the students asked me, given my own experience as a busy teacher, why I might not engage my students with the conference. I explained that it involved a lot of extra work. In response, they then considered ways in which we could make it easier for teachers to engage with the project. We worked together to create excursion templates and risk assessment documents that teachers could use. These strategies were effective in mobilising schools, and the students expanded their knowledge of marketing to different audiences.

The creation of these artefacts/resources was also evidence that this CoP was aligning with the requirements of the broader system. This was important to my design, as entrepreneurs require industry 'know-what', in this case, the ability to know how other systems work, and to align local activities with other processes. While 'imagining' is a CoP's way of

> YMI students spent many hours phoning schools to follow up on the Little BIGSOUND marketing material that had been emailed and sent out in the post. Given the inexperience and immaturity of the YMI students, they were not always able to respond to any difficult questions that teachers might have had. It was understandable that many teachers were reluctant to 'buy in' to the concept when it was being sold by young people. The situation improved after three iterations, as by then the brand had developed a track record and a credible reputation. Again, there were many instances where I had to respond to teachers on behalf of students, which was time consuming.

Fig. 6.2 Reflection Box 2: students meet teachers

travelling outside its boundaries, 'alignment' grounds this imagining in order to make its work effective beyond its zone of engagement. Having learned from their first *Little BIGSOUND* conference in Phase 2, the students were more strategic in the way that they created networks with a wider community of schools and teachers, and opened up new entrepreneurial opportunities to reach more young people (Fig. 6.2).

Building Useful Youth Networks

Throughout Phase 2 and Phase 3, the students increasingly built and expanded their youth networks. The bands that played at *Emerge* and *Four Walls Festival* were provided with the opportunity to build not only their fan base but also their friendships and networks with other young musicians. These networks became significant support structures within which bands were able to share their fans, their knowledge, and their ideas. In some cases, these networks lead to the formation of new bands. For the YMI team, such networking was a major goal that had been achieved. Their recognition of the benefits of their audience development and network growth are evident in the following extract from a YMI Four Walls Festival debrief session in Phase 2.

Tristan	Yes, I do think we support musicians by running live events, but I think our main goal like, is to support the bands, and if that's getting gigs elsewhere, and recording their stuff and all that sort of thing, we've done our job.
Kristina	do you reckon that's happened yet?
Tristan	we've definitely set up networks
Matt	[Band C], [Band D], [Band E], they've been doing gigs with each other for weeks now and they're all good mates now, and they're like, 'hey guys do you want to play with us next weekend'?

The networks that were shared by YMI and the bands they engaged opened up new possibilities for creative projects and audience exposure. In the following interview excerpt, Tristan recognises the importance of networking in building support structures for young musicians. He recounts:

However, it was never about the events at the start, it was about giving the younger musicians opportunities, and through these events we saw long term relationships develop with YMI and several artists, where we mutually supported each other. It was this idea of all youth musicians buying into the idea that excited us initially and was what gave us satisfaction as we saw it come to fruition. (Tristan, Interview, Phase 3)

These new networks did not simply see themselves as bands or audience members, but rather as part of the organisation, having a sense of pride and ownership of this youth initiative. Many young people from outside of the school volunteered at YMI gigs, giving up time to take photographs, lend equipment, share their ideas, and actively promote YMI activities via social media. This kind of external support enabled the YMI students to stage their events successfully as Indigo explained: 'Yeah there's a definite network and just people who come to all of our events, sort of, not a cult following, but we definitely have a following of people who really support us which is great' (Indigo, Interview, Phase 2). In a sense, the YMI community was successfully overlapping with other youth communities, thus enabling a culture of sharing and support for everyone involved.

On a more ambitious scale, the YMI team considered ways of leveraging their youth networks to connect with executive managers in the music industry, in order to acquire well-known Australian bands to headline acts at the *Four Walls Festival* (Phase 2). Brandon announces in the following Facebook interaction that he might have had a contact for a band that they had been discussing.

Brandon	Btw guys, my friend knows the [Band F] enough to get there number, so if you want, I'll ask her for it!
Hayden	We do, ask please!
Brandon	Aight

Three days later, Brandon posted on Facebook the results of his connection.

Brandon	dont you guys just love me? the phone number of [Band F] manager – Simon Mann – 0xxx xxx xxx these guys would bring such a huge crowd it would be worth it!

> *There were always risks involved in a growing youth network, especially when YMI engaged students from other schools to help out at their events. The principal was quite often nervous due to not knowing who and how many people were likely to attend the events. The events were not restricted to an under 18 audience, but there were clear entry conditions on arrival in regards to no alcohol on the premises. Even though we hired a security guard for each event, the principal still felt that he needed to attend the events (even if not for the entire evening) to safeguard the school property and his own students.*

Fig. 6.3 Reflection Box 3: real world meets school world

This lead did prove successful, with that particular act headlining the Phase 2 *Four Walls Festival* at a reduced 'youth'-friendly rate, negotiated successfully by the YMI students. This manager also proved a valuable contact as he managed other major headline acts that the students were able to book for the Phase 3 festival (Fig. 6.3).

Exploiting Opportunities Through Networking

While there was evidence that students recognised potential opportunities by networking with industry professionals, these 'discovered' opportunities were seldom exploited. In Phase 3, students recognised more and more external opportunities again, however, these opportunities were not always pursued. The students happily worked with these professionals and learned valuable skills. They were also able to expand their networks through the connections of their new partners. However, opportunities to use these partners for taking YMI in new directions were not a group priority at this stage. In a sense, the students had reflected on what the group could achieve based on their individual commitments, were realistic about what was doable, and prioritised. Ivan explains:

> So, I guess, we have the opportunity to really reach out to a lot of different people, I just don't think we've taken that step further. Strengths are we create a lot of opportunities, and our partners create a lot of

opportunities for us, whether we take full advantage of those is one thing. I think that is really, well, it's difficult cause we're at school, and being at school you have other milestones as well, so I guess, it's the same with my general life, it's a very narrow view I can only see specific things, it's not very regularly that I step back and look at the big picture…we're not ever really thinking big big picture. (Ivan, Interview, Phase 2)

CoP theory includes the idea that in order to keep the community's learning and momentum going, a group needs to connect with 'risky places' at the periphery to foster new interests, and build new repertoire. However, the risks of 'burn-out' and having too many projects on the go would ultimately affect the quality of the work they could achieve. Like any business, the students were constrained by their resources and, in particular, their lack of time. This is an example of these students developing a sense of entrepreneurial 'know-when': the ability to know when to exploit an opportunity, to know when the time is right for both the market and the organisation.

Bonding capital, which results from strong ties, makes it more likely for people to share their resources due to the trust built through frequent interactions. Bridging capital, or weaker ties, can open up novel opportunities. However, as was shown in the previous data excerpt, weaker ties require resources to cultivate them, and the students acknowledged that assembling these resources could be difficult. Both types of capital have their strengths and weaknesses for entrepreneurialism; however, the idea that bridging capital could further expand their enterprise continued to play a major role in my design (Fig. 6.4).

> *It was difficult to not get disappointed when the students did not embrace an opportunity that I had worked hard to facilitate. However, they made decisions that were sensible at the time, choosing to do events that they knew they could manage and do well. During Phase 2, I received a phone call from Hayden's father, who expressed concern over his son's YMI workload and stress levels. Again, this served as another important reminder that these students were still just adolescents, all trying to balance YMI with their academic studies, social lives and other interests.*

Fig. 6.4 Reflection Box 4: school workload versus real world workload

The Risks of Networking and Entrepreneurialism

Further evidence suggests that students were reluctant to build their bridging capital for fear of losing ownership over their work and intellectual property. Data excerpts show that some of the students expressed negative perceptions of working with their adult partners. In the Phase 2 Facebook interaction below, the students discuss a partnership brokered between YMI and the Queensland Music Festival (QMF).

Ivan	QMF GUIDE...wait for it (photo of Ivan with the Queensland Music Festival guide open at the Emerge advertisement)
Ivan	YEAH!!!
Indigo	:)fuckyeah.
Hayden	Ahaha YEAH!
Indigo	Nice face btw;)
Ivan	thanks
Faith	Haha so enthused Ivan:)
Tristan	INDIGO! That's the article which has "PRESENTED BY QUEENSLAND MUSIC FESTIVAL WITH THE HELP OF YOUTH MUSIC INDUSTRIES AND [the school]" or something like htat! [that] hahah
Indigo	BITCHES! ALL THEY DID WAS PUT AN ADD IN A MAGAZINE :(

In this excerpt Indigo and Tristan respond negatively. They take offence at the idea that their product and originality have not been acknowledged properly in this very public document. Others in the team, however, viewed the inclusion on the festival programme as an opportunity to expand their identity and enterprise, and to develop new repertoire (in this case, a state-wide document). Interestingly, students chose not to dispute this further, and it was not mentioned in any further Facebook posts.

In early Phase 2, YMI decided that they wanted to create a youth music industry conference to build on the 'education' component of their vision for YMI. The students pitched their idea to QMIA and it was agreed that the conference would go ahead, and that the students would work closely with QMIA to deliver this new event—*Little BIGSOUND* (Phase 2). Meetings occurred at both the QMIA office and the high school.

QMIA viewed their relationship with the students as being on the periphery of the QMIA community, the students were positioned as 'legitimate peripheral participants'. While the students had been granted legitimacy and given more responsibility than students their age would normally be given, there was a clear resistance from the students to being repositioned in this way.

One potential problem of a design built on bonding capital that gives such ownership to students is that they develop a 'big fish' mentality; that is, an over-inflated sense of self-importance, creating issues for developing bridging capital and new learning. For example, while the students did their jobs, the QMIA experience left a negative aftertaste for some. Their reluctance to make wider connections with industry 'adults', might have been due to the perception that they are thought of as 'kids' or apprentices, rather than as the experts they identified as within their own community. Indigo reflects thus on the group's relationship with the QMIA project manager:

> I think we definitely surpassed her expectations, which was good, but yeah, I don't know, I think there's a lot of attitude towards her because it almost feels like QMIA are slightly leeching off us a bit, which is true, but that's just what happens, but there is a lot of feelings about that within the group.
>
> I think she does treat a lot of us like we are kids, which I guess is a new feeling because we don't usually feel like that. (Indigo, Interview, Phase 2)

Again, Indigo refers to 'leeching' but, interestingly, acknowledges that this is 'normal'. In this situation, Indigo is learning about the nature of the music industry and is essentially managing risk for YMI, and demonstrating entrepreneurial 'know-when' and 'know-who' competency.

The YMI project gave the students a great deal of ownership and the experience to do 'adult' or authentic industry work, which was very motivating for them. In the QMIA community, however, they were apprentices and did not have complete creative control. This experience had great value for their learning as they began to explore the concept of aligning their practice with other processes. 'Alignment' in communities

> Given the success of YMI in terms of growing audiences, expansion of events and successful applications for funding, the students by the end of Phase 2 were outgrowing school rules, leading to clashes at times with the principal and industry partners. For example, the principal had enforced a 'no pass-out' rule for YMI events, which meant that once an audience member had entered the premises, they were not allowed to leave and come back. The YMI students argued the point with the principal, but eventually these rules and conditions became accepted as part of the YMI repertoire. While the principal enjoyed and created space for such negotiations with the students, I on the other hand, received sturdy instructions and would have to enforce these on the group without the luxury of negotiations.
>
> Managing the partnerships with industry proved to be hard work at times. A lot of work happened behind the scenes to ensure that students were safe and that industry partners were happy. The school timetable and holiday periods did not align with the workplace making it difficult to coordinate meetings. Our partners' expectations were also complex to manage at times. For example, my students tended to go quiet during the lead up to exams or school holidays. Unfortunately, when the students didn't respond to emails or meet deadlines, the industry partners would contact me. I would then have to chase students or do the job myself.

Fig. 6.5 Reflection Box 5: school culture versus industry culture

of practice theory, as earlier discussed, articulates with the concept of 'linking' capital, whereby the students learned to work across different contexts and, in this case, to align with others in positions of influence or authority (Fig. 6.5).

Understanding the Value of Networking

While the partnerships with industry remained solely around specific events, the students used the networks to accrue cultural capital for themselves. In the interview data, some of the students reported that they felt they were learning from these connections and that they would personally benefit. Tom explained: 'and working with the industry like QMIA – just knowing that I have that support now' (Interview, Phase 2). In an interview conducted one year (Phase 3) after YMI participation, Tristan reflected more broadly on the power of his learning about networking:

Networking can never be overstated at how important it is in the music industry, and meeting various professionals, emerging artists, and amateurs allowed for a broader understanding of the industry and a collective support that is still felt 3-4 years later...Although the professionals inspired - from artists such as [Artist 1], to managers such as [Manager 1] - the real connections were made with like-minded peers who were all understanding the exact need that YMI relentlessly saw to fulfil. These connections became tangible ways to support youth music in Brisbane and to be encouraged and motivated to pursue the art. (Tristan, Interview, Phase 3)

In YMI, the students accessed what they needed, using and developing the skills of networking to do so. In so doing, they walked away from the learning situation with skills and knowledge. While they did not focus on building strong industry relationships at that time, in a sense, they benefited from what Indigo had referred to in both a Facebook post and an interview as 'leeching'.

In the reflection above, Tristan comes back to the importance of networking with like-minded peers. YMI students developed strong bonding capital by connecting in such networks. However, the 'like-minded' peer network had structural holes or gaps in knowledge, which limited their access to resources, expertise and opportunities; in this case, performance opportunities and access to industry professionals. The benefit of bridging into the professional music industry networks, as Tristan discussed, was that students gained a greater understanding of the broader industry. The professionals provided a source of inspiration and energy, which YMI could use in their enterprise. This is a clear example of the process of 'imagining' in communities of practice; that is, being able to learn outside of one's immediate community and then bring back new knowledge, skills and perspectives, to enrich the enterprise and repertoire.

Summary: Networking Skills

In Phase 1 of the design, students began to grow their small business, and practised standard entrepreneurial strategy in this context by mobilising their personal networks. They formed much of the initial event audiences, and were useful in marketing YMI's events through word of mouth.

The diversity of expertise in the membership was a driving force behind the group, as were the tensions created by differing perspectives, which kept the community energy alive and moving forward. While the diversity of skills and perspectives was beneficial for the group's formation, 'like-mindedness' was a quality that the students felt brought them together around a common purpose and helped them to create the norms of the community.

Strong bonding capital was clearly developed throughout Phase 1 and, in particular, Phase 2. These strong ties allowed the group to create high aspirations, premised on norms of trust and reciprocity. The strengths in bonding capital could be seen in the skills that students acquired and the level of competence they developed.

In Phase 2 and Phase 3, I tailored my design to enable and encourage the students to work more collaboratively with music industry communities. There was some reluctance to build more substantial relationships with the industry partners. The rewards of bonding capital possibly inhibited more entrepreneurial risk-taking networking. First, they did not consider that they had the resources to exploit the opportunities to develop bridging capital. Second, they had become experts at the centre of their community, and moving to the periphery of another community could lead to a possible loss of identity and creative control. Third, there was a real risk of losing their intellectual property, of someone else taking their ideas and the credit for their work. While these concerns were real for the students, the limitations of bonding capital slowed down access to potential learning and innovations that can arise when people from different backgrounds come together.

However, there was evidence to show they were accruing their own cultural capital through these industry connections. This, in turn, provided further resources for the YMI community, and strengthened their bonding capital. These resources in the final phase became useful in helping the students to better engage with the industry, and allowed them to access further opportunities and resources through bridging capital.

Alignment in communities of practice refers to the bridging capital or exchange that occurs at the boundaries of the community. I wanted the students to work across different contexts, and they did demonstrate

Table 6.1 Learning about networking across the three phases

Phase	Networking skills
Phase 1 (Student phase)	Mobilising personal networks in the start-up phase
	Sourcing audience and musicians through school and personal networks
	Homogenous, strong internal networking (exploring each other's strengths, skills, and experience)
Phase 2 (Student to professional phase)	Expanding the youth network, sharing knowledge, and personal networks
	Homogenous networking
	Bonding capital possibly inhibiting entrepreneurial risk-taking behaviour
	Exploring bridging capital through industry connections
Phase 3 (Professional phase)	Bridging capital (recognising the learning and innovation that happens at the periphery of the community)
	Linking capital (being able to work collaboratively with stakeholders and benefit from those relationships)

an understanding of working together with schools and teachers by the time they got to *Little BIGSOUND 2* in Phase 3. They developed documents and strategies more suited to marketing to schools, as opposed to the focus on social media that they were using to target youth. Alignment, which is also associated with linking capital, is not always about compliance; rather, it is about developing resources to negotiate with the broader system. Table 6.1 provides a summary of the students' development of networking skills across the three phases of the design.

Interpersonal Skills

It became apparent that the students, throughout their time in YMI, consciously worked on improving their interpersonal skills. These skills included conflict resolution, improving productivity through clear communication and regular meetings. This section now addresses emerging themes from the data that provide evidence of learning about the importance of internal communication, open and honest dialogue, clear communication channels with stakeholders and audience, and an awareness of work–life balance.

Communication Styles

In Phase 2, the students decided that they should change the name of one of their stages at the *Four Walls Festival*. I had named the stage the *Jazz Café* in Phase 1, as I had more creative control at that point. When the YMI team took over the programming and booking of bands in Phase 2, they established that this particular stage was not solely focused on jazz, thus rendering the name inappropriate. Hayden used the Facebook meeting group to open up a forum for discussing three possible new names. There were over 250 posts for this one topic, and the discussion became heated. There were members who identified that the discussion was becoming confrontational and used humour to try and diffuse the atmosphere. Hayden, however, found the jokes to be unproductive and disrespectful, and made several remarks that everybody should be taking things more seriously: 'How about stop putting stupid comments and actually say something productive' (Facebook Excerpt, Phase 2). The Four Walls debrief meeting, (excerpt below) shows how the students reflected on this particular episode.

Hayden	It's more you just want to get things done, and other people do it, and you just get frustrated, it's not really a personal thing.
Tristan	Well, like the name of the basement, it all got a bit too serious. Like we had this argument about what we should call the jazz café, and like if we didn't joke around, it wouldn't have been as light-hearted it would have been aggressive, so yeah, people were arguing about what we should call it. But people are fine with it.
Faith	Do you think some people went a bit overboard? (everyone agrees)
Kristina	No grudges? (everyone agrees)
Hayden	Because we talk it out.

The students thus acknowledge that the light-hearted approach had saved the interaction from becoming overly aggressive. This style of interaction reflected the ethos of this community of practice, and created the conditions for building its social capital. Students were aware that grudges and unresolved conflict could seriously diminish the hard work that they had already undertaken.

In the excerpt above, Hayden makes reference to 'talking things out'. His report indicates that he valued open, honest communication, when dealing with internal conflicts:

> I just confront them, that's what I've learned, I mean that's what we do in my house, (speaking quietly and cautiously) that's our culture I guess, I just kind of confront them, not confront them, just talk to them about what the issue is, yeah, and a lot of people get annoyed with me for doing that, if I had an issue with somebody, the other YMI members would just tell me to leave it, because that's what they'd do. (Hayden, Interview, Phase 2)

In the context of YMI, these teenagers were still developing the skills needed to work through an issue. The learning environment enabled its members to be exposed to different communication models, and provided a trusting space to practise some of these skills.

Miscommunication

Phase 2 revealed miscommunication to be a weakness of the group. In a Phase 2 meeting, Hayden stated that: 'I think that at the moment there are too many ways of communication and we are not communicating efficiently'. Tristan attributed this to previously discussed issues around not having clear roles and jobs: 'It's just sorting out how we sort ourselves out, communication is always going to be a problem' (Interview, Phase 2). Chris highlighted that confusion occurred when the communication channels were not clear: 'Someone gets the wrong idea or a message doesn't get to someone, but we're working to improve it' (Interview, Phase 2). Miscommunication and confusion was later attributed to the lack of clear roles and job descriptions, which, in Phase 2, saw 'everybody doing everything'. In the following interview excerpt, Tom connects these communication issues with the implications for working with industry:

Weaknesses, definitely communication so far. Um it's hard, we've tried different approaches, like trying to get things to go through one person and that doesn't really work and sometimes it's like, well with Kevin [contracted for poster designs] for example – you know we've got Hayden talking to Kevin, and Ivan talking to Kevin, and people get mixed messages and that's in general, you know if someone is in charge of a band, and you got three different people talking to that band, they're going to think, this is kind of weird. I think, yeah, there's definitely communication issues. (Tom, Interview, Phase2)

Tom identifies how there are too many people involved in communicating with various stakeholders. He notes how this becomes confusing, and how it risks making the organisation look disorganised and unprofessional. This would ultimately affect their ability to build bridging capital and trusting relationships with industry. The benefits afforded to students in Phase 2 were that they were able to identify these issues through learning on the job, and to then refine and apply changes in Phase 3.

In the Phase 3 Facebook excerpt below, the students reinforce their new, clearly defined roles in order to improve their communication:

Brandon	So 17 days till Emerge…was thinking if we can start discussing the bands we want to play and then forward them to Tristan to start contacting them. I personally do think it would be okay to also approach bands :) So yeah? any ideas? discuss discuss discuss
Hayden	We spoke about this in the meeting. Only Tristan contacts bands. Or else it gets too confusing. If you have a band in mind tell Tristan. Don't approach them :)
Brandon	Thats what I said….I said we can discuss bands and then forward them to Tristan
Hayden	Ah okay. Well then, my bad. Tristan should be onto it already though

This interaction shows the temptation for the students to slip back into their previous mode while they are still refining their new professional enterprise and developing their repertoire. These new roles improved communication channels greatly and contributed to their efficiency and professionalism.

Internal Communication

The group was able to recognise how miscommunication could be detrimental to building bridging capital. However, it was recognised early on that internal communication was even more important for the group in building bonding capital and being successful.

At the end of Phase 1, for example, Ivan identified an issue related to internal communication, after certain YMI members chose not to stay after school to continue the set up for their first *Four Walls Festival*. This meant that a huge workload was imposed on a few students, who then had to negotiate a later pick up time with their parents. Ivan explained to the other members that: 'Not communicating that you aren't going to be in attendance lets the team down' (*Four Walls* Debrief, Phase 1). These became rules of engagement in YMI, and the norms of being a part of the YMI community—the building blocks of a team approach. This basic premise was not raised as an issue again, and internal communication improved significantly as seen in the Facebook interaction in Phase 2):

Tristan	Thanks so much to everyones effort last night!
	We pulled off another great EMERGE.
	We missed Brandon and Patricia who were sick (get well soon),
	but had the help of the [Band L] boys, so that was sweet.
	If anyone has details (i.e how much we raised) or photos from the night feel free to post it!
Hayden	hey man, how did the packing up go? any major sound issues?
Tristan	No sound issues at all, all bands were fantastic, packing up was cruisey! Hope you had fun at the 18th!

This excerpt shows that internal communication, such as advance notice of absence, allowed for solutions to be put in place to ensure smooth running of the event. Students also became proficient at communicating other issues that they felt might affect core business, such as notifying members of not having internet access, or not being available. These internal communication skills became a major strength of the YMI team as they moved from Phase 1 to Phase 2. Throughout Phase 3, it was embedded as part of their community repertoire.

Virtual Communication

The Facebook meeting group was established at the beginning of Phase 2 in response to the difficulty of finding time for face-to-face meetings at school. There were positive and negative outcomes resulting from the move to Facebook meetings. Indigo felt that it was a much more reliable and convenient method of communication:

> Everybody always replies, like if you text someone half the time they don't reply but if it's on Facebook, like I've deleted my Facebook now which I'm going to have to get back in order to communicate with people, but it's just so much easier than ringing someone, because everybody can participate in it, and you can have private conversations between two people as well. (Indigo, Interview, Phase 2)

Facebook became part of the way that the YMI members developed mutual engagement. These interactions also became their repertoire or tool for reflection. Hayden highlighted the convenience of the online group, and how useful it was in creating energy and momentum: 'It's just there to make everything quicker, to make decisions quicker, people get really proactive on Facebook, because that's really the only place where people discuss and communicate' (Interview, Phase 2). There was a substantial increase in momentum in Phase 2, with the implementation of the online group allowing for after school hours access. In addition, the students were comfortable in this mode, as Chris explained: 'It's our generation, how we've grown up, it's like we get a lot further as everyone is on the internet, and it's such a huge way to advertise and market something, hence why we are so efficient online' (Interview, Phase 2). However, for some students, this mode of communication became too demanding. Hayden explains:

> While it's fast, um I personally don't like it, just because I want to get off Facebook but I can't because of this, it's like I'm bound to Facebook. The only reason I check Facebook is to get onto this and I just don't think it gives you a break, like I'll be watching a movie, and somebody would be calling me, 'hey check your Facebook things are getting crazy' and I'll just have to go and do it cause it's always happening and I can't have a break,

and that's why I got really stressed out, cause it was always happening, twenty four seven. I'm thinking about it and there was just no way to get away from it. (Hayden, Interview, Phase 2)

This observation captures the intensity of student involvement during Phase 2, and their high expectations of connectivity, commitment and workload. While Hayden recognised that this level of intensity was a concern, by Phase 2, these norms and rules of engagement were well established. It was evident that, by Phase 3, these new professionals had become more organised, enabling them to create some distance between their own lives and the Facebook group. While they might not have interacted as much online, and their interactions were less intense, they were more productive and efficient.

Brandon	Tom - sorry to bug but when am I getting the doc? because I'm leaving the house in 2 hrs and I wanna click render before I leave and I wont be home till 5am
Brandon	LOLLL JUST GOT THE EMAIL
Tom	HAHAHAH AND I JUST POSTED A STATUS
Tom	freeeaaakkky
Tom	where da freak are you going?
Hayden	Brandon going clubbing??
Brandon	I am going to park road (la dolce vita) to watch Italy vs Croatia with few friends :)

In this Phase 3 Facebook excerpt, the students had moved from the Phase 2 high-energy, time-consuming environment where they were doing most things for the first time, to an environment that recognised work–life balance. As their new professional enterprise developed in Phase 3, this gave way to a new repertoire and new ways of engaging.

Summary: Interpersonal Skills

Throughout the project, the students developed their interpersonal skills within the overall category of project management. In particular, the students developed internal communication within their CoP, developed a culture of open and honest communication, improved communication channels with stakeholders and their audience, and developed an awareness of work–life balance.

Phase 1 was an 'establishing' phase, where the students came together to develop a shared enterprise and negotiate a vision. Internal communication issues were evident during this phase, as agreed communication processes and expectations had not yet become part of their repertoire. For example, they developed risk management strategies, which considered what they could physically manage, given the constraints of time and resources.

In Phase 2, the students were afforded greater autonomy. They established a culture of open and honest communication within a safe and constructive environment. Students undertook their positions in YMI with great responsibility, leading to better internal communication. As the students built trust over time and established strong bonding capital, they also developed the skills to confront and manage conflict within the group. They acknowledged that 'talking things out' prevented defensive behaviour.

The addition of Facebook as a meeting tool in Phase 2 presented a major step forward for the organisation. While Facebook enhanced communication, it also consumed an unreasonable amount of their time. Phase 3 was easier because students were refining their interpersonal skills. While Facebook was still their main form of communication, the threads were more succinct and thoughtful, demonstrating a better awareness of work–life balance.

The innovations created during Phase 2, together with the frequency of events, produced several episodes of miscommunication. Problems arose when YMI's audience, stakeholders and partners received conflicting information from the students. As they moved into Phase 3 with a new governance model and the allocation of specific roles, they were able to build bridging capital through reliable communication of information reflecting their new professional enterprise. Table 6.2 offers an overview of the learning of interpersonal skills across the three phases.

Table 6.2 Learning about interpersonal skills across the three phases

Design phase	Interpersonal skills
Phase 1 Learning and designing (Student phase)	• Communication processes within the group are not clearly established • All communication happens at school in person • Bonding capital developing
Phase 2 Learning skills (Student to professional phase)	• Open communication is established within the group to ensure adequate notification • Facebook group established and communication increases • Some negative effects of Facebook • Variety of communication styles helps to manage conflict • Open and honest communication acknowledged as best practice
Phase 3 Applying skills (Professional phase)	• Specified roles lead to better communication • Recognition of work–life balance • Succinct communication on Facebook

Chapter Summary

The findings of this chapter demonstrate that the design enabled the students to develop both bonding and bridging social capital, leading to opportunities for exploring linking social capital. By design, the YMI community moved through various contextual phases, beginning with a teacher-guided Phase 1, through to a more experimental Phase 2 with minimal teacher-guidance. The project concluded in Phase 3 with the students refining their learning in a more professional context with the teacher as an equal participant. The findings highlight the positive and negative impacts that social capital and social interaction had on the students' skill development.

During Phase 1, it was important that the students were offered legitimate opportunities to develop and implement their internal social norms of trust and reciprocity. Through mutual engagement, they were able to understand each other's strengths and weaknesses and discover the expertise that each individual possessed. Throughout this phase, the students realised the value of diversity within their network, including differing perspectives and opinions, which assisted them in solving problems and resolving conflict. Bonding social capital developed as the result of the strong ties that held the YMI community together. The benefits of bonding capital can be observed in the trust and reciprocity that YMI established, and in their strong sense of purpose.

Phase 2 introduced a more experimental approach and the students were given autonomy to develop and run YMI with latitude for learning from mistakes. The bonding capital was very strong in this phase, which helped them identify and develop their interpersonal skills. However, this bonding capital created substantial pressure for some students. This pressure occurred because the Facebook meeting group was active during and after school hours, leaving students unable to switch off and disconnect from the project. As a result, the after-hours nature of the project generated implications for the well-being of the students, in particular, for balancing schoolwork and a social life with YMI commitments.

This second phase provided the students with an opportunity to develop bridging capital through partnerships and interactions with music industry professionals. It was my intention that bridging capital would enable them to access further entrepreneurial opportunities. However, having built strong internal cohesion, the students were reluctant to invest time into building industry networks. They worked with the industry partners to produce quality events, however, they did not capitalise on those opportunities.

While my intention of broadening the students' networks in Phase 2 did not deliver all of the desired outcomes, there were other notable learning outcomes. Through their industry exposure, the students accrued cultural capital in the form of interpersonal skills, which they used to empower their community.

At the beginning of Phase 3, I engaged a professional facilitator to assist the students in formalising their organisation. The establishment of specific roles created a more professional working environment, which assisted their communication, efficiency, and productivity. As a result, the improved social cohesion enabled them to manage their stakeholders and partners with more success, and to negotiate confidently with industry professionals.

Throughout the three years, the transformation of 'student to professional' was assisted by the acquisition of new social skillsets. For entrepreneurial learning, the students developed 'know-who' and 'know-how'. These competencies were vital for the enactment of their vision as the students were able to mobilise their social capital in order to gain access to new knowledge and broaden the imaginative potential of their projects. Once the boundaries of these projects had been expanded, the students used their bridging social capital and improved outward interfacing with partners to align their new ideas with the broader industry.

7

Learning About Project Management for Entrepreneurship in the Music Industry

This chapter investigates the question, what negotiating and organisational skills do students learn through an education designed to foster entrepreneurial capacity in the music industry, and how did this learning occur? This chapter is broken into two main sections. First, I investigated the learned skills required to successfully execute a project. Second, I examined the reflective skills that students employed to refine their projects. In order to better understand the organisational processes of the students I examined the sequence of events in which the learning took place. As such, the findings are not presented according to individual learnings, but according to the experiences of the group and the learning that manifested when the group came together around a particular situation or event.

The category 'Project Management' refers to the skills that participants, as aspiring entrepreneurs, had to learn when staging public events. These events—as detailed in Chapter 5—included *Emerge*, *The Four Walls Festival*, and *Little BIGSOUND*. Each event took place a number of times over a three-year period.

© The Author(s) 2020
K. Kelman, *Entrepreneurial Music Education*,
https://doi.org/10.1007/978-3-030-37129-6_7

Setting Goals and Completing Tasks

The following section now focuses on the project management skills required (and acquired) to implement and complete a project. These skills include planning and scheduling, problem-solving, negotiating, risk-management, conflict resolution, technical skills, and budgeting.

Phase 1 involved discussion and planning, and implementation of the first YMI events. I was working hard behind the scenes to create the environment for these 'plans' to be realised. This involved negotiation with the school principal and facilitating regular meetings with the students. As previously discussed, the initial events were largely 'school-based', whereby students relied heavily on the members of the school community for support to build their audience and youth musician networks.

Making Decisions and Solving Problems Through Negotiation

In Phase 2 and Phase 3, the students were given more ownership over the organisation. After the success of the first year, their vision grew; this meant that the events became more frequent and larger in scale. As a result, the students' involvement became more time-intensive and the project management side of their work became more ambitious and complex. Tristan reflects on this:

> There was continued discussion in which we increasingly became more motivated to impact the music industry in Brisbane, and to create spaces for younger artists to perform, develop and achieve the goals that they set out to do with their music. These ideas then became plans, and the plans became events - Emerge nights, Four Walls Festival, Little BIGSOUND. Each event we created introduced us to new problems, which gave us new skills, and with the new skills we became more and more efficient at hosting and running these events. (Tristan, Interview, Phase 3)

Tristan's statement outlines how the students learned that project management involved setting goals and completing tasks and that, in meeting their deadlines, there would be many obstacles or problems to solve. When students engaged with these problems, they faced internal conflict, which had to be resolved through negotiation. They also encountered constraints working within the school and the wider music industry. Thus, they had to adapt in order to align with other processes. The following scenario surrounding poster design exemplifies their problem-solving, flexibility, negotiation, and planning.

In Phase 1, the students engaged a young graphic artist, who was a brother of one of the YMI team members. He designed the first *Four Walls Festival* poster (Fig. 7.1), which the students immediately embraced. However, in Phase 2, the design phase now granted the students greater ownership and responsibility over decision-making. They became much more involved in the process of the poster design, and invited the artist into the Facebook group so that they could work collaboratively to achieve the desired product.

During the phase 2 design process, the students moved ahead with a poster that the school principal and I later found inappropriate (Fig. 7.2). As I was not privy to the design discussions, the intervention came quite late in the process. This intervention created significant problems for the students, who were trying to meet tight deadlines for going to press, and for the artist who had now committed to other jobs. The following, lengthy Facebook interaction below captures the students and the artist dealing with my intervention.

Brandon	I personally think that the progression in the "character" is a good representation of how YMI is evolving.
	And at a time like this where we have the Conference and the YMI EP Competition, I think pressuring Kevin into making another poster will ultimately take away our focus from these events, which are just as important as 4 Walls.
	Also with the Poster already been distributed to some headliners, a change in character and design could possibly lower the professionalism of the organisation!
Kevin	I think if we're gonna soften the expression we need to make it super-cute so it has the same comedic value. These are fixups that should have been addressed in the drafting stage though. Perhaps we should have got Kristina involved a bit earlier.
Indigo	I honestly think it has enough continuity as is. as for the face, people are going to go for something that looks edgier anyway. We really appreciate you doing this for us, and i'm sure that everyone agrees that the design is perfect as is. If we'd had a problem we would have said something when you gave us the initial sketch.

Ivan	Please see this feedback from one of the headliners. Not saying we should follow it. But I think they are open to it changing. I received this feedback from one of the bands' manager
	"hey mate - I gotta say I'm not a big fan of the poster. I particularly don't like the way the bands are printed alongside that scary dudes head. I thought I'd give some feedback anyway. It just looks a bit immaturish and some of my colleagues have said the same. Also, I like List-based band line-ups with the biggest band first and the names getting progressively smaller. It creates excitement about the headline acts. Just my two cents - do with it as you will".
Chris	the dude has a point. however if we were to change the poster it would have to be done by monday at best (next wednesday latest), we can't afford to waste time. If you can make the small amendments to the poster by monday, Kevin, then by all means please do, but if not than i think we'll have to make do.
	thanks (fan of your art btw =P)
Brandon	well if the artist isn't happy with the poster, he doesn't have to be listed on it!
Indigo	Just out of curiosity, which artist was that?
Hayden	He was [Band H]'s manager and he has a point, but due to time restrictions, I believe we are going to have to stick with it guys
	It's not like the poster looks bad, it looks awesome, he just thought it didn't fit our festival,
Brandon	they don't even know anything about the organisation
Indigo	Let's not get personal haha, I dunno they can deal with it.
Hayden	No need to get personal dude, the guy was just giving his opinion, we can either take a constructive approach to it, or get personal
	i think we do what we can with our time, even if that means the poster stays the same, then we'll still have a sweet poster for a sweet festival
	just don't take it personally—toltec philosophy man *
Brandon	it's not personal
	they should just be informed that they are not the only band and other people may be like it!
Indigo	i dunno, let's just let it go…
Hayden	we'll chat on Monday, if there is a problem

*Toltec philosophy is an ancient set of spiritual guidelines that encourage awareness of the situation one is creating, essentially finding peace and contentment. This philosophy was laminated and hung on the back of toilet doors all over the school in order to remind students to think before making hasty decisions.

Fig. 7.1 Poster: *Four Walls Festival* (Phase 1) illustration by Ken Smith

The interaction in this excerpt was the students' first encounter with such a situation. They came up with three key arguments for not changing the poster: artistic judgement, professional identity, and deadlines. Indigo and Brandon reason with the group, saying that the image is a progression of how YMI is evolving and that it displays continuity. Most members of the group agree that it is too late to change the poster design due to advertising cut-off dates in Street Press, and the need to place an announcement on social media sites, with the festival only six weeks away.

It is evidenced in the interaction that they are gaining some grasp of the concept of professionalism, in this case, understanding the artist's

Fig. 7.2 *Four Walls Festival* poster: initial sketch (Phase 2) illustration by Ken Smith

workload and how it might reflect badly on YMI if they change the poster design that they have already shared with managers and booking agents.

Hayden, in particular, demonstrates skills in conflict management, using calming strategies such as, 'we can either take a constructive approach to it, or take it personally'. He also refers to Toltec philosophy, which was part of the school's repertoire, as a way to refocus the discussion, and move it away from the defensive stance. Indigo and Hayden seek to defuse the criticism for the artist in order to maintain a good working relationship and suggest that the group take a break in the meantime.

The next excerpt from the Four Walls Festival debriefing in Phase 2, also raises issues previously discussed (in the networking section of the previous chapter) that occur when working with adults in the industry.

Possibly, this greater sense of ownership enabled by Phase 2 of the design had created a more assertive attitude in the students, which is evident in their reaction to the band manager's feedback, and in their consensus that the poster should stay, even after being told it had to be changed in order to align with the school image. To some extent, the students had taken ownership of YMI, branding it 'for the youth by the youth', and considered themselves a separate entity from the school. Later, in a *Four Walls* debrief meeting, I raised this issue with the students.

Kristina	so when the issue came up you guys were pretty protective about it
Tristan	we went with it last year, and then suddenly it's not possible this year
Indigo	I think it's a loyalty thing too
Hayden	and the fact that we're teenagers and we don't want to be told what to do by old people. (others agree)
Tom	and it was a branding thing too… four walls has the same brand every year

This situation created challenges for my design, as I wanted my students to learn how to represent themselves in different situations. In this instance they were not only representing YMI but also the school and, ultimately, the Queensland Government and the guidelines that they set. At the Monday meeting, I instructed the students that the poster would have to be changed and there was to be no further argument.

The following Facebook interaction from Phase 2 occurred twelve days later after there had been time to consider the artist's new sketches for the festival poster.

Hayden	I know you all think that the bears are cute and stuff but I think the tapehead is way cooler, and gives much more of a sense of what the festival is about
Brandon	well not being rude, but what was the point of asking everyone if u are gonna pick the tapehead?
	I think we should just leave it to a pure vote!
Hayden	This is my vote man
Faith	i just don't think the tape head is particularly memorable compared to the bears. we've always had pretty unrelated imagery, in a way i think the bears flow more with the other posters because of that.

Hayden	I think that we are relating it too much to emerge
	because the poster for 4 walls last year had a guitar, to me that is pretty related
	So in a way the tapehead fits with last years' poster
Faith	That's a fair point, esthetically i still perfer the bears though
Brandon	Easiest way? (uploads a link to Easypoll website)
Hayden	Brandon, i think it should be more about what will work with the festival, than a simple vote - there has to be a valid point behind a vote man
Indigo	i honestly think if you can get kevin to put something vaugely musical in the bears one, then we should use that. the tapehead one isn't exactly memorable.
Hayden	what do you mean by not memorable though? in what way?
Indigo	i'm sorry no offense to kevin, but it's lame. the bears would work much better.
Faith	The tape just seems a little over-used and kindof cheesy in comparison.
Brandon	Well Hayden we all have given out reasons! And it seems more people want bear
Hayden	i personally have never seen a tapehead before, the 2 bears, although cute, seems completely unrelated, that's all
Tristan	(enters a weblink to a tapehead website)
Hayden:	Okay, Indigo I like that, I know that this is different to what he has already done, but what about the big bear playing a drumkit? Wearing the superhero outfit and Tristan, I get the point :)
Tristan:	I'm sorry Hayden:)
Brandon	btw, from what I know, when there is a like tape or something on a poster, its usually associated with hiphop/rap things
Tristan	Flip a coin
Indigo	We've established we're not keen on the tape, but let's keep it in mind in case the bears don't work…
Hayden	I'll email Kevin then

In this excerpt, the students demonstrate various ways of democratically negotiating their way through a problem, and coming to a final decision, Hayden was the project leader for *Four Walls* and, while he abides by the majority vote, he struggles to understand everyone else's reasoning. Having read the Facebook exchange, the artist produced another sketch, which incorporated animals, musical instruments, youth-style clothing, and the original Four *Walls* logo from the previous year (see Fig. 7.3). Three days later, the students were ecstatic about the new poster, and a final decision had been made, as evidenced in the following Facebook excerpt.

Hayden	Here is the drafter poster dudes!
Brandon	Holycanoly, amazing!!!!!!!!!!!!!!! And we keep the same top part as last years! AMAZING!!!!!!!!!!!!!!!!
Hayden	Yeeah
Faith	This is perfect! Awesome!
Indigo	Fuckyeahkeytar
Chris	Sweet looks awesome!

Fig. 7.3 Poster: *Four Walls Festival* (Phase 2) illustration by Ken Smith

> *Upon reflection, I should have intervened much earlier in the process in order to better manage the artist we had employed. While the students learned lessons about being adaptable and flexible, the decisions took a long time to be made, which cost the artist time and money. Fortunately, he was sympathetic to the learning environment and continued a working partnership with the students for the next few years. I learned that even though I was determined to create a 'student-owned' learning space in Phase 2, there were times when it was important to make timely leadership decisions in the best interests of all involved.*

Fig. 7.4 Reflection Box 6: teacher leadership and student limitations

The interactions around the poster design give an insight into the learning processes that students went through in order to achieve one of the goals of their project. While they were reluctant to align with industry expectations, they learned the importance of adapting and being flexible. In this process, they displayed maturity in maintaining their working relationships within the group and with industry professionals, as well as the ability to arrive at a decision (Fig. 7.4).

Decision-Making

Not long after the poster incident was put to rest, a further issue emerged with a band manager who disputed the billing. The manager was extremely hostile to the students on the phone, and demanded that YMI change the band's performance time. This meant that Hayden's band would have to move to the earlier spot and compete with a headline act that was scheduled to play at the same time. Hayden was angry about the rudeness of the band manager and proposed that they be taken off the festival billing. The team were opposed to this, and felt that Hayden was taking things personally. However, the group changed their mind when the manager wrote an email to someone outside of YMI, referring to Matt (artist liaison for YMI) in a derogatory manner. Unfortunately, this email had accidentally been sent to Matt. Hayden was furious and sent me an email asking me to take control of the situation and remove them from the program. See email excerpt below.

Hi Ms
I would like to report the [Band I], and have them banned from playing at 4 Walls immediately

They have already disrespected us enough, and this has nothing to do with a playing time
I would like to show you what they have called Matt - the file is attached
I personally think this is absolutely disrespectful, and I am sick of having to put up with their rudeness, and so is everybody else

Let me know your decision - I would like you to make the final decision
Hayden

Given it was Phase 2, and I had by then handed greater owner-ship over to the students, my response was to give them a choice as to whether they wanted me to intervene. They decided they wanted to sort it out themselves. In the end, they thought that it was in the best inter-ests of the festival that the band play. In the following Facebook excerpt, they share the project implications of this decision.

Brandon	if any other bands asks for time change they can piss off because of [Band I], now we have [Band J] angry he understands we cant do anything but yeah.....
Emily	ahahhahhahahahhahahahhahahha [Band J] is angry :')
Hayden	you should have listened to me ages ago
Indigo	can we not "i told you so"?
Brandon	why not, we desrve it :P *
Indigo	it's just negativeee, whatever happens happensss.
Hayden	sorry, i just really wanted to say it :) I will say it no more
	:P is a light-hearted emoticon which means poking the tongue out

This is an example of the students managing their decision, and its repercussions for other bands' schedules. They all come to real-ise that whatever the decision, there are going to be consequences. Unfortunately, in this example, the students allowed an overly assertive band manager to dictate the terms to them. They had programmed and

> *The email incident with the aggressive band manager was handled maturely by the students. However, given a different group of students, this could have had different consequences. Upon reflection, I should have spent more time working this through with the students face-to-face to show them my support but also to be more aware of potential threats that this could have posed for the students and festival.*

Fig. 7.5 Reflection Box 7: emergence of leaders

publicised the band [Band I], and felt it best not to change the line-up to maintain a professional face with their audience. However, they upset another band with yet another schedule change. Hayden is quick to quip with an 'I told you so' remark, and Indigo reminds the group that they need to live with their decision, move forward and not engage in any further negativity. Hayden apologises to the team and the students move forward. This excerpt demonstrates the students' ability to resolve conflict constructively as well as deal with an unpleasant situation.

In Phase 3, the poster and design decisions for the *Four Walls Festival* were efficiently coordinated. The poster was negotiated in a much shorter period, as evident in shorter Facebook threads, and these discussions took place much earlier in the year (April) for the festival in August. This leads into the discussion of the second project management skill: the importance of preparation and organisation when setting goals and completing tasks (Fig. 7.5).

Organisation

The students recognised that timely organisation was a major factor in executing project goals and that this involved not only personal organisation, but also clearly delegated jobs and responsibilities. Chris later identified learning about personal organisation from these experiences: 'Something I've learned, um, organisation, I'm a pretty unorganised person, but lately I've been, well when I was organising events, I'm really trying to pinpoint things that needs to get done' (Chris, Interview, Phase 2). In contrast, Hayden's interview reflection assessed YMI's ability to be organised:

Cause we haven't had much time, we kind of just do it, and we don't think about it, um, and we don't arrange it, we just do it, that's what I've been fighting to change for the past six months, just getting everybody to do a specific thing, instead of everyone just running around doing something. (Hayden, Interview, Phase 2)

Towards the end of Phase 2, the students aimed to improve their organisation skills to align with industry standards, and put in place clearly developed roles and responsibilities. This strategy led to an improved approach to organisation in Phase 3 involving a more professional governance structure with clearly defined roles. The students organised project deadlines and schedules earlier, and met each deadline well in advance of the equivalent milestones from previous years. They improved communication by providing me with updates and had 'touch base' meetings with the principal of the school every few weeks. This growing professionalism is evident in the following Phase 3 Facebook interactions below.
Facebook excerpt 1

Tom	Ethan, I'll have the run out of the day finished tonight and I'll let you know exactly how many volunteers we need. Everyone else I need some updates of your roles. We're 3 weeks out and I need to know what we're having issues with!
Ethan	sounds good
Tom	You should definitely send out some emails straight away though. Have you got any volunteers yet?
Ethan	Yeah I've got a few. I'll still send out some emails. How many approximately do you reckon we'll need? Lots or just a few?
Ethan	keeping in mind interns will also be helping
Tom	Yup, how many to be exact?
Tom	how many interns do we have I mean :P
Ethan	9 interns
Tom	To be honest we won't need a lot of volunteers. I will let you know tonight though. I'm now locking myself in my room and getting it finished. (uploads the schedule)
Tom	This looks so sick when looking over it
Hayden	Excellent man, looks cool
Tom	Such an amazing day this will be

Facebook interaction 2

Chris	Tom, Tristan, bro's. what's happening with band agreements? i haven't received any = D and no invoices either.
Tom	SOrry man I sent em to Kristina. Will forward them now.
Chris	ah sweet, not a problem man.

Facebook interaction 3

Tom	Indigo, Faith updates on your roles would put my mind at ease (:
Tom	Chris also
Faith	I've started contacting food, but no confirmations yet - I'll let you know when there are any. hellhound hotdogs haven't gotten back to me :(so I'm still looking for a hotdog vendour
Tom	Okie doke, let me know if it's still not looking good at the end of the week and we'll have a chat about it.
Faith	ok sounds good
Indigo	got 5 people keen to do photos

As Hayden points out at the end of Phase 2, there are still organisational issues resulting from members just 'doing it' rather than having it all arranged. The above Phase 3 excerpts provide evidence of the students showing greater organisational maturity in the way they approach their project goals and deadlines. In the second excerpt the improved reporting and accountability is also effective in clearing up communication issues regarding band agreements. These kinds of Facebook interactions in Phase 3 contrast with those in Phase 2, where the students all tend to be involved in every issue, which at times creates confusion and the need for lengthier periods of time to solve problems.

Learning to Negotiate

This new business-like attitude and professionalism adopted by the group in Phase 3 played an important role in their ability to negotiate with band managers and booking agents. It also marked an important aspect of learning about project managing a festival, especially when working within a constrained budget. The students went from two or three headliners in Phase 1 to engaging at least ten major headline acts in Phase 2 and 3. The following Facebook excerpt from Phase 3 shows the group discussing their negotiations with headline acts for the *Four Walls Festival.*

Chris	I love the [Band K], they have some quality music. I'm not aware of how big they are, I came across them by accident and I suppose the reason theyre askin for so much is cause they are like a 7-8 piece band
Hayden	they do have 21,000 likes on facebook, whereas [Band F] had 7000
Hayden	4K
Tom	Really!?
Tom	wow
Tom	Well anyway I've pushed for 3000, they're doing Bigsound for free so obviously the travel isn't that annoying for them…
Hayden	How are they charging 4K if they do Bigsound for free?
Tom	Hahaha because Bigsound is one of the biggest music conferences in QLD if not Australia
Tom	You know how QMIA are, they make bands come to them
Hayden	geniuses

The students continued to share weblinks and Facebook statistics as tools to help them gauge the fees they should be negotiating with band managers. In the interaction above, they successfully negotiate a deal with Melbourne Band, [Band K] for $3000. Soon after, they discuss another potential headline act in their Facebook interactions:

Tristan	The [Band L] are hoping for $4k. They would be a headliner. What do you all think about that?
Indigo	not worth 4k, they're not that big atm [at the moment]
Tristan	alternative price?
Indigo	mergh, i'm bad with money. they've only 6 thousand likes in comparison to [Band K] 22 thousand, and we're not even willing to pay them 4 grand. mightbe like 2?

The students successfully negotiated with the [Band L] manager for a $2000 fee. They were very pleased with themselves and managed to acquire six headline acts for $11,000. The Phase 3 festival was programmed well in advance and there were more efficient negotiations

> *While we had grant funding to help raise the profile and quality of our festival, we still relied on ticket sales to contribute to the overall running costs of the festival. We received no financial assistance from the school (beyond in-kind support and use of the facilities). The students felt the risks involved but they were always confident and optimistic that the event would be a success. The risks were much more real for me, given that I would ultimately be responsible.*

Fig. 7.6 Reflection Box 8: risk management realities

with managers compared to the previous year. This is attributed to the experience that the students had gained from working on two festivals prior to Phase 3, and to the confidence they had developed through the refinement of their practice. Specifically, the way they organised themselves (mutual engagement) lead to a new improved sense of professionalism (joint enterprise); and the further developed tools, planning documents, words, and resources (repertoire) gave them the credibility and confidence to negotiate with the industry (bridging capital) (Fig. 7.6).

The strong bonding capital that the students had developed over the past two years had created an environment of learning, where they were helping each other to become more competent. In terms of their learning about entrepreneurship, the students were increasingly demonstrating entrepreneurial 'know-why': they had a clear idea of who they were, what they were trying to achieve, and what they valued.

Problem-Solving on the Job

While the students developed the ability to set goals and complete tasks in the lead up to a project, problem-solving on the job was equally important to learning. One young YMI volunteer comments on his experience of working at the *Four Walls Festival* in Phase 2:

> It was really good how we had that chat together before Four Walls opened, that if problems came up throughout the day, we were to stay really calm and not create big dramas for everyone to see, and people kept really calm! (Volunteer, *Four Walls* Debrief Meeting, Phase 2)

> *At times, I found it quite difficult to not interfere, jump in and solve problems. In the early days of YMI, my students would quite often let me know if I was being over-bearing. On one particular occasion, the students were setting up and performing a sound-check for a new band for an Emerge (2011), and I was quizzing the band about logistics such as parking and where to leave their gear. Matt stopped me halfway through a sentence, and said "Miss Kelman, can't you see we're trying to finish a sound-check? Could you please go and do something else, we have everything under control here."*

Fig. 7.7 Reflection Box 9: learning my boundaries

Tristan reflects on how he dealt with issues at *Emerge 2*, Phase 3:

> Yeah, well last night, the last band were late, and so I got [Musician A] from an earlier band to perform a solo set, and they still weren't there, and then they came and they had a film crew which we hadn't known about, so I had to quickly think about what to do, and two other people were missing from the band and so I just had to think of what to do, and that's a challenge, so I got Indigo to look after their film crew and then I just, I wasn't angry, but I was assertive to them and just saying I need you to do this this and this, and get your stuff on stage and get ready to play, and then, so I did that, it was fine. (Tristan, YMI Meeting, Phase 3)

The major difference between Phase 2 and Phase 3 evidenced in the above quotes was that, in Phase 2, they were explicitly rehearsing how to behave and respond should a problem arise. In Phase 3, this behaviour had become embedded and they could automatically move into problem-solving mode. As a community of practice, the students developed their enterprise over time, and the repertoire they built reflected this enterprise. By Phase 3, they had established their enterprise as highly professional and adult-like, which was the image they wanted to project (Fig. 7.7).

Summary: Setting Goals and Completing Tasks

In this section, the data provided evidence of the students developing their project management skills, specifically those related to setting goals and completing tasks. In particular, issues around problem-solving,

Table 7.1 Learning about setting goals and completing tasks across the three phases

Design phase	Setting goals and completing tasks
Phase 1 Learning and designing (Student phase)	• Largely lead by the teacher in the role of mentor • Students develop their community of practice
Phase 2 Learning skills (Student to professional phase)	• Exploring each other's expertise and sharing these skills with members of the community • Learning to negotiate and solve problems • Reflecting on the need for clear roles and job descriptions to keep a project moving forward, and improve organisational skills
Phase 3 Applying skills (Professional phase)	• Clear roles and job descriptions give students greater independence; project goals understood by everyone, leading to more efficient and organised planning and implementation • Clearer communication and reporting strategies allow for potential problems to be identified • Efficiency and professionalism enable students to better negotiate, and to develop trusting relationships with their stakeholders

negotiating, managing stakeholders, communication of clear goals, were evidenced as opportunities for learning. With iterations over phases and events, students developed the skills needed to execute a project through the opportunity to build an enterprise, with interventions that caused students to realise these attributes in practical industry experiences. The progression of learning from Phase 1 to Phase 3 displays a significant growth as the students transitioned to a more professional identity. This progression is summarised in Table 7.1.

At the end of Phase 2, the students were able to acknowledge that their productivity and efficiency would improve if project goals were clearer, and if they each took responsibility and ownership for a particular aspect of the project. It was evident in Phase 3 that they had developed clearer processes in regards to their particular roles in the project. They were thus able to refine their repertoire of documents, processes, procedures, words, and gestures to reflect a more professional, mature and confident enterprise.

The negative aspects of bonding capital that were evidenced in Phase 2 included the potential for the group to become inward-looking and resistant to the opinions and processes of others outside the group. On the other hand, the strengths of bonding capital (as evidenced in Phase 2) could be seen in the trust and reciprocity that developed and enabled a culture of learning from each other, and from their mistakes. This had enormous benefits for Phase 3, where the strength of bonding capital served as the premise for the creation of the resources (repertoire) for garnering bridging capital. Table 7.1 provides a summary of the students' learning about setting goals and completing tasks across the three phases of the design.

Reflection Skills

Throughout all three phases, reflection became an everyday part of the community's repertoire, whether through formal debrief or Facebook interactions. As a process, the ability to reflect assisted the students to complete their projects by:

- learning from both successes and failures
- gaining knowledge and understanding
- developing effective forms of action
- cementing relationships and building trust to enable community maintenance
- sharing thoughts and ideas.

Debriefing

As the leader of YMI in Phase 1, I did not hold a *Four Walls Festival* debrief. In Phase 2, the students were handed complete ownership. Even though several months had passed since the first *Four Walls Festival,* the students recognised the importance of reflecting on the event in preparation for the second festival. In the meeting excerpt below, students reflect on the lack of media coverage and the loss of their video footage as significant issues in Phase 1.

Indigo	Media coverage - was a disaster.
Ivan	There just wasn't enough time, we needed more time, we only marketed three or four weeks before the festival. I mean by the time we contacted MX the issues were closed.
	We need to start now, we need to target that market, it's huge.
Faith	I know someone at Bats magazine - so we could probably get a word in there? She's a family friend.
Indigo	We had lots of interviews, Shane had it all, and now we don't have the footage, it was heartbreaking, we got so many great interviews - like what advice would you give to other young musicians? That kind of thing.
Ivan	I just don't think we put enough emphasis on how important those videos were I mean that is basically what we were doing the festival for.
	I mean when it comes down to it, that was it.
Faith	We won't make the same mistake again. (everyone agrees)
Kristina	What did we do wrong?
Ivan	I don't think we followed up?
Indigo	We kind of just left the festival and all went home to bed, and like I was thinking about it, we could look at getting something like a nightlife - they like go to clubs – it's a service.
Ivan	If we have the interviews again, is there a way that we can have a laptop there where everyone can dump the files?
Indigo	On the day we just don't have time to do that but we need to at least invest in an SD card - so that's what goes on there for YMI.

This excerpt is an example of an effective retrospective reflection. The students are able to identify areas of concern, attribute explanations, and offer solutions. Some of these solutions involved simple technicalities such as finding ways to store data, and mobilising social capital. While the debrief introduced the students to the importance of reflection for project management, it also instilled an emotional engagement. This was evident in Indigo's remark about how heartbreaking it was to lose their valuable footage. While not all students attended this debrief session, reflection became part of the community's repertoire in Phase 2.

Informally, the creation of a Facebook meeting group enabled continuous discussion and reflection at any time. This helped the students to develop more formal approaches to reflection, as previously acknowledged by the group. The students retrospectively compared the Phase 1 and Phase 2 *Four Walls* festivals and drew similarities, such as a lack of time. It was suggested that 'rushing things' was part of the group's practice; however, this was disputed. Hayden explicitly referred to the design phases, reminding the group that, as opposed to Phase 1, the students largely ran Phase 2 without any assistance. Reflection in Phase 2 had now become not only a way of helping the students to improve the way they worked, but also a way of helping them to see how they learned about how they worked.

Reflecting on Reflecting

As the students moved to a more professional enterprise in Phase 3, they had developed the skills of reflection as a way to problem solve. In the Phase 3 Facebook excerpt below, Brandon announced to the group that the promotional video he created contained footage of a different band with the same name. The main concern was that the video had already been posted online for one day.

Brandon	omg i wanna die....i used the wrong video of [Band K]...i used the video of another band called [Band K] :(
Chris	....
Hayden	Are you serious? well, lets hold back on the video man, just announce tickets - update the video, and wait for [Band L]'s song – [Band L] would work so much better,
	I don't know if we need to release the promo just yet - what do you guys think - Indigo?
Brandon	what a freaking rollercoaster!!!! sorry guys, my bad"
Hayden	(Two hours later) Okay - I think we need to hold back on 4 Walls... Every decision we're making on facebook is super hasty. We need Tom's input and he doesn't have a computer someone needs to be liaising with him - Tristan, we haven't even finalised early bird or final ticket prices, I'm pretty sure we all want [Band L]'s song to be in the video, so why don't we announce ticket sales for now - if they become early birds, then be it so, but as for the video Brandon - update it and see if we can get the [Band L]'s song
	The festival is still 2 months away, I understand that we want to get it out as quickly as possible, but we need to make sure we have it right
Chris	fair call

The excerpt shows evidence of meta-reflection. In the past two years, the students had reflected on their rushed and last-minute festival preparation. Here, in the final phase, the students respond by rushing to get things done earlier. After stepping away from the situation for a couple of hours, Hayden acknowledges that, while the group is trying to improve their timelines, it is better to get things right. Hayden is demonstrating entrepreneurial 'know-when', and shows a more mature approach in reflecting on situations rather than trying to come up with a solution in the first instance. The excerpt is also further evidence of the trust and reciprocity that have become the norms of their community. In particular, Brandon feels comfortable admitting to a mistake, taking responsibility for the situation and apologising to the group.

Summary: Reflection Skills

The students identified the need for reflection as a core part of their practice and repertoire in moving forward from one event to the next, and between iterations. I discussed three pieces of data that captured the students developing these skills.

Students implemented formal reflection processes such as debriefing sessions from Phase 2, and these became a routine expectation of community involvement. They learned how to critically analyse their projects in detail, share ideas for moving forward, and to learn from mistakes (and the emotional connection to those mistakes) to make improvements. The act of sharing ideas through the reflection process assisted them to articulate new knowledge, and to gain greater awareness and control over their enterprise. These skills in Phase 2 were indicative of growing entrepreneurial 'know-how', and demonstrated entrepreneurial 'know-when'. Table 7.2 offers an overview of learning about reflection across the three phases.

Table 7.2 Learning about reflection across the three phases

Design phase	Reflection skills
Phase 1 Learning and designing (Student phase)	• No formal reflection processes in place
Phase 2 Learning skills (Student to professional phase)	• Formal reflection or debriefing starts early in the phase • Identifying, explaining and solving • Learning from mistakes • Understanding emotional engagement • Cementing relationships—community maintenance • Sharing ideas and developing action strategies • New knowledge and understandings • Learning how they work together
Phase 3 Applying skills (Professional phase)	• Reflecting on reflecting • Stepping back and taking time • Paying attention to what has been created • Developing entrepreneurial 'know-when'

Chapter Summary

The findings of this chapter demonstrate that the design enabled the students to develop organisational skills relating to project management using real-world projects. By design, the YMI community moved through various contextual phases, beginning with a teacher-guided Phase 1, through to a more experimental Phase 2 with minimal teacher-guidance. The project concluded in Phase 3 with the students refining their learning in a more professional context with the teacher as an equal participant. The findings from this chapter highlight the positive and negative impacts that social capital had on the students' skill development.

During Phase 1, it was important that the students were offered legitimate opportunities to develop and implement their first events without the pressure of the more formal processes such as budgeting, reporting to the principal, and negotiating with industry stakeholders.

This allowed the students to develop their enterprise and repertoire. At this early stage, the students were able to set and achieve goals using the school as a resource to achieve some early successes. These early successes bonded the students together and established early organisational skills. The benefits of these learned organisational skills can be observed through the organisational structures that YMI established, and in their ability to deploy their organisational structures and manage events.

Phase 2 introduced a more experimental approach and the students were given autonomy to develop and run YMI with latitude for learning from mistakes. During this phase students began designing new projects and interfacing with industry with less teacher engagement. Students developed organisational structures in reaction to mistakes and began to design governance hierarchies to adapt to the more ambitious projects. The ambitious projects and the bridging capital developed through partnerships with industry bodies, enabled the students to observe different organisational structures and bring new ideas back to the community. This resulted in improved communicational structures and the ability for the students to solve complex problems with autonomy. However, the autonomy that occurred during this phase meant that there were some issues (such as aggressive band managers) that I was unable to shield the students from. Through their industry exposure, the students accrued cultural capital in the form of organisational skills, which they used to empower their community. During this phase, students participated in decision-making, learned to negotiate with industry and stakeholders, became more autonomous problem-solvers, while using reflective skills to improve and refine their project management.

At the beginning of Phase 3, I engaged a professional facilitator to assist the students in formalising their organisation. The establishment of specific roles created a more professional working environment, which assisted their communication, efficiency, and productivity. As a result, the improved processes enabled them to manage their stakeholders and partners with more success, and to negotiate confidently with industry professionals.

Throughout the three years, the transformation of 'student to professional' was attributed to successful acquisition of skills required for project management. For entrepreneurial learning, the students developed 'know-how' and 'know-when'. These competencies were vital for the enactment of their vision.

8

Acquiring Domain Knowledge for Entrepreneurship in the Music Industry

This chapter continues to present the findings of the YMI study, addressing questions related to knowledge and learning. First, what music industry knowledge did students acquire in an environment designed to encourage entrepreneurialism in the music industry? Second, how did this learning unfold? There are four key specific knowledge themes related to the music industry: knowledge of the music business, knowledge of industry expectations, knowledge of music and musicians, and knowledge of sustainability. As the result of acquiring this knowledge, the students had more resources with which to leverage further social capital, and to work towards greater alignment with industry processes.

Learning About the Music Business

As discussed in Chapter 4, music students need to have a broad understanding of the dynamic environment that they will eventually inhabit as professionals. The design provided students with a contextual experience, which allowed them to develop their 'know-what' through a

© The Author(s) 2020
K. Kelman, *Entrepreneurial Music Education*,
https://doi.org/10.1007/978-3-030-37129-6_8

greater understanding of various music industry practices such as copyright, contractual agreements, budgeting, and marketing. The content that they needed to understand these concepts occurred through learning 'on the job'.

The Emerging Professional Learning Model allowed students to acquire this knowledge in a staged process. In Phase 1, they were engaged with building their audience and staging events, while I took on administrative roles. In Phase 2, they were handed greater responsibility of the tools including; the budget, band contracts, and marketing. The addition of further industry partnerships and collaborations revealed the knowledge that they would need to acquire to efficiently run their own events.

Learning About Copyright

The students used the creative work of musicians in the marketing tools for their events. The Facebook excerpt below, for example, refers to Brandon's promotional video for the *Four Walls Festival* (Phase 2). Here, we see that he has not sought the correct permission for using another musician's song as an accompanying soundtrack to the film clip. As demonstrated in this excerpt, the students explicitly learned about copyright issues through their own errors:

Indigo	Brandon, did you see the email from the oceanics manager? not cool, we need to be really careful about this stuff in the future.
Brandon	yes and its fine! cause Hayden had sent them a message last night anyway! so it was just bad timing in how we sent emails! all sorted! did someone reply to them? if not, I will again
Indigo	we need to make sure we get permission before release…
Brandon	we thought it was a creative commons licenced download as it was available for free on triple J
Indigo	yeah, i dunno that is something we should probably actually learn abouttt
Brandon	which we just did
Indigo	I mean like the legit techniqucalities

In this excerpt, it is evident that the band manager, who operates in the wider music industry, has played a significant role in teaching the students about a serious legal issue. This role can be understood through the theoretical concept of 'imagining' in communities of practice, in particular the concept of 'legitimate peripheral participation'. In this sense, Brandon's competence has been extended by the band manager. Indigo is encouraging Brandon as he develops competence and brings this competency back to the YMI community. For Brandon, lacking certain knowledge puts him at the periphery of both YMI and the wider music industry, a risky place where mistakes can be made. However, he increases his expertise and returns to the competency centre of the YMI community.

Within legitimate peripheral participation, these mistakes are considered a significant aspect of learning, and the students have acknowledged this explicitly. This could have become a much more serious situation; fortunately, the manager was aware that the students were learning about the industry, and offered them retroactive permission to use the song. Learning about copyright is particularly pertinent to the music industry, as the students themselves will one day have their own copyright to understand and protect.

This new knowledge changed their community's enterprise to become more industry-compliant but also allowed them to build new repertoire. To further contextualise this learning, the students later displayed competency in copyright issues during Phase 3 as evidenced in the Facebook interaction below:

Brandon	now gotta just wait for [BAND M] ! HURRY UP [uploaded the video without soundtrack]
Tom	Yeah I'm speaking with their management at the moment... don't know why its taking so long
Brandon	what are they saying!
Tom	I think it should be fine... just need to hear from the band themselves... Which is kinda weird these days... haha
Brandon	if I was a band I'd easily be like sure play my song ANYWHERE
Hayden	[commenting on the video] Looks so sick man!!!! but yeah, get their permission first

> *While the copyright incident was a significant learning experience for the students, there could have been serious consequences. Due to the more student-directed focus in Phase 2, I was not aware of this incident until weeks later when I gained access to the Facebook interactions. I learned that a 'real-world' learning environment offers enormous possibilities for on-demand learning, but has 'real-world risks'.*

Fig. 8.1 Reflection Box 10: risks of 'real world' learning

Brandon was renowned for his previous mistakes, which arose from his enthusiastic and impatient need to do things 'now'. In this excerpt, Brandon is still showing his pressing desire to upload their promo video to YouTube; however, he holds back in applying the soundtrack to the video. The community's new repertoire of industry 'know-what' is evidenced in this excerpt by their condition to 'get their permission first'. Given this change in their enterprise and the development of new repertoire, we can also see the emergence of an entrepreneurial disposition, exemplified in their knowledge of copyright law (know-what), but also the ability to make judgements about when to act on their ideas and the appropriate action sequence (know-when) (Fig. 8.1).

Learning About Marketing

During the YMI project advertising and marketing became a significant and ongoing aspect of the students' responsibilities. Throughout Phase 1, the students spent their time advertising their events through Facebook, and an advertisement was purchased in the local press. In Phase 2, I engaged a publicist to develop a campaign for the Phase 2 *Four Walls Festival* and, as part of the arrangement, they agreed to mentor and work with the students. In Phase 3, we worked with QMIA's publicist to ease the work burden for both the conference and the festival.

In Phase 2, the publicist encouraged the students to maximise the benefits of advertising their product on Facebook and offered them strategies to help improve their ticket sales. In the following, Phase 2 Facebook excerpt, Hayden experiments with these techniques.

Hayden	And the effect our marketing has on people..[enters a screenshot of his post]

Hayden
Only 150 tickets left guys!!!
http://www.facebook.com/event.php?eid=118916928201514
http://www.moshtix.com.au/event.aspx?id=49010

4 Walls Festival
Location: High School A
Time: **Saturday, 06 August 2011 14:00**

📋 7 hours ago · 🔒 · Like · Comment · Share

Mary   **awwwwww shit**
7 hours ago · Unlike · 👍 1 person

John   **Fuck.**
6 hours ago · Like · 👍 1 person

Brendan   **Serious?! That was fast!**
6 hours ago · Unlike · 👍 1 person

Bradley   **Ticket acquired!**
5 hours ago · Like

Hayden   **Tickets were bound to sell with a lineup like that!**
4 hours ago · Like

Write a comment...

Brandon	we are amazing
Matt	bahahahaha YES
Brandon	we should start another batch promotion tonight around 8 pm when there is a lot of people on facebook
Brandon	also, im gonn send a bulk email to all people who have clicked attending
Brandon	Start online promotion in about 20 mins Most people should be on by then
Angus	So we just advertise like crazy?
Brandon	Yepyepyep
Angus	Okay, I can do that;)

The common theme that threads through marketing conversations is the students' reliance on, and exploitation of social media as a marketing tool. They are strategically planning Facebook announcements and considering the specific times when their social networks are online. The aim here is to maximise the potential audience by increasing the visibility of status updates, and event invites.

The key word in the above excerpt is 'advertise', which reflects only one aspect of marketing. In Phase 3, the students were still heavily reliant on Facebook, but there was evidence that they had acquired a broader concept of marketing. For example, Brandon explained that, "users need a reason to follow us" (Facebook, Phase 3), and suggested small competitions throughout the year. This broader concept of marketing is further demonstrated in the Facebook interaction below.

Brandon	Tom Anyone like the idea of making a status when we announce 4 walls tonight and say if you share the status you can win 2 free tickets?
	Then hopefully we will all share it and get more people to share it and get the status EVERYWHERE
	Also if we are announcing tonight. can we get every youth band ready to announce at the same time
	i think it would be awesome to have so many people post it at once
Tristan	Good idea, we will have to do it tomorrow though as we are delaying the announcement.
Indigo	I think it might be Monday, but good idea, mightbe only 1 ticket and for the first 10 people to share it

In this excerpt, Brandon identifies two possible strategies for the promotion of *Four Walls*: rewarding their audience if they share the Facebook status, and coordinating the bands to announce the festival line-up on their Facebook pages at the same time. Students' more strategic approach was evidence of a growing understanding of marketing, as opposed to just advertising, and indicated their developing entrepreneurial competency in 'know-how', 'know-when', and 'know-what'. Their evolving repertoire—in this case, the protocols—were clear, which allowed them to hold each other accountable through honest and open interactions.

Summary: Learning About the Music Industry Business

This section investigated copyright and marketing. The Emerging Professional Learning Model did not include explicit teaching about copyright law, but rather, provided opportunities for them to come to acquire that knowledge. Due to the high stakes environment of my design, students were driven to research and learn independently. For example, they booked a representative from APRA (The Australasian Performing Rights Association) to speak at *Little BIGSOUND (2011)*.

Each member in YMI was accountable to the group, in Phase 3 they were double-checking their facts with each other before making specific moves. In this sense, their enterprise was clearly defined by the way they pooled, refined, and applied their knowledge. These skills equipped them with new repertoire that better aligned with the broader music industry community. The bonding capital and the norm of high expectations established by the collective enabled the students to drive their own learning.

Marketing was the primary focus of YMI's work. While social media was the platform for much of their advertising, the students learned new ways of engaging with their audience across the design phases. Phase 1 saw them mostly focused on advertising through Facebook posts. In Phase 2, they worked with a publicist, who provided them with strategies to engage audience emotion and reach a wider audience. By Phase 3, students were more sophisticated in their approaches to motivating their audience.

Students developed knowledge about the business side of the music industry through experience, discovery, and trial and error. While they were given greater control of the budget throughout Phases 2 and 3, no formal learning in accounting or budgeting was provided. However, I believe that this should be considered for future designs. While no formal budgeting processes were in place, several incidents in the data capture students considering financial matters. Table 8.1 offers an overview of learning about the music business across the three phases.

Table 8.1 Learning about the music business across the three phases

Phase	Learning about the business
Phase 1 (Student phase)	• Using social media and personal networks to advertise events • Designing and creating marketing material appropriate to the audience
Phase 2 (Student to professional phase)	• Copyright knowledge gained through experience • Knowledge acquired through interactions with industry professionals • Marketing strategies
Phase 3 (Professional phase)	• Recognition that marketing via social media is more than advertising; greater audience awareness • Applying knowledge gained in previous phases with greater control and care

Learning About Industry Expectations

There are several incidents that capture the students displaying increased knowledge and awareness of the music industry environment. This chapter specifically examines what it is that students learned about working within the music industry; this particular section highlights how their work behind the scenes gave them a greater understanding of what it takes to be successful in the industry. The foci of this section include professionalism, industry expectations on responsiveness and punctuality, the ability to take initiative, the understanding what happens behind the scenes, the music industry structure, and the different career pathways. This section explores how students arrived at critical realisations.

Learning About Professionalism

Throughout Phase 2, the students became more aware of the industry environment. This awareness played a significant role in their emerging understanding of professionalism. In the Facebook excerpt below, Matt reports that with only two weeks to go before the *Four Walls Festival* (Phase 2), only four out of more than fifteen of the youth bands had returned their contracts, which included vital information required by the technical team for planning.

| Matt | btw only 4 bands have replied with stuff.....WOO for them emailing back hahaha |
| Hayden | holy shit they are lazy, no wonder bands need managers |

In this excerpt, Hayden shares his appreciation of one less visible aspect of the music industry's structure: band management. The excerpt also shows Matt's frustration with the young bands not returning emails and other important information necessary for the operation of the festival. This conversation displays students developing important knowledge about working in the music industry. Such learning is significant for developing the entrepreneurial competency of 'know-what' and demonstrates a more nuanced understanding of what communication strategies are required in a music festival. It also makes students aware of a gap in music industry knowledge for young performers; in this case, the need to respond to an opportunity and to be professional and punctual. Tom later explained:

> Musicians definitely need to know the business management side, you don't need to know specifically how to run a festival, but I definitely think that there are a lot of musicians who just think that opportunities will just come to them. (Tom, Interview, Phase 2)

As a singer-songwriter, Tom learnt that a musician should know how the industry works in order to participate successfully. A similar moment of explicit learning about the nature of the industry, albeit with extra layers of complexity, occurs in the Facebook excerpt below (Phase 2).

Brandon	Hayden - [Band M] dont know when they need to be there
Brandon	email them
Matt	I HAVE EMAILED THEM
Matt	HOLY CRAP ARE THESE BANDS RETARDED
Matt	I EMAILED [Band M Manager] LIKE I DO EVERY TIME
Matt	HE NEVER USUALLY HAS A PROBLEM REPLYING OR GETTING EMAILS SO I DON'T KNOW WHY THERE'S A PROBLEM NOW.
Matt	but seriously. I can't be held accountable if bands don't chek their shit
Matt	so don't blame me for anything when I've been doing my job............................
Hayden	alright - i'll talk to him on fb
	[an hour passes]
Hayden	not to worry, Matt has done it already
Hayden	Matt, you are an efficient worker ;)

This excerpt is significant for two reasons. First, it addressed the gap of knowledge that young bands have about the music industry and, second, it addresses YMI's own community roles, rules, and expectations. Being on the other side of the music industry (producing an event) showed the YMI students, as musicians themselves, what not to do—another entrepreneurial 'know-what'. This learning is acknowledged by Tristan:

> It has shown me that with my own band you just have to be on the ball, cause I know that other people who were trying to organise an event, they'd just cut you if you're not like responding to emails, you're not just there waiting to be directed, you just have to be on the ball. (Tristan, Interview, Phase 2)

Matt has now experienced the frustration that event managers have with young bands' attitude towards concert logistics and the number of people working behind the scenes. The excerpt also exemplifies their own expectations about community norms and roles. In this excerpt, Matt, quickly responded to the post displaying his frustration through the use of capital letters and preemptively defending his competency.

In this phase of their learning (Phase 2), the students nurtured a strong sense of commitment and held each other accountable. This is particularly evident in the excerpt above when Hayden affirms for Matt that he is an 'efficient worker'. Through the process, they were able to experience first-hand the gaps in young people's music education and the consequences of these gaps, and thus learn for themselves what is expected of musicians in the industry. They were also able to acquire knowledge of the music industry structure, its regulatory environment, and the various roles and careers available. As Hayden explains:

> I've learned a whole lot as a musician, knowing how people pick bands for a concert, like how tech people work, knowing that people that run the event put in a lot more effort than you know. Knowing how to work with other bands and other musicians and how to promote yourself, how to speak to other music industry people. I know all of the different careers and how roles work and intertwine with each other. How to approach managers, agents, festival organisers, and promoters successfully to be able form a connection and begin a working relationship. There is an art to the email, and that bit of extra effort can make the difference between being rejected or given a chance. (Hayden, Interview, Phase 2)

Hayden was proactive throughout his time in YMI, making sure that he extracted the most out of every experience. His understanding of the entrepreneurial competencies—'know-why', 'know-how', and 'know-what'—are articulated in the interview excerpt below that was conducted at the end of Phase 2. His understanding of how the music industry works continued to deepen, as he explains two years later in reflection:

> I've also learnt that a lot of people will give you a chance, if you show them that you are making an effort to do something. This is especially true in the music industry, as it is all very fickle, people come and go and false promises are common. I feel that I was treated with respect, instead of being treated like a school student, by some of the industry professionals simply because I showed them that I was making an effort. (Hayden, Interview, Phase 3)

Here, Hayden describes common practices in the industry, in particular, the making of false promises (For example, he was offered several job opportunities at the end of Phase 3, and only one job offer was real). The experience and entrepreneurial competencies that he developed over the three years allowed him to move from the periphery towards the centre of the professional music industry (Fig. 8.2).

Through his leadership within YMI, Hayden was able to bring his boundary knowledge back to that community to develop the competence of other members. This process can be evidenced in the following extract. It is taken from a PowerPoint that Hayden presented to the YMI team at a meeting in early Phase 3.

This is how the organisation will run in the future:

- When we work at meetings and online, we are all professional, we all know what is going on, we all know the purpose of what we are doing and why we are meeting.
- We should surprise other organisations, not only with our awesome events, but with our clear sense of direction, professionalism and communication skills.
- If something important happens. E.g. important meeting, then we need to share this with each other so that we all know what is happening.

The significance of this extract is the explicit statement and reinforcement of the community's norms of engagement that the students had been working towards from the beginning. However, by this stage—the transition from Phase 2 to 3—the students were able to articulate

> *Hayden pursued opportunities outside of YMI time. He developed very 'adult-like' working relationships with people in the industry through our partnerships, which had its benefits and risks. I was not aware that during Phase 3, Hayden was being invited to industry events and became quite social with industry key players. While he was 18 and recognised the 'networking' potential of attending these events, they did blur the line between what is 'school-activity' and what is 'personal-activity' which raised concerns around 'duty of care'. I did have an open and honest conversation with Hayden's father who was fully aware and supportive of Hayden's involvement in the industry.*

Fig. 8.2 Reflection Box 11: growing beyond the school walls

and refine both their enterprise and their repertoire of industry knowledge to reflect how other successful music industry organisations operated.

Summary: Learning About Music Industry Expectations

I was always concerned with how the students, as young musicians themselves, would translate formal school knowledge into actual music industry engagement. Through the Emerging Professional Learning Model, therefore, I deliberately fostered an environment where the students would not be functioning solely as musicians, but as music industry workers, producers, and managers. However, the Facebook interactions and interviews displayed how the students learned through engaging with professional scenarios.

Some students could translate the experience of working behind the scenes to their own bands. In Phase 2, the students' growing frustration over young bands not returning contracts, emails, and other necessary information helped them to see what they should not do in their own bands. They also acknowledged that an awareness of what happens behind the scenes was a valuable experience, as it provided them with a broader set of skills and knowledge with which to communicate with industry professionals. This knowledge was important in refining their own, more professional enterprise in Phase 3. In this final phase, the students adopted a structure, and created job descriptions for an organised community capable of running a music festival.

The deliberate design of partnering YMI with other professional music industry communities was the means by which their industry knowledge was acquired. The experience of partnering on projects such as *Little BIGSOUND*, and working with a professional publicity company on the *Four Walls Festival*, provided the bridging capital that allowed students to move across the boundary of the YMI Community of Practice into other Communities of Practice. Observing at the periphery of other communities and, in some cases, having the opportunity to deepen their experience through legitimate participation, gave students useful knowledge to take back into the YMI community.

Table 8.2 Learning about music industry expectations across the three phases

Phase	Learning about music industry expectations
Phase 1 (Student phase)	
Phase 2 (Student to professional phase)	• Learning about music industry structure and roles • Learning about the responsibilities of musician through working on the other side of the music industry (event management)
Phase 3 (Professional phase)	• Learning about the nature of the music industry • Learning about professionalism (emails, presentation, effort)

Towards the end of the design, some students were able to critically reflect on detailed elements of the industry. Table 8.2 offers a summary of the ways in which the students learned about music industry expectations across the three phases.

Learning About Music and Musicians

Programming music events and festivals requires research and careful planning for the event to be successful. The music has to be of high quality, and it should appeal to the target audience. To program several gigs a year, as well as an annual festival, YMI needed to access a significant number of bands. While they were initially able to engage their own personal networks to source bands, they later relied heavily on broadening their networks to access new musical acts. Ivan explains: 'I've been educated a lot on different types of music through YMI, for example when we sat down and started to plot out Four Walls, I was like, who are these bands' (Interview, Phase 2). Exposing students to a wide range of music is a crucial aspect of music education, and this new knowledge produces a more industry-aware music student. As Ivan articulated, each individual in YMI brought a unique body of knowledge of music and, when pooled, this knowledge, which is quite often questioned or ignored in traditional music classrooms, allowed each individual to learn more about musical styles. In the Phase 2 Facebook excerpt below, the students discuss strategies for sourcing new bands for their events.

Brandon	In terms of emerge applicants
	the girl is the only new one
	other bands like [Band N] and [Band O] have played before any ideas?
Ciaran	we find bands and suggest it to them?
Chris	I know 2 acoustic acts, real fresh, never done gigs
Chris	just go on triple J Unearthed *look for bands from brisbane and contact them
	go to the charts, mightbe we can score a good band, [Band P] were there before they became big
Ciaran	yeah, go and like 'headhunt' people.
	*Unearthed is an online competition designed to find and 'dig up' hidden talent from across Australia

This excerpt from Phase 2 is further evidence of how strategically YMI was looking to expand their network of young bands. They had exhausted their personal networks and were looking for something fresh. Chris suggests that the YMI team do a thorough research of the (radio station) Triple J website for 'Unearthed' bands and, in their words, 'headhunt' appropriate acts. It was a common practice for YMI members to post suggestions in the Facebook threads with a link to the Triple J Unearthed website. This, in itself, is an entrepreneurial approach; in this case, garnering 'know-who'. The students developed the confidence and professional skills needed to initiate contact with prospective bands, as well as the ability to approach bands in person.

This strategy worked well for the students when they staged an *Emerge* event in the regional town of Cairns (Phase 3). Having no personal contacts there, meant that they needed to search for bands via the internet, including the Triple J Unearthed website. The event in Cairns was a success, and a subsequent collaboration between Hayden and a Cairns artist has since seen them perform around Australia. While these loose and unfamiliar network ties involve a degree of uncertainty and risk, this strategy is also an example of the necessary risk-taking behaviour associated with entrepreneurialism. If successful, risk-taking can open up a whole new level of opportunities and resources. In the year after this study finished, YMI were able to reconnect with their newly acquired Cairns network, and offer them opportunities to perform at events in Brisbane.

In Phase 3, YMI were inundated with applications to perform at their events. In this more professional iteration of the design, the students were more strategic in the selection of bands to best reflect their brand, or their enterprise. In the Facebook excerpt below, the students discuss bands and musicians that had applied, by providing YouTube links for perusal.

Brandon	Band Suggestions :)
	[Band Q] – [YouTube link entered]
	[Band R] – [YouTube link entered]
Brandon	Not the best, but she will be applying [enters a YouTube link to 'Band S']
	She will bring more numbers then [Band O] and [Band T] mixed. Not even kidding, her image and friendship and all her people are just so huge, what do you guys think?
Hayden	I think we should be focusing more on bands this year, I dont really think we should get people like that gold coast chick which was just her and an acoustic guitar.. it's too awkward for our mega stage
Brandon	Thats what me and Tristan were talking about.....usually with 3 bands 1 acoustic singer, the crowd quiets down or sits down etc. and its awkward for the next band.
	So mightbe the best idea would be is if we find good acoustic bands and they apply, tell them their application has been reserved for the chillout emerge at the parklands
Ethan	And I don't think we should get people to play just because they'll bring a crowd
Indigo	[Band U youtube link entered]
	he'd bring people
	even if his timing is awful...
Tristan	[Band V] [youtube link entered]
	[Band W] [youtube link entered]
Brandon	Also [Band X] applied
Tristan	[Band X]? Dude they are amazing...they have won multiple band comps.

Sharing knowledge is a strong feature of the way the students engage in their community and build their bonding capital. Sharing weblinks was the most common form of research and sharing knowledge in the YMI community. In this particular excerpt, YouTube examples are used as tools to drive their discussion.

Indigo's remark about musical quality—in this case, a criticism of the artist's timing—is counter to the aims of audience building. However, it displays long term thinking, and an ability to consider the reputation of the festival beyond the short term gain of audience numbers. Ethan reinforces the concept that bringing a crowd to a concert is not the sole criteria for building the reputation of a music festival. Tristan shares his knowledge of the success of one of the bands in winning several band competitions. For the students, this was considered a legitimate indicator of the quality of a band. This approach demonstrates that the students were developing and modifying their enterprise, nuancing their 'know-what' and 'know-who' entrepreneurial attributes by diversifying.

As young emerging professionals, students were also aware that expanding their networks would increase their financial viability and profit. In order to expand in Phase 3, they employed strategies that would achieve a better experience for both audience and performers, as well as create more opportunities for emerging musicians. Specific strategies included the improvement of their *Emerge* product, and the addition of an acoustic event. The new stage afforded the students new challenges and goals, which, in turn, provided more learning opportunities.

The students' capacity to grow business through bridging capital was evidenced in Phase 3. Hayden mentions in a Facebook post: "[Band Z] could be a good option to go with, I think, they are super popular to our teenage girls indie audience" (Facebook, Phase 3). This idea allowed the bands themselves to become effective marketing tools for the YMI events. This 'know-what' competency was further demonstrated throughout Phase 2 and Phase 3. Specifically, the students were able to procure headline acts at the *Four Walls Festival* that were on the cusp of breaking through to the next level of popularity in the market. This approach saved money and added to the cultural capital of the festival, and the students considered their curation to be a key feature of their enterprise and success.

In Phase 2, the students were able to negotiate a deal with a young Australian musician and entrepreneur who had been slowly building his popularity by conducting 'secret garden' shows throughout Australia. The students were happy with their ability to negotiate a deal with his manager and have him perform at the *Four Walls Festival* in Phase 2. Faith commented at the festival debrief: "Some festivals are renowned for picking the best bands that next year are blossoming, we can totally do that!" (*Four Walls Festival* Debrief, Phase 2). This entrepreneurial mindset of not just 'know-who', but also 'know-when', helped the students grow their enterprise. This combination of who and when became a significant part of the students' repertoire, as discussed in the below Facebook excerpt from Phase 3:

| Indigo | [Band K] are in this months rollingstone. Yeh yeh! |
| Brandon | I think we found our next famous band guysss ;) |

Students procured this particular band for a very reasonable fee. Here, Indigo states that the band had been featured in *Rolling Stone* magazine, an influential industry publication. This is proof for the students that they had accomplished their goal of finding the next up and coming band.

Summary: Learning About Music and Musicians

Throughout the three learning phases the students managed the programming of their events by developing relationships and exploring new music. They developed criteria for choosing bands and created strategies for finding new musical acts. This work diversified their events to cater for different musical styles, and generated an ability to host events in other cities. In Phase 1, the students relied heavily on their personal networks when sourcing bands. They spent this period pooling networks to learn more about the local music scene. As a start-up venture developing their community of practice, they were mobilising social capital to build resources.

By design, Phase 2 gave greater ownership to the students, who chose to expand the size and frequency of their events. Students had depleted their personal networks to source bands, and they now had to develop other strategies. This involved operationalising networks built on looser ties, such as tapping into the 'Unearthed' network, or identifying and approaching musicians at events such as band competitions.

While working with artists that were unfamiliar presented a risk for YMI, it also created a learning opportunity for them to develop new criteria for their programs. These criteria placed heavy emphasis on how popular the band was and how many people they would bring to a YMI event. There was also a strong focus on whether a band could engage an audience effectively in a live performance. These are interesting criteria, new to the field of music education, but highly relevant to the music industry. Students also integrated musicianship in their criteria and relied on recommendations from trusted sources in their personal networks, feedback/reviews from industry experts, and music publications.

For a community of practice, a fine balance had to be struck between deep expertise at the core, where the students were very comfortable, and the unknown riskier place at the boundary or periphery where new learning occurs. This has been referred to in Chapter 4 as 'imagining' in CoPs, where the tension created by convergence at the centre and divergence at the periphery perpetuates a learning community by enabling the development of new repertoire, which, in turn, allows the community to refine their enterprise. In this case, the students explored the unknown by conducting research, sharing weblinks, and applying agreed criteria. This approach became part of their growing repertoire. The ability to cross boundaries and access bridging capital had a significant impact on their learning and development.

In Phase 3 of the Emerging Professional Learning Model, I brokered a partnership between YMI and the Cairns Regional Council and Performing Arts Centre to host an *Emerge* event. This would be preceded by a workshop and networking session, hosted by YMI, for high school students around North Queensland. The benefits of working at the boundary of their community created the potential for innovation and learning, where they were taking the risks of weaker ties or bridging capital to open up new opportunities and resources.

During this time, YMI was able to develop repertoire in the form of resources, which would later enable them to interpret, challenge and

Table 8.3 Learning about music and musicians across the three phases

Phase	Learning about the business
Phase 1 (Student phase)	• Broadening knowledge of musical styles • Researching and getting to know the local music scene
Phase 2 (Student to professional phase)	• Developing criteria for programming • Using external feedback for judging the merits of a band • Developing strategies for acquiring new bands for events • Developing research skills by using social media, sharing knowledge and experience
Phase 3 (Professional phase)	• Diversifying events to cater for various musical styles • Applying knowledge for hosting an event in a regional centre • Leveraging loose connections to create new events and new music

negotiate with the broader industry. These entrepreneurial competencies were crucial aspects of the students' learning and for the overall expansion of YMI as an organisation. Table 8.3 offers a summary of YMI's learning about music and musicians across the three phases.

Learning About Sustainability

The final category of entrepreneurial knowledge for the music industry presented in this chapter deals with the sustainability of the YMI organisation. Sub-categories emerged from the data that displayed how the students reflected on, and developed strategies and objectives for keeping themselves motivated to continue their work, understanding how the organisation would grow and remain competitive. Considering these objectives, sustainability became an important aspect of the design as YMI expanded.

For Phase 2, bringing the new Year Ten 'intern' students into YMI was not only important in assisting during the events, but also for succession planning. In Phase 3, the students were increasingly attached to what they had grown, and exhibited a strong desire to continue the organisation after they finished Year Twelve. Therefore, Phase 3 was designed to assist them in becoming more professional, and to formalise their activities. The emerging sub-categories of the broader 'sustainability' category included succession planning, roles and governance, and maintaining a community passion and vision. Each of these sub-categories is now discussed to demonstrate how the students considered these issues, and the implications of their decisions.

Succession Planning

With everything that had been achieved in each phase, and the growing strength of the students' bonding capital, there was always an underlying question of what would happen after these students finished Year 12, and how they would implement strategies for 'handing over' to the next generation. Early in Phase 2), the students and I discussed the idea of bringing the newly arrived Year 10 students into YMI, given the expansion and ambitious frequency of our events. The data presented here shows the students struggling with the idea of bringing new people into the organisation and their community of practice. This section explores their reflections in this regard, and the varied strategies and conditions they applied.

Ivan played a major role as producer in Phase 1, and approached Phase 2 with a broader perspective. In Phase 2, in the Facebook forum, he raises the need to bring in younger students:

Ivan	Also :) I think that it is really important that we really start to foster a new committee who will eventually take over. I feel like if we can find suitable people in gr 10 we can make sure that the organisation is sustainable not just a one hit wonder. yeah!

While Phase 2 was deliberately designed to hand ownership to the students so that they could discover what they needed to learn in order to enact their vision, I did recommend that they consider recruiting new students at this stage. This excerpt shows Ivan explicitly trying to raise internal awareness of sustainability within the YMI group.

This post received little response, however, it provided the starting point for future exploration. One possible interpretation of the lack of response could be students' reluctance to hand over what they had built. At the beginning of Phase 3, students explicitly expressed sentiments to this effect. This turn of events is discussed further on in this section.

Later in Phase 2, the team advertised in the school's student notices for students to join YMI. They received an overwhelming response, and YMI grew from a core team of eight to twenty-five. The first idea that they implemented was to set up a new 'Junior YMI' Facebook group, where the new members could be updated on what the core team were doing. The Facebook interactions from the 'Junior YMI' group were not collected as part of the dataset for this study. These new members were not involved in the strategic planning or decision-making processes; rather, they helped out at events by selling tickets, ushering, selling drinks, meeting and escorting bands, and with stage set up.

In the following Facebook excerpt from Phase 2, Hayden declares that it is time to include the Year Ten students in the core YMI Facebook group.

Hayden	Hey guys, just letting you know I am adding all of the grade 10's to this group
	It's about time they become a part of YMI
Indigo	this is about to get hecticcc
Hayden	it'll be good, they are keen as beanz to become a part
Indigo	yeah, it'll just be hard to keep track. it'll be fine

For the first half of Phase 2, the Year Ten interns had been separated from the core team and were not granted legitimacy or full membership. This had further implications for the development of their competency. This positioning also limited their opportunities for learning, and for eventually moving to the centre of the community. In this excerpt above, Hayden explicitly acknowledges the fact that up until this point, they have not been a part of the YMI team. Hayden displays an awareness of YMI's sustainability, and the importance of granting the new students legitimacy by being involved in the Facebook group.

For a community of practice, bringing new members into the group is also an opportunity for reinvigorating their enterprise, creating new repertoire, and building more social capital. Indigo, always the voice of caution, expresses mixed feelings about the decision, and demonstrates an awareness of the risk involved. She is most concerned about how the increased number of participants will be managed. While her caution balances Hayden's optimism, both students are behaving with entrepreneurial 'know-when' and 'know-how', as they consider how to stage the incorporation of new people. This episode also reinforces the importance of sustainability through legitimate peripheral participation.

As the planned merge unfolded, the new members were reluctant to join in the Facebook conversations, and the older members were not sure of how to involve them. Three days later, as seen in the Facebook excerpt below, Brandon rather abruptly instructs the new members in how to participate.

| Brandon | grad 10's need to comment as well...i had a grad 10 from ymi tell me what she thinks but was to scared too post in the convo.... |
| | SO PARTICIPATE |

The younger members, who had been granted access to the official Facebook meeting group, continued to occupy a peripheral position, and to lurk rather than participate. This could be considered a usual phase for any newcomers who have yet to grasp the community norms and rules of engagement. These conditions, internal to the community of practice, need to be understood for legitimate participation to occur or develop. The older students were simply expecting that the new members would automatically become a part of the democratic processes that had been established over the past 18 months.

One young student had confided in Brandon that she felt uncomfortable sharing her ideas. Brandon's way of dealing with this was to make public that information, followed by an instruction to participate (given in capital letters). Due to the strong bonding capital and trust built over time, these unmoderated styles of conversation were accepted among the older members; however, they were foreign, and confronting, to the newcomers. While Brandon's instruction was well intended, the implications for not granting the newcomers the time to get to know the community had risks for their full integration and learning. It also posed problems for the intended sustainability of the YMI organisation.

After the *Four Walls Festival* in Phase 2 a debrief meeting was held, where the younger students were more confident about contributing to the conversation. I asked a few questions unrelated to the festival, as I was interested in how the Year Tens were feeling about their involvement. In the excerpt below (Phase 2 Four Walls Festival debrief) a combination of 'old' and 'new' student input, I discuss the effectiveness of the Facebook meeting group for communication purposes. Older members take the opportunity to celebrate the work of the younger students at the festival.

Kristina: communication between the young members, your best methods of communication—tell me about how that's evolved?
Faith: now we have all the grade 10's that's working
Tom: I think since the Facebook thing started that's when we've gotten better
Hayden: it's evolved a lot
Tom: cause every night you get home you talk about YMI
Kristina: what about the grade 10s?
Ethan: yes!!
Kristina: do you still feel like you're on the outer?
Ethan: no it's a lot more inclusive now, that it's not the 'YMI junior team' before I was like, well, but now its a lot better, because you feel like you're contributing now
Hayden: and you are! Like you just did Four Walls, and it would not have run without you
[they all clap and cheer for the year 10s]
Tristan: and thanks for being excited about it too.
Hayden: and now you know how awesome and exciting it is so you can do it next year.

In this excerpt, students acknowledge that Facebook is the most effective means of communication and the Year Tens feel that the situation has become more inclusive. Ethan feels that their earlier placement as the 'Junior YMI team' Facebook group was somewhat demeaning, but now their contributions are valued.

The restructured communications marked an important step towards achieving legitimate participation. Also significant is the enthusiasm that the older members show for their joint enterprise, and the celebratory way that they engage the Year Tens. Hayden again creates awareness of sustainability through succession planning in the conversation, when he extends an invitation to the younger students to take more control and ownership of the festival in Phase 2.

Phase 2 was about the students finding their own way. While they did not have the strategic knowledge or skills related to succession planning, their first step was to become aware of the issue of enterprise sustainability, and the need to bring newcomers into the group. The interview data captured at the end of Phase 2, however, told a different story in relation to the new members in the YMI team, as Indigo explains:

> I think having the committee was really good, but as soon as we added the Grade Tens it added an extra layer of confusion and even more people were getting into it, like there were more comments posted, and more opinions to take into account and it made deciding things just so much harder, yeah, the name of the jazz cafe - it was ridiculous there was about 280 comments on the same post, and I really wanted 'the den' so I was like 'the den' and then it was just irritating…At Four Walls I saw one of our grade 10s sitting in the lift with a boy, like you just don't do that… it was definitely a social thing and image for the grade 10s. (Indigo, Interview, Phase 2)

Indigo's complaint in the excerpt above is evidence of the students not having clear strategies for managing the expansion of YMI. The older members had high expectations of themselves as a community; however, by the end of Phase 2, it became clear that the new students did not share those same expectations. This can be attributed to the strong bonding capital that the older members had built previously when first growing their community's vision. The newcomers would not share the sense of achievement that came from being a foundation member, and this would have been a barrier to full inclusion and motivation. The older members tried to implement a democratic approach, and, while they had more physical support for their events, the extra bodies created more work.

Indigo also believed that some of the new members were not involved for the right reasons, but because it was 'cool', and provided them with a great opportunity for socialising. While these are valid reasons for participation, the current model was not built on these values, and this created a tension between the older and younger members. Reasons for membership are a difficult issue. YMI was born out of a group of students who, together, expressed a need for greater industry knowledge and skills. For the new students, YMI was not born out of their particular needs and vision, indicating that a new model might need to be considered.

Roles and Governance

As part of the Phase 3 design, there was a full-day, facilitated workshop, which included the original YMI team; one of the younger members, industry stakeholders and partners, and the principal of the school. I include some of the facilitator's reflections (below) to assist in providing some context to Phase 3 of YMI. The facilitator listened to the stories of the students for the first hour, in order to help them identify the issues and see a broader picture. In the following comments, she relays her summation of the issues back to the students.

> So this is broadly the challenges, and so far the challenges are 'bringing new people along' and 'some resources stuff' and so what about this one, 'supporting new people distracted us from the big picture' is that about 'bringing new people along' - the challenge? (everyone agrees) and 'it's easier to just do it yourself' (all nod heads) and some of this stuff – 'it's hard having too many people organising the event' (everyone agrees), so it's hard to bring people along on the road when you just need to get stuff done (all agree). (Workshop facilitator)

Brandon elaborates by conceptualising the previous model's roles:

> It was pretty much like, an organisation saying that volunteers were part of the organisation like it ended up being, or the easiest way to describe them was they were volunteers and the way we categorised them or treated them was like they were part of the organisation. (Workshop)

Here, Brandon reflects on the way they handled the process of bringing the new students into the community, highlighting the confusion over what exactly constituted community membership. Brandon believes that they treated the new students as regular members, but did not provide them with genuine opportunities for being a part of the strategic or decision-making processes. As a result, they then perceived that their lack of participation at this level gave them volunteer status only. Ethan discusses what it was like becoming a new member of YMI:

> Coming into the organisation, especially in the first term, when everyone was trying to give us opportunities it wasn't easy speaking up because you guys were like, you had a rapport. You knew each other very well and we didn't know what to say or how everything worked yet, and then we learned that you guys were telling everyone what to do. (Workshop)

Ethan's explanation sheds light on why the process of bringing new people into YMI had been so difficult. The younger students were intimidated by the strong rapport that the older members had. This capacity to exclude others constitutes one of the downsides of bonding capital. As Ethan explains, they did not know how things worked, and that made it difficult to contribute. He also points out that the older members were not necessarily open to new ways of doing things, but rather gave instructions.

For full acceptance into a community of practice, the members must all be provided with opportunities to contribute, and to feel that their contributions are valued. However, in their own accounts, the older members of YMI were reluctant to accept the opinions and ideas of new members. Indigo confessed, and the others agreed: "we're not so sure how much we want to hand it over" (Workshop), indicating both the ownership they felt and the potential threat of newcomers wanting to change what they had worked so hard to achieve. The facilitator, in listening to the students, reflected back to them:

> Sustainability is about bringing new peeps in and I'm hearing a lot of 'us and them' and to be honest hearing 'us and them' - and people are kind of saying that a lot, and it's not intentional, but if that's how it was felt, then possibly coming in is probably hard (Tristan agrees) and there's a sense that people were coming to you, in this kind of chaos stuff, and it feels a bit like people were coming and they kind of didn't have a role so they didn't quite know what to do. (Workshop facilitator)

The students identified that formalising roles was something they had struggled with in the past, and that they hoped they could achieve some clarity around their organisational structure by the end of the workshop. The facilitator agreed that formalising roles would help 'take the weight off', and asked the students what they had already considered. They presented a new model in which they saw themselves as a small committee, with each member allocated a specific role. They separated the new students into two levels of membership, intern, and volunteer. Brandon explained to the group that volunteering was considered a "one day thing" and internship was to be a "long term thing" (Workshop). Tom suggested that "volunteering is about doing jobs on the day such as selling drinks, while interning is sitting in on meetings where you actually skill yourself up" (Workshop).

The students came to the realisation that sustainability requires support structures, where each person knows what they are responsible for, and has the support to be successful in that responsibility. Being successful and having the need for achievement were the values that underpinned participation in YMI, and can be recognised as part of entrepreneurial 'know-why' competency.

Factoring organisational sustainability into strategy emerged as a crucial issue and, by the end of the workshop, the students not only had a clearer model for organising themselves, but also could see the value of involving their stakeholders and partners in the process. In other words, building linking capital and aligning communities of practice would

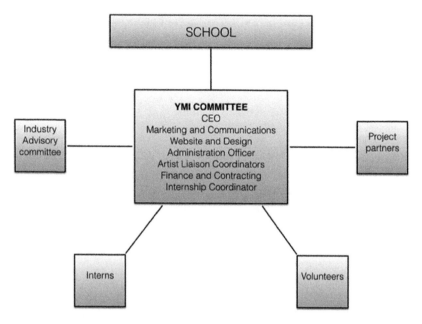

Fig. 8.3   YMI governance model, Phase 3

now be an explicit part of YMI's repertoire and enterprise. By the conclusion of the workshop, the students and partners had devised a formal governance model, which is presented in Fig. 8.3.

Hayden moved into a CEO role, managing stakeholders and partners, and creating further partnership opportunities. Other roles included:

- marketing and communications (Indigo)
- website and design (Brandon)
- administration officer (Faith)
- artist liaison coordinators (Tom and Tristan)
- finance and contracting (Chris) and
- internship and mentoring coordinator (Ethan)

The students agreed that project management would be a floating role for each event. Interns would be selected and appointed to the

> *The internship program was not successful, and as a result the new students were not as skilled and as emotionally invested in YMI for Phase 4. The Year 12s were confident that they would continue to grow YMI, but a few months after leaving school, most of them had moved on to their own projects, careers and university studies.*

Fig. 8.4 Reflection Box 12: succession planning

committee by an application process. Once appointed, they would be involved in all meetings, and shadow a specific YMI committee member for the duration of the year with the intention of taking over the role the following year. Volunteers would only be required on the day, with training and briefing provided prior to the events. The students felt that having an intern selection process would separate those who were serious and those who were not.

It was also recommended, that YMI must be accountable to the school, with Hayden responsible for regular reporting to the principal. An industry advisory committee would be put in place and include four industry professionals, one YMI member, the school principal, and myself to guide the students in overall decision-making processes. The project partners, such as QMIA, would work directly with YMI to continue to deliver events such as *Little BIGSOUND* and workshops and events in regional towns. Interns and volunteers would fall directly under the YMI committee.

Working with stakeholders and partners at the workshop proved beneficial for the students as the model they proposed was shaped and refined to meet the needs of all involved. The formalising of roles within YMI was effective and improved the organisation and communication between the students and partners, and the delivery of their events. However, the internship process later proved unsuccessful. Hayden reflected, "it was very difficult to transfer this sense of ownership to the younger cohorts, and we were so busy with grade 12" (Interview, Phase 3). This is possibly attributed to the committee members lack of mentoring skills. While the professionalism and benchmark of YMI was raised, issues around sustainability continued the following year (Fig. 8.4).

Awareness, Vision, and Passion

For a community of practice to be sustained over time, its members require the opportunity for mutual engagement. The challenge and learning that occurs at the boundaries of other communities keeps their own enterprise from becoming stale. It is also essential for sustainability that an organisation understands the realities and broader context of the industry in which it operates, and can take advantage of the emerging gaps in the market. Finally, to ensure sustainability, the entrepreneur needs 'know-why' competency, and the motivation and passion to drive an innovation.

Towards the end of Phase 2, the students reflected on the need to refine their enterprise to remain competitive in the market. In the Facebook excerpt below, Indigo keeps the group informed about a similar organisation based on the Gold Coast.

Indigo	young kickstarters are doing really well...
Chris	whats that?
Indigo	[enters a link to the kickstarters website]
Indigo	read the top post
Chris	mm
Hayden	yeah, they are pretty proactive
Indigo	keen to start work again
Brandon	working on the site and a new video as we speak....
Ethan	Young kickstarters managed to get the basement for their gigs, we need to start doing stuff again D: D: D:
Hayden	We are man, we just need to sort out our position within the school first – which we are trying to fix tomorrow ☺

At the time of this excerpt, the events had been completed for the year, and the YMI team was considering their next steps in order to organise themselves the following year. This appeared urgent, given the emergence of other youth organisations. Hayden demonstrates entrepreneurial 'know-when', particularly at this point in their journey as they seek to redefine their enterprise and build new repertoire. Tom also demonstrated 'know-when' a few weeks earlier when he suggested that they need to take a step back, "remember when we first had that meeting about what YMI should be, I think we need to have that again, scrap everything we've known, and decide what we want to be" (*Four Walls* Debrief, September, Phase 2).

The discussions demonstrate two opposing approaches: keeping up with the competition, and taking a step back to get things right. These contrasting perspectives and knowledge exchanges demonstrate the maturing procedural repertoire that sustained and renewed their enterprise.

A couple of weeks later, as seen in the Facebook excerpt below, Brandon suggests that someone from YMI attend an event being hosted by another group of young people outside of the school.

Brandon	is anyone going to soundsesh tomorrow?
	if so, take a camera and take few pics of the place. would be interesting to see how they set the whole thing up. the two people are running it, Carly and Connie have messaged me etc.
	and they are running it by themselves…just them two
	but I wished them good luck and posted the event on the YMI page
	nice peoplee
Hayden	I'm going, and I'll be saying hey
Chris	I should be there

The feature of interest in this excerpt is the idea of not only raising awareness of the competition, but networking and learning from them. The harvesting of social capital and entrepreneurial 'know-who' is evident here, where both parties leverage resources and ideas from each other. In this case, Soundsesh was promoted through the YMI networks, and YMI were able to acquire new 'know-how' and bring that back into their own community.

In Phase 3, the YMI team continued to demonstrate awareness of the broader industry in which they were operating, and would regularly inform each other of what they had discovered. For example, Hayden posted a weblink to the program guide of a major music festival, commenting: "such a smart way to advertise the bands…Brandon, could be inspiration?" (Facebook, Phase 3). This comment, together with the previous excerpt, are evidence that awareness of industry practices, improved their competitive edge and sustainability.

Building on this notion that sustainability requires an awareness of the broader context, the students needed to understand the opportunities in the market. Having entrepreneurial 'know-who' and 'know-when' competencies enabled them to address these gaps in YMI's sustainability and success. At the end of his time in YMI, Tristan reflects:

> The first discussion was based around the frustration that there were no underage gigs for us as collective musicians to play and be involved with.
> This spurred to excitement at the idea that we could change that - that we as a group of motivated youth could combine our collective skills to put on events to cater towards people just like us. (Tristan, Interview, Phase 3)

The students demonstrated entrepreneurial competencies by identifying the gaps, and aligning these gaps with their collective skills and the school resources—inner city location, recording studio and performance spaces. The students mobilised this social capital to build YMI as a platform for creating products that would fill the gaps in the broader music industry.

Part of the students' vision to be competitive and sustainable was to provide experiences of the highest quality. They realised early on that this required substantial funding. Thus, the goal of financial independence was another issue they raised, and one that demonstrated their growing awareness of sustainability.

Each year, the *Four Walls Festival* cost approximately $25000 AUD. These events were financed by a combination of the profits from *Emerge* events and grants. Chris explained: "In the long run we're looking to overcome any need for grants, financially that's where I would like to see YMI, not just making money, but not having to rely on grants" (Interview, Phase 2). In Phase 3, he proposed that they increase the ticket price for *Emerge* from $5 to $10, explaining that they were reputable enough now to charge this kind of money, and that the fee was comparable to smaller events around town. He also highlighted that the ticket price reflected the quality and value of their product, and that the group should not underrate themselves. As it eventuated, audience numbers did not change with the increase in ticket price, and the public seemed quite happy to pay the difference.

Entrepreneurial 'know-why' was evidenced by the students' vision. They demonstrated a sense of purpose and an awareness of how to be sustainable. This 'know-why' competency is derived from passion and motivation, and these qualities manifest as key motivators for sustainability. In YMI, these qualities were consistently nurtured by the group's ability to provide encouragement and support. In Chris's words: "it's definitely not a thing I have to do, I enjoy it, I'm all for everything we're about!" (Interview, Phase 2).

By the end of Phase 2, the students had developed a strong emotional response to their achievements. Chris explained: "When you do an event and there's people there and they look happy, and things are going smoothly, and things just work, yeah, it just feels great" (Interview, Phase 2). Chris acknowledges that they knew they had been successful when they saw others enjoying the outcome of their hard work. Ivan echoes this sentiment, describing how he felt seeing the audience "moshing" when the headline band was on stage at the *Four Walls Festival*: "It was a highlight because it was 'real' and we worked so hard and we actually accomplished it" (Interview, Phase 2).

This external reinforcement, was a significant factor in keeping the students connected emotionally to their vision. External reinforcement from other sources, such as reviews by the media and endorsements from the bands that had played at *Four Walls*, were also very powerful indicators of achievement. Indigo discussed how she felt seeing articles and reviews about YMI and the *Four Walls Festival* mentioning that, "I have them all in a scrap book I've got to admit, I just thought that was really nice" (Interview, Phase 2). Brandon also proudly posted a screenshot, showing an endorsement that [Band L] had publicly shared online:

> Youth Music Industries are the way to go! They don't need to sell any tickets and the crowd is always top notch. They are definitely the way to go for young bands in Brisbane if you ask us. They've been so good to us and have supported us through the thick of things. (Facebook post on band L's page)

Sharing these reviews and endorsements became a significant part of the enterprise's repertoire, they were reminders of how far they had come. The positive feelings and emotions that students experienced contributed significantly to the bonding capital they had developed, and manifested in the mutual support and encouragement that had also become part of their repertoire. Indigo was able to articulate this sense of support: "After the first *Emerge* this year, that was a great feeling, cause it was the first event of the year and we had so many people, and we had this giant group hug afterwards cause everyone was just so happy" (Interview, Phase 2). Keeping the workplace positive can be a challenge for most adults; however, this was an element that the students seemed to intuit naturally. In the Facebook excerpt below, Hayden takes the time to post a celebratory message to remind the group of their achievements:

Hayden	BTW guys, just wanted to say how proud I am of what we are doing. You shold all be super proud, our event will be in all magazines next week! Tell your friends! And show them how cool we are, and that we are literally running a youth festival! You should all be super proud, and excited for the festival
Brandon	this is cute! haha
Hayden	ahaha, just had a proud moment
Brandon	hahah WEW
Indigo	aww YAAAYYY goo usss!!!

Celebrating achievement and making time to build morale and pride among the group became part of their ongoing procedural repertoire and, thus, the foundation of building bonding capital.

Summary: Learning About Sustainability

At the end of Phase 1, my design intervention was to encourage the students to consider opening up YMI membership to younger students. My aim was to assist the students to start considering how they might grow and maintain YMI in the future. In Phase 2, the students developed a greater awareness of enterprise sustainability as they sought to manage the inclusion of new members into their group; however, they struggled with the question of how best to do this. For legitimate peripheral participation, the new members required legitimate access, with authentic opportunities to contribute and participate.

Later in Phase 2, the students decided to bring the new members into their Facebook group. In this way, the group grew from eight to twenty-five members. However, the downside of the bonding capital that the older students had accrued was that it intimidated the new members. Eventually, the latter became more comfortable with contributing to the Facebook forum, but their contributions were limited.

As the students moved into Phase 3, they reflected on the difficulties of working with a large group, and wanted to explore organisational sustainability as a way of moving forward. In response to this need, I created an intervention in the form of a workshop day. The workshop produced a structure, which saw younger students move into either intern or volunteer roles, and the older students move into formalised roles. The formalising of roles improved communication channels and their ability to build better bridging capital with the wider industry; however, they still lacked the skills and time to mentor their interns.

While intergenerational encounters proved difficult for the YMI team, they demonstrated other strategies related to sustainability, particularly an awareness of the market. Notably, in Phase 3, they demonstrated the ability to not only keep an eye on the competition, but also to time their reactions to the competition. They also strategically mobilised social capital by learning from their competition. The value in their being able to see development opportunities manifested in a potential for financial independence.

For community maintenance, the students were conscious of keeping their workplace positive and supportive. These intuitive ways of engaging took the form of celebratory posts, highlighting the work of the team, and reporting to the group whenever positive feedback from external participants was received. This created bonding capital, which fed the enterprise's strength of purpose. Table 8.4 provides a summary of the students' learning about sustainability across the three phases.

Table 8.4 Learning about sustainability across the three phases

Phase	Learning about sustainability
Phase 1 (Student phase)	• no evidence presented from the data
Phase 2 (Student to professional phase)	• developing awareness of enterprise sustainability • developing strategies for merging new members • developing a safe, supportive and positive workplace
Phase 3 (Professional phase)	• learning about organisational sustainability • understanding the market and competition • mobilising social capital in building sustainability • reinvigorating the enterprise • learning about financial independence

Chapter Summary

This chapter highlighted four key learning areas related to entrepreneurial knowledge for the music industry: learning about the business, learning about music industry expectations, learning about music and musicians, and learning about sustainability. The findings highlight the positive and negative impacts that social capital had on the students' acquisition of knowledge within these four entrepreneurial knowledge areas.

During the first phase of the learning design, without any formal knowledge of programming bands, students looked within their own community for solutions. They spent several months analysing their own and each other's personal networks to learn more about the local music scene. They were able to source and program most of their artists through their own networks.

Marketing is a complex field that is constantly changing, and contextually dependant, as such, the students had no formal instruction in this area. During this early phase, they used strategies such as word of mouth, and advertising on Facebook. These strategies were appropriate at this stage in their development, particularly because they were more focused on establishing their community of practice, and connecting with the knowledge that already resided within the group. The bonding capital that resulted from these strong connections gave the students a sense of purpose, which provided the impetus for sustaining their community and vision.

The experimental nature of Phase 2 allowed the students to identify what knowledge they would need to acquire in order to run their own music organisation. I specifically wanted them to learn about the industry by being producers and event managers rather than as entry-level musicians. Through their engagement with booking musicians, students gained knowledge about the various careers and roles that comprise the music industry structure. The frustration of working with young bands made them aware of the knowledge that young musicians lack, in regards to professionalism, intellectual property, and legalities.

As part of my design, I never set out to explicitly teach the students this content. Rather, my aim was to provide realistic opportunities that would create a need to develop important skills and knowledge. This approach presented some risks of potential mistakes. However, the problems created by not knowing something were highly valuable opportunities for the students in assisting them to identify their own knowledge gaps. While developing entrepreneurial 'know-what' was essential for the community, 'know-when' was an important competency that ensured that the students had their facts right before making hasty decisions.

When students had exhausted their personal networks for sourcing musicians, it became necessary to learn by stepping outside of their interpersonal networks. The idea of researching and head-hunting bands through distant and unknown networks became an important part of their procedural repertoire. This opened up opportunities for developing new repertoire in the form of band selection criteria. Exposure to industry professionals working on larger music festivals helped the students to recognise and establish certain band criteria as important for their purposes. The students' discovery and analysis of new music in this way was an important element of the Emerging Professional Learning Model, as it opened up new ways for them to engage with musical content that was useful and had authentic application.

The success of each event brought the group closer together, and provided the impetus for them to continue to learn and grow. However, further strengthening and reinforcing of their bonding capital created a culture of exclusivity. I raised the sustainability issue early in Phase 2. While the group did open up membership, they struggled throughout both Phases 2 and 3 with ways in which to engage new members and give them access to legitimate participation.

By Phase 3, the knowledge they had acquired was now being pooled, refined and applied; however, they also now had a greater sense of ownership of the knowledge, enabling them to create new ideas and strategies. Exposure to constitutive roles within industry organisations informed and influenced the students. They now had a strong desire to formalise their own organisation and set up a governance model. However, the governance model generated a hierarchy that fought against the nature of CoPs. These are key issues to consider for further Emerging Professional Learning Model iterations.

While succession planning was not successful, the students did learn about the importance of organisational sustainability. They kept an eye on the competition, while also considering the right time to respond to the market; in this case, developing entrepreneurial 'know-when'. They also learned the importance of working with their competition to leverage social capital in the pursuit of new knowledge and resources. Finally, for organisational sustainability, the students demonstrated a strong understanding of how to keep their workplace positive.

9

Design Principles to Plan Entrepreneurial Learning in Music Education

Review of Earlier Chapters

This concluding chapter establishes the design principles that can be distilled from this project, and then focuses on the implications of the Emerging Professional Learning Model for practitioners in the creative industries and for future research. The discussion highlights the iterative and collaborative nature of the learning design underpinning the emerging professional learning model. The design principles distilled can also support alternative learning models to assist students' transition to creative careers. To more effectively position the discussion of findings, implications, and contributions, the chapter begins with a review of the preceding chapters.

The project came about after working with students who were undertaking a highly academic and rigorous international curriculum in a newly established school. As an educator, I was concerned about the mismatch between student interests and aspirations, and the heavy content-driven curriculum, which could potentially lead to the development of inert knowledge (Freudenberg, Brimble, & Vyvyan, 2010); that is, knowledge that is not immediately useful. The students in this

© The Author(s) 2020
K. Kelman, *Entrepreneurial Music Education*,
https://doi.org/10.1007/978-3-030-37129-6_9

study were inspired by a newspaper article about a young Brisbane girl discussing the lack of opportunities and resources for young people to perform their music, and to attend live music events. This article resonated with the students who addressed the gaps in the music education they were being offered, that is, the skills and experiences that would equip them to participate in the wider music industry. YMI, a student-driven organisation was created in response to these gaps. The aim of this project was to develop a learning design that provided meaningful opportunities for students to learn about the music industry, and to develop the necessary skills and attributes required for sustainable careers in that industry and in the broader creative industries arena. In order to conceptualise a way forward, the literature review considered studies that broadly framed issues in contemporary education, before turning to studies of music education in particular.

Chapter 3 reviewed the body of literature addressing the implications of modern economies for teaching and learning processes. The commonalities in much of this research refer to the need for students to be better equipped for a world that is constantly changing. Employers criticise educational institutions for not preparing students to be self-directed, flexible, adaptable, creative, problem-solving and collaborative. Various researchers (Ito et al., 2013; Lebler, 2008; McWilliam, 2005; Siemens, 2008) critique conventional models of teaching and learning, and propose new approaches. These new approaches include considering students and teachers in a form of pedagogical exchange or co-creation; embracing error; and breaking away from the constraints of set curriculum. Studies—such as those by Tinto (2000), Freudenberg et al. (2010), and Kisiel (2010)—suggest that community learning environments offer the most practical contexts for exploring these new approaches to teaching and learning. However, most of these empirical studies were still situated within formal regulated environments and heuristic settings rather than authentic industry contexts. In contrast, online learning communities (Browne, 2003; Ito et al., 2013; Salavuo, 2008) are more organically formed, and ownership remains with the users who generate knowledge through their interactions. Work-integrated learning programs are also useful for giving students opportunities to experience the world of work (Freudenberg et al., 2010).

This study extended these approaches and advocated a design that enabled students to become a part of the wider industry through meaningful and collaborative engagement, whereby they could contribute and act on their own innovative and creative ideas. The literature review of studies regarding music education in industry contexts raised similar issues to those arising from the review of the more general studies. The changes in the music industry structure over the last decade now require musicians to be multiskilled and responsible for all aspects of their career development. Researchers have addressed the resulting gaps between the music industry and music education, revealing that most musicians face a future of self-employment or freelancing (Bennett, 2007; Forrest, 2001). These conditions require musicians to be entrepreneurial. This includes having not only industry knowledge, but also knowing how to leverage opportunities through networks, and having the right attributes and skills to act on ideas. While these gaps in music education have been acknowledged, there have been few empirical studies offering principles or designs for new approaches to address these gaps.

Other researchers (Folkestad, 2005; Green, 2002; Jaffurs, 2004; Westerlund, 2006) have studied popular music and musicians, and the informal and self-directed approaches reported by Green (2001) and Jaffurs (2004) were useful starting points for my study; however, their studies still focused on how the students learned music, not on their industry skills. However, it was difficult to find studies reporting on programs that enabled young music students the opportunity to develop skills and knowledge in authentic music industry contexts, with a focus on developing entrepreneurship. While many studies recommended that music students develop business skills and entrepreneurship (Beckman, 2007; Bennett, 2004; Oakley, 2007), there is limited research on how this might be embedded in their education, rather than simply included as an 'add-on'.

Chapter 4 presented a theoretical frame for the study's design and its analysis, drawing on communities of practice, social capital, and entrepreneurialism. I built on Lave and Wenger's (1991) argument that learners should engage directly and productively in target communities (or CoPs), as opposed to being taught simulated practice in a separate learning environment. Social capital plays an important role in developing a shared purpose, which is vital for a successful CoP. Putnam (2000) emphasises the concept of bridging capital and its role in broadening people's opportunities. On the other hand, Coleman (1994) considers that closed networks offer stability, and a common shared ideology leading to an enhancement of 'bonding' human capital in the form of knowledge and skills.

Social capital can mobilise a community of practice by providing a sense of cohesion and shared purpose, and thus creating a conducive space for learning. Members' learning results from the community's ability to refine their enterprise and develop new repertoire, which, in turn, builds more social capital. In this way, social capital becomes the driver for a community's sustainability. However, social capital can have negative consequences when the strong ties between members create non-porous boundaries around the community, making it difficult for newcomers to access knowledge and accrue skills. Bridging capital, if leveraged, can create opportunities for members to gain new perspectives and new knowledge, and to challenge the community norms. The benefits of bridging capital can lead to linking capital, whereby the community can better align with the broader system, and be more effective.

The authentic context in which the CoP emerged was entrepreneurial at heart. This was attributed to the venture of launching a new enterprise where the students responded to their environment by designing and implementing new and innovative industry products. The emerging professional learning model synthesised relevant theories, and provided a framework for investigating how social capital influences a CoP's ability to develop the skills and knowledge to be entrepreneurial, and to be better prepared for a future within the music and broader creative industries. The key entrepreneurial knowledges included in the model were drawn from Johannisson's (1991) five 'know' competencies: *know-why*, *know-how*, *know-who*, *know-when*, and *know-what*.

Chapter 5 presented a methodology to address the aims and purpose driving this research: Brown's (1992) design-based research (DBR), and its mode of theoretically informed exploration of innovative learning environments. DBR has the capacity to account for the 'messiness' of real-world practice, with the context being a core consideration. As the design required students to learn through experience, it was important that I chose a methodology that allowed for flexibility, with the opportunity to revise the design iteratively, and to capture evidence of learning through social interaction. Most importantly, and key to this study, is DBR's treatment of participants, not as subjects, but as co-participants in the design (Barab & Squire, 2004).

The design phases outlined in Table 5.1 grew out of constant reflection and ongoing discussion with the students. Facebook data captured the students working together, and provided naturally occurring data of implicit and explicit learning moments and events. In addition, the interviews and group meetings were able to serve as both a part of the learning process, and as important occasions for data generation. These dialogues were beneficial for students to reflect on their journey, and to identify what would assist them to move further along the 'student to professional' continuum. These reflections informed the subsequent design phases and interventions. The information produced and collected during this collaborative journey has led to the development of a set of transferrable design principles that can inform practice in other creative industries. These design principles respond to the research aims and questions, as discussed below.

Learning Entrepreneurialism: What and How

During this project, the students developed project management skills including networking skills, the ability to set goals and complete tasks, interpersonal skills, and reflection skills. In this section, I detail each of these four categories as 'findings'.

Networking Skills

Students quickly learnt that mobilising their own personal networks, and developing their 'know-who' competency, would be key to starting the YMI venture. This enabled them to access musicians for their events, as well as build their audience. As a collective responsible for the initiatives of YMI, the students were quick to recognise each other's strengths, skills, and expertise, and realised that, they were better able to succeed as a collective. In this sense, the expertise of individuals resourced the collective enterprise. This ability to mobilise personal networks is indicative of a community learning approach, where the students were able to shift their attention from their own individual performance to their capacity to learn through their own networks; that is, to connect, access information, and forge relationships (McWilliam & Haukka, 2008).

Falk and Kilpatrick (2000) suggest that learning through interactions with others in one's community can build social capital. This study demonstrates that the interactions between the students built strong bonding social capital, which provided a sense of collective cohesion. This capital contributed to the development of community norms of trust and reciprocity, which fostered a strong common purpose or vision. Langston and Barrett (2008) assert that trust is a precondition of social capital, which, if enabled, will lead to the achievement of collective goals. In the case of this study, a high aspiration culture was fostered. Social capital was fundamental to the development of the students' joint enterprise and, subsequently, their repertoire (artefacts, events, resources, processes, words, and actions).

While bonding capital has been evidenced as facilitating a common purpose or vision and enabling a culture of high aspiration and learning, Putnam (2000) identifies the potential for strongly bonded communities to become overly inward looking. He explains that bridging capital developed through weaker or more indirect ties across different social groups can open up greater possibilities for learning and resources. Wenger (1998) similarly explains that strongly bonded CoPs can become hostage to their own history. He argues that boundary crossing through imagination can create opportunities for communities to be revitalised.

The findings of this study highlight that students were reluctant in the early stages to engage with external networks, which were introduced through the facilitating partnerships. While the students and partners collaborated on a successful innovation, *Little BIGSOUND*, they did not explore the possibilities of these networks beyond this one annual project. This had both positive and negative consequences for the students' entrepreneurialism. First, it could be seen as the students developing business acumen in managing both the constraints of time and resources, and potential risks such as loss of their intellectual property. However, it can also be seen that bonding capital can inhibit risk-taking behaviour, and restrict new ways to create business opportunities.

There were successful learning outcomes for students when they engaged with external industry networks. The knowledge and skills within these networks did resource the YMI community, enabling them to develop more effective repertoire and processes, which eventually aligned them more successfully with the broader system. This exposure to, and collaboration with industry had a significant impact on the ability of YMI to redefine the enterprise as more professional. This, in turn, enabled YMI to build more trusting and meaningful relationships with their partners and stakeholders. The exposure also increased their understanding of the risks involved in entrepreneurialism. For example, students' concern over the loss of intellectual property and potential exploitation.

The students mobilised their own personal networks to access information and make important connections, and they learned how to successfully distribute expertise across the community to achieve collective goals. Coulson (2012) highlights networking as a proactive strategy commonly used by musicians for finding work, and these skills are necessary to becoming entrepreneurial. Young (2018) refers to this mobilising of networks as a 'hunter gatherer' approach to musical entrepreneurship, and argues this mindset is crucial for the future of employment in the arts (p. 88). Opportunities that reside in networks, such as finding employment, resonate with the conditions of a flatter world (Friedman, 2005), where value is now created less within vertical silos, and more through horizontal collaboration.

Interviews with YMI members, revealed that students recognised the learning opportunities of collaboration with external networks. Kilpatrick, Barrett, and Jones (2003) argue that learning through collaboration with people and groups external to the community introduces new ideas, raises awareness of new practices, and exposes

DESIGN PRINCIPLE 1: Networking is fundamental to learning and developing entrepreneurial 'know-who'.

- The learning community should value the knowledge and expertise that resides within the students' own networks.

- The learning community must involve communities of professionals in such a way that collaborations are authentic, beneficial, and meaningful to all involved.

- Learning activities should be authentic and owned by the community, and require networking for sourcing information, making connections, and accessing resources.

Fig. 9.1 Design principle 1: networking

community members to new norms and value sets. Such learning was evidenced in YMI's transition from 'student to professional' across the design phases.

In recognising that industry networking capabilities ('know-who') is a fundamental skill for musicians and creative industries practitioners, future learning designs must place these at the centre of the curriculum, rather than concentrating on more conventional ways of teaching. In this light, the first design principle I propose is presented and elaborated in Fig. 9.1.

Setting Goals and Completing Tasks

Students learned the skills needed for executing a project through the opportunity to build an authentic enterprise, and to develop their own industry products: in this case, music festivals, a youth music venue, and a youth music industry conference. With iterations over phases and cycles of events, the students learned skills in problem-solving, negotiation, stakeholder management, time management, clearer communication processes, and organisational skills.

The discoveries in Chapter 7 show how the students were able to develop more effective processes and procedures for executing their project goals, thus developing their 'know-how' competency. The transition from student to professional was evident through their refined enterprise and new repertoire. There were several factors that enabled this development in student learning. First, it can be attributed to the environment that was established, and the building of strong bonding social capital, which provided a culture of trust and reciprocity, thus facilitating learning. Second, as the teacher, I created opportunities for the students to work in unfamiliar situations, which invoked a 'need to learn'. This afforded the students the chance to develop their skills by 'discovering and using new terminology, [and] key concepts' (Ronkin & Alhadeff, 2016, p. 27). Westerlund (2006) refers to this as 'on-demand learning'. Similarly, McWilliam (2005) recommends that unfamiliar situations align better with a fluid, scriptless world. She argues that the best learners will be the learners who can make 'not knowing' useful.

A common theme in the literature is that potential creative industries employees must have a high level of problem-solving skill because this leads to fresh opportunities, ideas, and products. Therefore, learning tasks should involve obstacles that need to be overcome. The YMI learning environment continually challenged students with problems they did not 'know-how' to solve.

Having trust, enabled the students to feel confident in sharing ideas as they negotiated solutions. This learning was evidenced in episodes where students were able to let go of their own personal beliefs in the best interests of the group, making the right decisions to move forward. They were not afraid to acknowledge mistakes, and quite often explicitly used these mistakes as ways to design better processes in future iterations.

Bonding capital, in turn, opened up opportunities for garnering bridging and linking capital. In this sense, the professional enterprise to which they aspired (and eventually achieved) gave them the confidence to bridge into the wider music industry community. It also gave stakeholders and partners more trust and confidence in the students, which eventually led to more meaningful and authentic collaborations. These relationships, created further opportunities for learning, and later

DESIGN PRINCIPLE 2: Setting goals and completing tasks is fundamental to learning and developing entrepreneurial 'know-how'.

- Students should be able to develop their own projects that are based on their interests, and actioned in authentic contexts.

- In the process of developing authentic products, students should be able to set their own goals and objectives.

- Teachers should create unfamiliar situations that generate a need to learn.

- An environment of open and honest communication is paramount, where all opinions and ideas contribute to community initiatives.

- The environment must welcome error and reflection so that students can develop their own organisational processes.

- Students should work with minimal guidance, but have recourse to the support structure of the wider community of teachers and professionals.

Fig. 9.2 Design principle 2: goals

proved important for the careers of some of the YMI students. While the learning environment was focused on nurturing informal learning processes, bonding and bridging capital provided the support structure for such learning. In this sense, the usual 'subconscious' or implicit nature of informal learning was rendered conscious and explicit, as evidenced by the knowledge and skills intentionally communicated by the group members.

In recognising that the skills involved in setting goals and completing tasks are highly desired by employers within the music and broader creative industries, future learning designs should involve authentic opportunities for students to design and implement industry products and initiatives. This leads to the second design principle (Fig. 9.2).

Interpersonal Skills

While interpersonal skills are fundamental to networking, and setting goals and completing tasks, the findings of this study reveal that the students deemed these skills valuable in themselves, which contributed to their 'know-how' competency. This was evident as they consciously worked on improving their interpersonal skills including, conflict resolution, clear communication and regular meetings, and team building. Facebook played a central role in the students' interpersonal interactions as the chosen communication platform.

As the students improved their interpersonal skills, they became more confident and adaptable, and were able to engage more effectively with their industry partners and stakeholders. The importance of these skills is noted by Temmerman (2005):

> Today's demanding workplace and knowledge-based and ideas-focussed economy expects young people to not only have certain scholastic abilities, but to increasingly demonstrate capacity in creative thinking, problem solving, flexibility and communication ... businesses are progressively requiring well-rounded, original thinkers and adaptable, confident and self-motivated knowledge workers to give them the edge in today's competitiveness market. (p. 34)

Facebook interactions captured explicit moments where students acknowledged problems with communication, and this awareness was reinforced in the interviews. While bonding social capital had enabled a democratic, horizontal approach to working together, the students revealed that it became messy at times, with 'everybody doing everything'.

Through their exposure to industry practice, the students decided that adopting a more formalised structure would improve their communication and productivity. The student ownership over specific aspects of the organisation forced them to improve their modes of communication, which enabled the community to refine a more professional enterprise with repertoire that reflected more efficient processes. While there was a focus on individual roles, the findings also show that each YMI member still actively contributed to the bigger picture, including decision-making and visioning.

The study highlighted that students had very different communication styles, and they recognised this as an important aspect to consider, especially in moments of tension. Bonding capital had enabled strong norms of trust and reciprocity, and this enabled an environment of honest communication, where students acknowledged that they felt comfortable 'talking things out' and resolving conflict.

Students also became aware of their own traits, such as stubbornness and the inability to listen to the views of others. As a result, they consciously improved these aspects of their own behaviour with the support of the group. Developing the skills to be a better collaborator and team player were successful outcomes of the learning design.

The project also revealed that engaging in virtual communities, in this case, via Facebook, was highly regarded by students as a factor contributing to their enterprise's success and their own learning. Salavuo (2008) argues that social media tools for community building offer great promise for the distributed development of knowledge and sharing practices. This value of tools like Facebook are reinforced by Li (2016) who frames social media as a form of 'collective intelligence' and as a crowdsourced community of learning (p. 346). In my study, the students were able to teach each other important technical skills and share all their research and ideas by uploading web links to various musicians and festivals as impetus for their online discussions.

In their interviews and event debriefs, students also reported that using Facebook group was convenient, enhanced their productivity and communication, and enabled them to do YMI work at any time of the day or week. They also acknowledged that the platform suited them. As Salavuo explained: 'Students have been using social network platforms in ways that weren't planned for by teachers' (2008, p. 13).

The project displays how the autonomy and ownership provided to users in online communities of their own making, enhanced their bonding social capital. However, this bonding social capital increased the already high expectations of the community, and some students revealed that they couldn't get a break from the relentless flow of YMI business on Facebook. The students also felt that some students' online communication styles were harsher than their 'in person' styles. In this way, the group revealed a subconscious sense of 'netiquette', and negotiated ways to moderate the community's practices.

Design Principle 3: Effective interpersonal skills can enhance community learning and develop entrepreneurial 'know-how'.

- The learning environment recognises the value of students engaging in both virtual and face-to-face contexts.

- Online social network platforms should be chosen and moderated by the students, and legitimated as a valuable workplace.

- Exposure to professional organisations can model various approaches to improving communication channels, both internal and external.

- Student ownership of authentic industry initiatives builds their greater sense of responsibility and accountability. This provides the impetus for students to develop community norms such as open and honest communication, leading to more effective conflict resolution, teamwork, and productivity.

Fig. 9.3 Design principle 3: interpersonal skills

Browne (2003) acknowledges that the asynchronous nature of online communities allows for reflection, thus making more thoughtful communication possible. This was also evident in the YMI study, where students would quite often post at a later time and, therefore, give a more considered response. The YMI Facebook group also revealed that newcomers required time to observe and learn the community rules before actively participating.

In recognising the value of developing the effective interpersonal skills desired by employers within the music and broader creative industries, future learning designs should involve authentic opportunities for students to become aware of their own interpersonal skills, and of ways in which these might be adapted in the pursuit of meaningful collaboration and teamwork. This leads to the third design principle (Fig. 9.3).

Reflection

The transition from student to professional is enabled by the skills and habits of reflection. Not only were the students able to improve their products from one iteration to the next, but they were also able to refine their enterprise to become more professional, thus receiving industry recognition and credibility. Forms of reflection included learning from successes and failures, developing effective forms of action, and sharing their thoughts and ideas. For example, debriefs regularly occurred after events, where typical questions raised were: 'What did we do wrong?' and 'Is there a better way we can do …?'.

In the process of reflection, the students were able to cement their relationships and thus maintain their community. The findings also demonstrate how students developed their critical thinking skills, which may have attributed to their growing ability to take more risks and exploit their creativity. The students' ability to engage in processes of reflection is indicative of entrepreneurial 'know-how', a skill that enhanced their ability to take action.

Too often in the formal classroom, assessment instruments are final, and students are not given the time and space to critically reflect and try again. This is not the case in the contemporary world of work where, as Bauman (2000) explains, what we know today is likely to be irrelevant tomorrow, and students need to be able to adapt. In this study, by the time students arrived at the final phase of the design, they were able to adapt and rethink their approaches. This was especially evident when aligning with industry partners.

Reflection became a standard practice and expectation in the YMI community. Due to the collective and supportive environment that the students had developed, failure was embraced as a learning experience, and an opportunity to improve. This is a successful outcome of the learning design as, too often, students give up when something does not work. The students' growing professionalism was evidenced as they transitioned from overenthusiastic students, who at times made hasty decisions and miscommunicated important information, to professionals who showed a more thoughtful and considered approach. This points to the development of 'know-when' competency.

DESIGN PRINCIPLE 4: Reflection and self-feedback enable students to create effective strategies for action and improvement, and develop entrepreneurial 'know-when' and 'know-how'.

- The learning environment should give students opportunities to repeat their initiatives, with space and support for meaningful reflection in between.

- Learning from failure should be embraced as an opportunity for improvement.

- Reflection should focus on both success and failure.

- Formal debriefing opportunities involving students, teachers, industry partners and stakeholders should be created.

- Teachers and students should work together to improve designs for future iterations.

Fig. 9.4 Design principle 4: reflection

Reflection was key to the community's successful transition from students to professionals. Adaptability, flexibility, and critical thinking are highly valued by employers. In a world of rapid change and uncertainty, the ability to learn from failure, and the willingness to 'de-learn or forget' and start again, are attributes that will assist young people in the creative industries and modern economies in general. This leads me to the fourth design principle (Fig. 9.4).

Industry Knowledge: 'Know-How' and 'Know-What'

The students developed industry knowledge and 'know-what' competency, plus a greater understanding of 'how' to participate in the music industry throughout the design phases. In particular, the students learned domain knowledge such as copyright considerations, budgeting strategies, and suitable criteria for talent searching. They also gained an understanding of industry expectations and professional standards, and of the importance of sustainability.

Domain Knowledge

While there was no explicit content provided for students, they were able to acquire and learn relevant knowledge 'on the job' in order to carry out their tasks. Disciplinary knowledge is arguably less important in today's economies, as knowledge requirements change rapidly. Claxton (2004) argues 'knowing what to do when you don't know what to do' is more relevant for learners today, while McWilliam (2008) suggests that students become 'prod-users' of disciplinary and interdisciplinary knowledge, rather than consumers of teacher knowledge. My design did not include explicit teaching about copyright law; rather it provided opportunities for students to be exposed to that knowledge. Due to the high-stakes environment produced by my design, the students were guided to research and learn on their own.

The industry partnerships and collaborations gave the students greater exposure to the music industry, and gave them the knowledge that they needed to run their own events successfully. In some cases, the students made mistakes that were highlighted by industry professionals; however, these situations provoked the students to research further to avoid making those mistakes again. In a sense, while the students were experts in the centre of their own community, they were novices on the periphery of the wider music industry community. Learning through exposure to the industry developed their competence.

Over time, the industry professionals granted greater legitimacy to the students, enabling a learning environment based on mutually beneficial relationships and industry projects. The experience had therefore become more than 'work experience' or peripheral participation, and had developed into a synergy between peripheral and core memberships. Bringing new knowledge and experience back into the YMI community assisted the students to refine their enterprise, build new repertoire, and become more professional in their practices. For example, the mistakes made in relation to copyright were addressed by the students the following year.

The students acquired knowledge about the business side of the music industry through experience, discovery, and mistakes.

They recognised this as 'relevant' knowledge, and refined this knowledge through multiple iterations. Not only did they acquire relevant knowledge on a 'need to know' basis, but were also able to pool their knowledge to generate new knowledge. For example, they were able to build on the knowledge of marketing strategies they had learned from their industry partners.

Students challenged traditional domain knowledge in an effort to engage with entrepreneurial industry practice. For example, they established new criteria for programming musicians at their music festivals. Rather than focusing on the traditional 'music education' criteria for assessing quality, such as technicality and precision, they developed their own criteria. These included musicians' audience engagement, and band popularity (based on the number of Facebook 'likes' or the size of the audience they attracted at a previous show). These criteria were informed by their developing industry knowledge and entrepreneurial mindset. Their process for selecting these criteria was evident in many Facebook exchanges where they shared previous research, such as YouTube links to bands or critiques of concerts. This also exemplifies what McWilliam (2005) refers to as the 'cut and paste' strategy of the creative assembler (p. 19), to acknowledge how knowledge is constantly changing, forcing learners to look beyond their main discipline. For the students, working across different disciplines such as law and marketing was vital for them to construct a music industry knowledge base or 'know-what' competency.

The highly networked and authentic environment that underpinned YMI made learning challenging but motivating for the students. This way of learning aligns with Dede's (2005) profile of millennial learners who, due to their digital lifestyles, expect education environments to be similar; that is, participative, engaging, and active. Recognising that knowledge is in a constant state of change, and that students need to 'know-how' to access relevant up to date knowledge, leads me to the fifth design principle (Fig. 9.5).

DESIGN PRINCIPLE 5: *Students acquire domain knowledge through an engagement in authentic contexts to develop entrepreneurial 'know-what'.*

- The teacher should create opportunities for students to 'need to know'.

- Opportunities for learning should focus on knowledge that is current and relevant.

- Students should have opportunities to apply their newly acquired knowledge and refine it over multiple iterations.

- Legitimate knowledge can be sourced from any node within the network of industry partners, stakeholders, teachers and students, and virtual platforms.

- Students can construct new knowledge through the pooling of resources and sharing of knowledge.

- Knowledge can be acquired through trial and error, or accidentally encountered.

- Recognising that knowledge needs to have currency and relevance, no predetermined curriculum or body of content should be stipulated.

Fig. 9.5 Design principle 5: domain knowledge

Professionalism and Industry Expectations

Students developed 'know-what' and 'know-why' competency and a nuanced understanding of the music industry by actively working in roles 'behind the scenes'. This included taking on roles such as project manager, event manager, artist coordinator, technical advisor, marketing officer, and administrator. The analysis of the Facebook data demonstrates students' growing awareness of industry roles, expectations, and professionalism through their frustrating experiences in working with young bands. In their interviews, they explicitly articulated what they had learned from such experiences, and how this had influenced their own behaviour as working musicians. They reported an understanding of the wider structure in which the musician sits, and of how all these roles interact. Most importantly, they learned about the logistical efforts behind the scenes through their own involvement in staging opportunities for young musicians.

The interviews, revealed how the students had learned the importance of punctuality, returning emails, cooperation, effort, manners, initiative, and attending to special requirements. These experiences gave the students an understanding of the variety of careers available within the music industry.

While the literature speaks of the broader skill set required by musicians today, including the benefits of networking, it does not include professionalism and knowledge of industry standards as a part of this skill set. As the students demonstrated throughout their time in YMI, compliance with industry standards and professionalism are vital for young people to make meaningful connections for their future. Operating behind the scenes in non-performer roles was fundamental for the students to grasp this knowledge ('know-what'), and to develop the attitudes, dispositions, and habits of the professional ('know-why').

This experience produced benefits for the students as individuals, and for the YMI community. The findings also display that students were able to articulate and refine their own enterprise and procedural repertoire to reflect on how other successful music industry organisations operated.

Bridging capital was fundamental for the students' transition to the professional phase. Exposure to industry practices was not always positive; nevertheless, it provided experience that gave students a more realistic understanding of the industry. For example, one student showed an awareness of some of the negative realities of the industry, including its uncertainty and the possibility of false promises being made. For some students, learning about professionalism and industry expectations earned them music industry jobs straight out of high school.

Having a greater understanding of industry expectations and realities, and knowledge of the broader structure of various meshed and interdependent roles, is necessary for successful participation in the music industry. These considerations lead to the sixth design principle (Fig. 9.6).

> *DESIGN PRINCIPLE 6: Students learn about industry professionalism, standards, and cultural practices by working in a variety of roles 'behind the scenes' to develop entrepreneurial 'know-what' and 'know-why'.*
>
> - The learning environment should require students to actively work in roles behind the scenes in order to gain a better understanding of how the industry works.
>
> - The learning environment should offer opportunities to engage in authentic industry initiatives.
>
> - Students should have the opportunity to engage with industry professionals who are working in different roles.
>
> - Opportunities must be created for students to reflect on, and make the connection to their own work and future as creative practitioners.
>
> - Students should have several opportunities to apply their knowledge in different contexts over time.
>
> - Students should have the opportunity to enter, develop, and maintain ongoing partnerships with industry professionals.

Fig. 9.6 Design principle 6: professionalism and industry standards

Sustainability

The findings of this study show that students had developed an awareness of issues relating to enterprise sustainability, which contributed to developing 'know-why' and 'know-when' competencies. This awareness of sustainability was acquired through both explicit and implicit learning. The issues considered by the students were around succession planning, organisational structure, understanding the market, keeping an eye on the competition, striving for financial independence, and creating a positive workplace for community maintenance.

The students initially struggled to recruit new members into the community. While they recognised that succession planning was necessary, they did not trust that anybody else could do their job.

This negative effect of the strong bonding social capital the students had developed created an almost exclusive culture, which intimidated and deterred younger students. The YMI students did invite new students into the community, but these new students were never given opportunities to participate as legitimate members with equal status within the community. Without some degree of legitimate peripheral participation, the new students could not learn as the others had, and as a result, lost the motivation to contribute. This, in turn, justified the older students' reasons to deny the younger students' legitimate opportunities to participate. The consequences of this pattern were evident a couple of years later, after the study period, when new students struggled to maintain the YMI enterprise. Arguably, the school interface, which turns students around in 2–3 years (a much shorter period than any industry organisation), creates particular stresses around sustainability.

The students were strategic about organisational sustainability in other ways (that is, beyond recruiting). As the result of building bridging capital, they learned how other industry enterprises organised themselves, then adopted ideas to improve the delivery of their products, to become the professionals they aspired to be—thus demonstrating 'know-why' competency. They developed their own new governance structure and workshopped the final model with their industry partners. Over time, the students improved all aspects of their organisation and enterprise, and learned to more effectively manage their stakeholders. However, their incorporation of newcomers was not successful. In a sense, the new structure served to reinforce their bonding capital and reject younger voices.

Students became more strategic about the sustainability of the YMI brand, as they acquired more awareness of how the market worked. For example, they initially designed their initiatives by identifying gaps in the market. They were later able to observe the competition, while managing the timing of responses—thus demonstrating 'know-when' competency.

The students strategically mobilised social capital, by working with their competition in order to leverage ideas and resources. Coulson (2012) notes the unique nature of competition in the creative industries:

DESIGN PRINCIPLE 7: Students learn about career sustainability through maintaining and renewing their own enterprise, thus developing entrepreneurial 'know-why' and 'know-when'.

- The learning environment should be designed around student interests and passions.

- Students should have the opportunity to initiate, and then maintain, their own authentic organisation.

- The learning environment should be situated within the industry in order for students to develop an understanding of the realities of the market, for better and for worse.

- Students should be supported in their efforts to improve organisational sustainability.

  There must be multiple opportunities to reflect on, and improve their industry products in the interests of enterprise sustainability.

- Students should be encouraged and assisted to mentor new community members.

- New students require authentic opportunities in order to successfully participate.

- Industry partners and stakeholders should be involved in strategic processes related to enterprise sustainability.

Fig. 9.7 Design principle 7: sustainability

while musicians must compete for scarce resources, they also need to recognise that the music profession is essentially cooperative.

To maintain their community, the students intuitively developed a repertoire of processes, including mutual encouragement, celebration of achievement, emotional support, and motivation. These skills are downplayed in the music education literature; however, the challenges faced by artists would be well served by supportive networks that model persistence, resilience, and passion. The positive impacts of bonding social capital were seen in the creation of a positive working environment, which sustained the community for three years. My attention to social capital has helped to foreground the importance and ramifications of these capital-building processes, and this leads to the seventh design principle (Fig. 9.7).

Design Principles for Nurturing an Entrepreneurial Creative Mindset

Entrepreneurial 'knowledges'—or competencies, skills, values, and attributes—were demonstrated by the students. This demonstration makes a case for the value of an entrepreneurial approach as a valid learning experience, leading to the development of an entrepreneurial mindset. Scholars provide various definitions of an entrepreneurial mindset. These include:

- Ability to rapidly sense, act, and mobilise, even under uncertain conditions (Ireland, Hitt, & Sirmon, 2003)
- Cognitive adaptability: ability to be dynamic, flexible, and self-regulating (Haynie, Shepherd, Mosakowski, & Earley, 2010)
- Possession of attributes (intuition, lifelong learning, tenacity, risk-taking, passion, vision, persistence, and motivation); skill proficiencies (communication, negotiation, conflict resolution, and networking); and knowledge (deep knowledge of organisational structure and protocols) (Johannisson, 1991; Kriewall & Mekemson, 2010).

Gibb (1993) and Sogunro (2004) advocate 'hands on' enterprise experience, with exposure to real businesses and entrepreneurs. The design principles that have emerged from the YMI study offer evidence-based ideas for orchestrating entrepreneurial learning for high school students. These principles nurture the creative entrepreneur or, more specifically in the case of this study, to develop the musician's entrepreneurial mindset. A summary of the seven design principles is provided in Table 9.1.

Table 9.1 Summary and description of design principles

Design principle	Description
Design principle 1	Networking is fundamental to learning and developing entrepreneurial 'know-who'
Design principle 2	Setting goals and completing tasks is fundamental to learning and developing entrepreneurial 'know-how'
Design principle 3	Effective interpersonal skills can enhance community learning and develop entrepreneurial 'know-how'
Design principle 4	Reflection and self-feedback enable students to create effective strategies for action and improvement, and develop entrepreneurial know-when and 'know-how'
Design principle 5	Students acquire domain knowledge through engagement in authentic contexts to develop entrepreneurial 'know-what'
Design principle 6	Students learn about industry professionalism, standards, and cultural practices by working in a variety of roles 'behind the scenes' to develop entrepreneurial 'know-what' and 'know-why'
Design principle 7	Students learn about career sustainability through maintaining and renewing their own enterprise, thus developing entrepreneurial 'know-why' and 'know-when'

Researchers suggest that there is a need for colleges, universities, and conservatories to deal with the authentic world of musical experience, not withdraw from it (Seaton, 1997, p. 4). However, research that addresses this need is lacking (Bennett, 2007).

Education and skills are crucial in today's changing economy; however, there is no specific advice on how to develop creative approaches to entrepreneurship in school curricula. In particular, music industry respondents in Ninan, Hearn, and Oakley's (2004) study of the Queensland music industry argue for the inclusion of industry 'know-how' and practical skills in school curricula.

The need for broader skill sets is also recognised as vital for musicians. D'Andrea (2012) calls for research to identify the knowledge, skills, traits, and ways of operating that music students need. Bennett (2007) suggests that if these musicians had a broader skill set, a wider range of more satisfying, high-paying jobs within the creative industries would be available to them as secondary or alternative positions.

Ito et al. (2013) explain that youth are entering a labor market different from earlier generations; that is, a market where there is 'a chronic shortage of jobs relative to those who seek them' (p. 15). They also argue that a college degree has become a requirement for most good jobs, but is no longer a guarantee of acquiring one. Ito et al. (2013) suggest that we need to look to education as a way of building capacity and meaningful participation, rather than as 'a pipeline to a shrinking set of opportunities' (p. 19). To address these issues, the National Research Council (2012) identifies twenty-first-century skills such as systems thinking, problem-solving, critical thinking, adaptability, self-direction, and perseverance as necessary for sustaining careers within the modern economies.

The YMI project developed and trialed a design that realises the potential for young people to be self-directed learners, capable of undertaking entrepreneurial ventures through acquiring and mobilising social capital. It demonstrated that it is possible to develop a twenty-first-century learning environment that more effectively prepares young people for entrepreneurial careers within the creative industries.

My role as a teacher was to create the conditions of possibility that allowed learning to take place. The students were required to critically evaluate and reflect on their learning, and the cycles afforded by DBR allowed them the opportunity to develop from 'student' to 'professional' over several iterative phases. I extended the static notion of teaching students about the music industry, by contextualising and situating students within the industry. Entrepreneurship, like all the other elements related to business and project management, were not abstracted or decontextualised, but embedded in a dynamic, authentic context.

Pragmatic Limitations of the Design

There are many pragmatic considerations for practitioners interested in adopting or adapting the YMI design. As the designer, researcher, and teacher, I faced many challenges, which are potential design limitations to be considered. In particular, there are limitations around teacher workload, risk management, and balancing school/industry cultures. I reflected on these challenges in the reflection boxes throughout Chapters 6, 7 and 8.

Teacher Workload

It is important not to underestimate the workload in innovative practice. In recognition of the workload that teachers of music and other
arts already carry, I recommend that teachers consider what is realistic
in terms of the scale of the project to which the design is applied. The
YMI organisation expanded each year in terms of the frequency and
scale of events, as well as the inclusion of industry partners. This had
a significant impact on the amount of time I was obligated to invest in
the project. As a teacher, I was responsible for not only the core group
of YMI students but also their team of volunteers and interns.

Aside from my role as designer of the learning experiences, I had
to manage a heavy administration load (see Reflection Box 1). This
involved risk assessments; preparing excursion letters and consent
forms; negotiating the school calendar of competing events; managing
school staff who were also competing for the students' time and attention; ensuring that events were planned well in advance; ensuring that
YMI work did not conflict with the academic calendar; preparing travel
itineraries, flights and accommodation for regional trips; and continuous reporting to the school principal.

Enacting the design on a larger scale required extra funding (see
Reflection Box 4). While the students were very successful in generating
profits, I spent a considerable amount of time in grant writing to procure funding for a few of the headline artists for the festival, and to enable the YMI students to travel around Queensland to share their work
with other young musicians. Beyond the time spent writing grants,
more time was spent administering and acquitting them to ensure that
all guidelines were followed stringently. Aside from the grant budgets,
I was also responsible for overseeing the YMI budget in general. This
involved budget tracking, managing invoices, and keeping a record of
expenditure.

In order to create the YMI learning environment, and to realise its
potential as an entrepreneurial venture, I sourced the funding, and
worked hard to broker partnerships between the students and the
industry (see Reflection Boxes 3 and 5). This involved coordination
and attendance at meetings additional to student-industry meetings.

For industry partners, I was the first point of contact for all issues relating to the students. If a student had not completed a task or was not able to be contacted, it would fall on me to intervene. This would either involve me searching for the student or doing the task myself, simply to manage stakeholder expectations and obligations. It was also necessary for YMI to pitch its events to schools throughout Queensland. Students were responsible for managing this communication, but it was difficult for teachers from other schools to trust or accept information being provided to them by high-school-aged students (see Reflection Box 2). This then required further support from me in the form of follow-up phone calls to teachers.

Being the only teacher on the project, I was expected to be at every event, not only to observe as a researcher, but also to co-manage events, and to supervise students. This meant that some aspects of the design were neglected. For example, succession planning (see Reflection Box 12) was impacted because the volume of work made it impossible to prioritise the engagement of the next generation of YMI students. Time is a precious commodity for teachers, so this level of personal subsidy of the project may not be sustainable for others. However, I do not apologise for this, as the growth of the design leads to growth of student development.

Risk Management

There are similar student workload realities to be considered. As this design was in addition to the students' classroom curriculum, there was a lot of pressure on them as they managed the YMI role on top of their academic commitments. This required careful management, not only in looking out for the students' welfare but also in managing other teachers' and parents' priorities (see Reflection Box 4). Industry professionals are not school teachers, and do not necessarily display the same sensitivities. For example, some of the students were confronted by angry booking agents when their artists were not paid on time. Another example involved a band manager who was upset at the order of band line-up on the festival (see Reflection Box 7). While these may be the realities of the professional world, some may question whether school-aged students are ready to handle such friction.

There were other very significant risks. For example, errors in aspects of copyright law (see Reflection Box 10) and communication with contractors (see Reflection Box 4) could have had serious consequences. There were also financial risks for me personally, as the school did not fund the events and grant funding did not cover all the expenses (see Reflection Box 8). Students worked tirelessly to ensure their events were well attended; however, a capacity audience was not always guaranteed. In addition, there were significant risks for the school in opening its facilities to large public audiences, particularly in terms of maintenance and security of facilities and equipment (see Reflection Box 3). Risks involving student safety at the events had to be carefully managed (through conditions related to the entry), especially given that the audience population had increased in size, and included a greater number of people not connected to the school. None of these pragmatic limitations should be underestimated and, while each had its own field of influence, each also impacted on the students' workload.

Balancing School and Industry Cultures

Bringing the industry and school environments together presented challenges, some of which cross over the issues of student workload. Despite the investment of my time in facilitating the partnership, aligning two very different cultural institutions proved difficult at times.

Communication was a challenge, firstly because there was limited space within a rigid school timetable to facilitate meetings and, secondly, because of the unavoidable agendas and objectives of the two institutions. The school agenda was primarily about education first; in particular, its dominant focus on the individual's international curriculum score. The industry partners' agendas were about business, deadlines, and reputation. It was difficult for the students to please both the school (in both academic and extracurricular pursuits) and industry partners. Learning how to manage the partnership was complex, and needed constant attention throughout the design phases (see Reflection Box 5).

The aims and objectives of the design were to develop students' entrepreneurial mindset. Having had exposure to the world of the music industry, the students began to outgrow the institution of school, in particular, its rules and limitations. They had a strong desire to think outside the box, make changes, act fast, and expand their networks. These ways of thinking and working were often restricted by the institutional nature of the school. The principal and students were often in disagreement about various processes (see Reflection Box 5). This put added pressure on my relationship with the principal, especially as I was accountable to him.

Students' growing entrepreneurial mindset created further challenges for me. It was important for the design to let them have independence and control. Letting go and trusting that the students would make the right decisions and solve problems was difficult but became easier over time. However, I also learned that there were times that required my leadership or intervention. Even by the end of the project, I still felt that I did not quite achieve the right balance (see Reflection Boxes 6 and 9).

Finally, with their new entrepreneurial mindset and wider exposure, students wanted to push beyond the four walls of the school and actively network with industry in pursuit of their own careers and personal goals. This networking included attendance at social functions. While two of the students were 18, the boundaries between school and 'not-school' were blurred. While this was difficult to monitor outside of school hours, I ensured that I had open and honest communication with parents at all times (see Reflection Box 11). Translating between the two institutional cultures was challenging, and the issue provides the impetus for further research.

Future Research

School-industry collaboration emerged as one of the most difficult aspects of the research, not only in terms of logistics but also in terms of inherent culture. However, the data does not include the industry partners' perspectives. Future iterations or implementations of the design would benefit from acknowledging a range of perspectives from both students and industry professionals with regard to developing effective partnerships. Issues relating to student workload could also have been addressed, had the perspectives of teachers, administrators, and parents been captured. Developing solutions to both of these limitations might have produced very different findings with regard to student learning. This makes a case for revisiting the design from a methodological point of view.

This research can be extended in a number of ways. In particular, future research is needed to track how students apply knowledge beyond the school. Evidence suggests that the students valued the opportunities they received through the YMI project in terms of skills and knowledge gained, as well as the opportunities to collaborate and network with industry professionals. It would be of value to conduct a longitudinal study, which investigates any long-term influence that the YMI project might have on the students as they move through their future music/creative industries education and/or careers. An investigation of ways of formalising the design as a curriculum offering, or seeking accreditation/certification for students who participate in the design, would also provide new insights and outcomes, which could further support the design's potential in future contexts.

The role of the teacher was considered throughout the design; however, my own professional development was not documented. My own entrepreneurial capacity was extended as the result of facilitating a design involving risk-taking and leveraging professional networks. Investigating the potential that teachers can play in developing school-industry partnerships, and the influence that these partnerships can have on teaching practice is recommended as an avenue for future research. Future research could also consider how learning in this design might have an impact on student achievement in not only their music studies but also in all other areas of academic life.

Concluding Remarks

The YMI experience was a rich one for the participating students, industry partners, stakeholders and myself as a teacher. The students developed a shared identity around a music enterprise that required them to grapple with complex problems and entrepreneurial issues. They took ownership of their learning and explicitly worked towards achieving a professional identity. Hayden was featured on the front cover of a Queensland magazine, with the headline 'CEO at 17', and was offered a position of responsibility within a prominent music industry organisation in Australia in his first year out of school. Indeed, two years on, all of the YMI students are either working or studying within the creative industries. This detailed documentation and analysis of the YMI design experiment will help to seed similar work in other schools.

Fundamentally, this book provides a foundation for solutions to a question raised by many researchers within the creative industries over the last decade: How do we more effectively transition students into careers within the creative industries, and within contemporary economies more broadly? While this work demonstrates an idealistic vision for the future of education, the reality is inevitably less optimistic. YMI does offer a promising set of goals; however, the challenge for educators will be to determine how this generative approach can be implemented within the formal structure and systematic constraints of schooling or higher education settings, if they continue to be governed by conventional templates. I conclude with a reflective statement from Tristan, a year after he finished in YMI. His narrative speaks confidently and resonantly about his learning, and provides an insight into the ways in which YMI benefitted him:

> The experience was incredibly fruitful in that it taught me not just industry specific skills, but broader life skills that apply to various careers ... I took a step into a more stable career path which still incorporated the creative skills that I'd accumulated – into advertising. Studying Business majoring in advertising, I have seen these skills of networking, communication and collective projects play a fundamental role in the industry ...

Alongside this, I have been performing, writing and recording with artist [Tom] (another past YMI student) now rebranded as [Band V]. This allows me to still access the music industry knowledge I learned to help the band to make wise decisions in recording, management, brand image and much more…My aspirations are to become a copyright director for an advertising firm, using the initiative and innovative qualities to engineer well thought out advertisements, a career that ultimately fulfils the need to be both creative and yet stable. (Tristan, Interview, November, Phase 3)

References

Barab, S., & Squire, K. (2004). Introduction: Design-based research: Putting a stake in the ground. *The Journal of the Learning Sciences, 13*(1), 1–14. https://doi.org/10.2307/1466930.

Bauman, Z. (2000). *Liquid modernity*. Malden, MA; Cambridge: Polity.

Beckman, G. D. (2007). "Adventuring" arts entrepreneurship curricula in higher education: An examination of present efforts, obstacles, and best practices. *Journal of Arts Management Law and Society, 37*(2), 87–112. https://doi.org/10.3200/JAML.37.2.87-112.

Bennett, D. (2004). Peas in a cultural pod?: A comparison of the skills and personal attributes of artists and musicians. *Australian Journal of Music Education, 1,* 53.

Bennett, D. (2007). Utopia for music performance graduates. Is it achievable, and how should it be defined? *British Journal of Music Education, 24*(2), 179–189. https://doi.org/10.1017/s0265051707007383.

Brown, A. (1992). Design experiments: Theoretical and methodological challenges in creating complex interventions in classroom settings. *The Journal of the Learning Sciences, 2*(2), 141–178. https://doi.org/10.1207/s15327809jls0202_2.

Browne, E. (2003). Conversations in cyberspace: A study of online learning. *Open Learning: The Journal of Open, Distance and e-Learning, 18*(3), 245–259.

Claxton, G. (2004). *Learning is learnable (and we ought to teach it)*. Ten Years On, The National Commission for Education Report, 237–250.

Coleman, J. (1994). *Foundations of social theory*. Cambridge, MA: Harvard University Press.

Coulson, S. (2012). Collaborating in a competitive world: Musicians' working lives and understandings of entrepreneurship. *Work, Employment & Society, 26*(2), 246–261. https://doi.org/10.1177/0950017011432919.

D'Andrea, M. (2012). The Ontario curriculum in the arts and the creative economy agenda. *Arts Education Policy Review, 113*(2), 80–88.

Dede, C. (2005). Planning for neomillennial learning styles: Implications for investments in technology and faculty. *Educating the net generation, 5.*

Falk, I., & Kilpatrick, S. (2000). What is social capital? A study of interaction in a rural community. *Sociologia Ruralis, 40*(1), 87–110. https://doi.org/10.1111/1467-9523.00133.

Folkestad, G. (2005). Here, there and everywhere: Music education research in a globalised world. *Music Education Research, 7*(3), 279–287.

Forrest, D. (2001). *The odyssey of music industry education.* Paper presented at the ASME XIII Conference, Adelaide.

Freudenberg, B., Brimble, M., & Vyvyan, V. (2010). The penny drops: Can work integrated learning improve students' learning? *e-Journal of Business Education and Scholarship Teaching, 4*(1), 42.

Friedman, T. L. (2005). *The world is flat: A brief history of the twenty-first century.* New York: Farrar, Straus and Giroux.

Gibb, A. A. (1993). Enterprise culture and education: Understanding enterprise education and its links with small business, entrepreneurship and wider educational goals. *International Small Business Journal, 11*(3), 11–34.

Green, L. (2001). *How popular musicians learn: A way ahead for music education.* Burlington, VT: Ashgate.

Green, L. (2002). From the Western classics to the world: Secondary music teachers' changing attitudes in England, 1982 and 1998. *British Journal of Music Education, 19*(1), 5–30.

Haynie, J. M., Shepherd, D., Mosakowski, E., & Earley, P. C. (2010). A situated metacognitive model of the entrepreneurial mindset. *Journal of Business Venturing, 25*(2), 217–229. https://doi.org/10.1016/j.jbusvent.2008.10.001.

Ireland, R. D., Hitt, M. A., & Sirmon, D. G. (2003). A model of strategic entrepreneurship: The construct and its dimensions. *Journal of Management, 29*(6), 963–989. https://doi.org/10.1016/S0149-2063(03)00086-2.

Ito, M., Gutiérrez, K., Livingstone, S., Penuel, B., Rhodes, J., Salen, K., ... Watkins, S. C. (2013). *Connected learning: An agenda for research and design.* Irvine: Digital Media and Learning Research Hub.

Jaffurs, S. E. (2004). The impact of informal music learning practices in the classroom, or how I learned how to teach from a garage band. *International Journal of Music Education, 22*(3), 189–200.

Johannisson, B. (1991). University training for entrepreneurship: Swedish approaches. *Entrepreneurship & Regional Development, 3*(1), 67–82. https://doi.org/10.1080/08985629100000005.

Kilpatrick, S., Barrett, M., & Jones, T. (2003). *Defining learning communities*. Paper presented at the Joint New Zealand Association for Research in Education (NZARE) & Australian Association for Research in Education (AARE) International Conference, Auckland, New Zealand.

Kisiel, J. F. (2010). Exploring a school-aquarium collaboration: An intersection of communities of practice. *Science Education, 94*(1), 95–121. https://doi.org/10.1002/sce.20350.

Kriewall, T. J., & Mekemson, K. (2010). Instilling the entrepreneurial mindset into engineering undergraduates. *The Journal of Engineering Entrepreneurship, 1*(1), 5–19.

Langston, T., & Barrett, M. (2008). Capitalising on community music: A case study of the manifestation of social capital in a community choir. *Research Studies in Music Education, 30*(2), 118–138. https://doi.org/10.1177/1321103X08097503.

Lave, J., & Wenger, E. (1991). Situated learning: Legitimate peripheral participation. New York: Cambridge University Press.

Lebler, D. (2008). Popular music pedagogy: Peer learning in practice. *Music Education Research, 10*(2), 193–213. https://doi.org/10.1080/14613800802079056.

Li, Z. (2016). International students' employability: What can we learn from it? In *Graduate employability in context*. https://doi.org/10.1057/978-1-137-57168-7_9.

McWilliam, E. (2005). Unlearning pedagogy. *Journal of Learning Design, 1*(1), 1–11.

McWilliam, E. (2008). *The creative workforce: How to launch young people into high-flying futures*. Sydney: University of NSW Press.

McWilliam, E., & Haukka, S. (2008). Educating the creative workforce: New directions for twenty-first century schooling. *British Educational Research Journal, 34*(5), 651–666. https://doi.org/10.1080/01411920802224204.

National Research Council. (2012). *Education for life and work: Developing transferable knowledge and skills in the 21st century*. Washington, DC. Retrieved July 24, 2012, from http://bit.ly/14ZNmbf.

Ninan, A., Hearn, G., & Oakley, K. (2004). *Queensland music industry trends: Independence day?* (CIRAC, Trans.). Kelvin Grove, QLD: Queensland University of Technology.

Oakley, K. (2007). *Educating for the creative workforce: Rethinking arts and education.* Australia Council for the Arts. Retrieved from http://bit.ly/1xLDDB1.

Putnam, R. D. (2000). Bowling alone. In R. T. LeGates & F. Stout (Eds.), *The city reader.* New York: Routledge.

Ronkin, B., & Alhadeff, P. (2016). Music & entertainment industry educators association budgeting for crowdfunding rewards. *Journal of the Music & Entertainment Industry Educators Association, 16*(1), 27–44.

Salavuo, M. (2008). Social media as an opportunity for pedagogical change in music education. *Journal of Music, Technology and Education, 1*(2–3), 2–3.

Seaton, D. (1997). *Music and American higher education.* Retrieved July 14, 2012, from http://www.music.org/InfoEdMusic/HigherEd/SumSeaton.html.

Siemens, G. (2008). *Learning and knowing in networks: Changing roles for educators and designers.* Retrieved May 4, 2011, from http://itforum.coe.uga.edu/Paper105/Siemens.pdf.

Sogunro, O. A. (2004). Efficacy of role-playing pedagogy in training leaders: Some reflections. *Journal of Management Development, 23*(4), 355–371.

Temmerman, N. (2005). The role of arts education in advancing leadership life skills for young people. *Australian Journal of Music Education, 1*, 33–40.

Tinto, V. (2000). What have we learned about the impact of learning communities on students. *Assessment Update, 12*(2), 1–2.

Wenger, E. (1998). *Communities of practice: Learning, meaning, and identity.* Cambridge, UK: Cambridge University Press.

Westerlund, H. (2006). Garage rock bands: A future model for developing musical expertise? *International Journal of Music Education, 24*(2), 119–125.

Young, S. (2018). A work of art in the age of technological disruption: The future of work in the music industry. *Journal of the Music and Entertainment Industry Educators Association, 18*(1), 73–104. https://doi.org/10.25101/18.3.

Index

A

Adaptive capacity 44, 56
Align 65, 72, 87, 104, 121, 127,
    194, 199, 220, 234
Alignment 71, 72, 82, 104, 122,
    127, 130, 131, 167
Art and culture 12
Artefacts 66, 71, 95, 121, 212
Artistic judgement 147
Aspiring musicians 12
Authentic 6, 50, 63, 84, 112, 230
Authentic activities 39
Authentic application 204
Authentic collaborations 215
Authentic context 29, 48, 210, 231
Authentic enterprise 214
Authentic environment 223
Authentic evaluator 15
Authentic experience 5, 37
Authentic industry 83
Authentic industry contexts 208
Authentic industry participation 56
Authentic industry work 127
Authentic learning 38
Authentic learning context 40
Authentic learning environments 39
Authentic music industry 53
Authentic music industry contexts
    209
Authentic opportunities 202, 216,
    219
Authentic organisation 7
Authentic projects 15, 37
Autonomy 34, 76, 84, 138, 140,
    166, 218

B

BIGSOUND 104, 108
Bonding 78–80, 86, 139, 210, 216
Bonding capital. *See* Bonding social
    capital

© The Editor(s) (if applicable) and The Author(s), under exclusive
license to Springer Nature Switzerland AG 2020
K. Kelman, *Entrepreneurial Music Education*,
https://doi.org/10.1007/978-3-030-37129-6

Bonding social capital 78, 80, 82, 102, 104, 140, 212, 215, 217, 218, 227, 228

Boundary 13, 68, 70, 71, 103, 118, 178, 179, 185

Boundary crossing 70, 72, 73, 212

Boundary objects 71

Bourdieu, Pierre 74, 75, 80, 81

Bridging 78, 83, 86, 87, 129, 215

Bridging capital. *See* Bridging social capital

Bridging social capital 78, 79, 104, 139, 141

Broker 71, 232

Budgeting 108, 144, 165, 168, 173, 221

Business plan 105

Business skills 45, 46, 209

Business venture 9, 56

C

Co-creating authentic 56

Coleman, James 74–77, 79, 80, 102, 119, 210

Collaboration 6, 14, 15, 29, 35, 37, 38, 63, 70, 72, 108, 168, 181, 213, 219, 222, 235

Collaborative learning environments 14

Collaborative pedagogy 35

Collective learning 51, 65

Communication 14, 25, 31, 33, 34, 50, 108, 110, 118, 131, 133, 134, 136, 138, 140, 155, 156, 160, 166, 175, 190, 191, 196, 202, 217–219, 229, 233–235, 237

Communication skills 45, 135, 178

Communication styles 132, 217, 218

Communities of practice (CoP) 6, 14, 52, 63–77, 79, 82, 83, 86, 87, 95, 96, 102–104, 118, 121, 125, 127, 129, 130, 137, 159, 169, 179, 184, 185, 187, 189, 193, 194, 197, 203, 205, 209, 210, 212

Community 3, 13, 23, 31–33, 35, 37–40, 45, 52–54, 56, 63, 65–71, 73, 74, 77, 79–83, 85, 87, 95, 98, 102, 104, 111, 119, 122, 123, 125, 127, 129, 130, 132, 139, 140, 144, 161, 162, 164–166, 169, 170, 173, 176, 178, 179, 183, 185, 188–191, 193, 198, 202–204, 208, 210, 212, 213, 215, 217–222, 225–228

Community cohesion 12, 80

Community development 45

Community membership 193

Community passion 187

Community repertoire 69, 135

Competence 31, 44, 65, 66, 68–70, 73, 118, 130, 169, 178, 222

Conflict resolution 109, 131, 144, 217, 229

Connected learning 31

Copyright 42, 109, 168–170, 173, 221, 222, 234, 238

Creative 2, 3, 11–13, 15–17, 23, 28, 43, 46, 49, 53–55, 80, 105, 119, 130, 132, 168, 208, 209, 223

Creative curriculum 10

Creative enterprise 55

Creative industries 3, 6, 9–17, 19, 23, 41, 43, 45, 55, 56, 99, 100, 105, 207, 208, 210, 211, 214–216, 219, 221, 227, 230, 231, 236, 237
Creative practitioners 13
Creative skills 24, 46, 237
Creative workforce 15
Creativity 5, 11–17, 24, 50, 51, 54, 63, 71, 76, 83, 84, 101, 220
Cultural and entrepreneurial economy 10
Cultural capital 74, 82, 119, 128, 130, 140, 166, 183
Culture and creativity 12
Curation 183
Curriculum 2–4, 10, 16, 24–28, 36, 39–41, 43, 44, 48, 50, 53, 54, 56, 82–84, 96, 97, 207, 208, 214, 233, 236

D

Debriefing 148, 161, 164
Decision-making 145, 152, 166, 188, 196, 217
Design-based research (DBR) 18, 95, 96, 101, 112, 210, 211, 231
Design-based research methodology 94, 95
Design principles 19, 95, 96, 105, 207, 211, 214, 216, 219, 221, 223, 225, 229
Digital economy 24
Digital era 42
Digitalisation 41
Diversity 14, 25, 39, 46, 48, 119, 130, 139
DIY culture 43, 56

E

Educational practice 94
Education and Experience 27
Education partnerships 3
Embedded activity 84
Emerge 6, 19, 56, 94, 103, 105, 107, 108, 118, 122, 126, 134, 135, 143, 144, 150, 159, 181–183, 185, 199, 201
Emergent structures 68, 70
Emerging artists 42, 129
Emerging professional learning model (EPLM) 85–87, 102, 113, 168, 173, 179, 185, 204, 205, 207, 210
Emerging professionals 183
Employment 2, 5, 11, 12, 36, 47, 209, 213
Engaging 23, 31, 36, 52, 65, 87, 102, 137, 157, 173, 179, 202, 218, 223
Enterprise 7, 14, 15, 18, 25, 55, 65, 67, 69, 83, 84, 125, 126, 129, 134, 137, 138, 159, 160, 163, 164, 166, 169, 170, 173, 179, 182–185, 189, 191, 195, 197, 198, 201, 202, 210, 212, 213, 215, 217, 218, 220, 222, 225–227, 237
Entrepreneurial behaviour 83, 84, 118
Entrepreneurial capacity 7, 18, 87, 117, 143, 236
Entrepreneurial characteristics 83, 84
Entrepreneurial competence(ies) 83, 84, 87, 112, 172, 175, 177, 178, 186, 199
Entrepreneurial curriculum 10
Entrepreneurial identity 84

Entrepreneurial initiatives 86

Entrepreneurialism 4, 17, 42, 53, 85, 86, 117, 125, 167, 181, 209, 213

Entrepreneurial mindset 10, 84, 184, 223, 229, 235

Entrepreneurial training 84

Entrepreneurs 2, 9, 14, 84, 95, 121, 143, 184, 197, 229

Entrepreneurship 14, 17, 44–46, 56, 63, 83–85, 158, 209, 213, 230, 231

Entrepreneurship education 6, 17

Experience 2, 4, 5, 12–15, 25–28, 31, 32, 40, 43, 44, 48, 50, 64–66, 68–70, 72, 73, 75, 83, 84, 97, 104, 108, 111, 121, 127, 143, 158, 160, 167, 173, 177–179, 183, 199, 208, 211, 220, 222, 224, 225, 229, 230, 232, 237

Experiential learning 13, 29

Experimental 28, 139, 140, 165, 166, 204

External community 13

F

Facebook 18, 105, 109, 118, 123, 126, 129, 135–138, 145, 149–151, 153–157, 161, 163, 170–175, 179, 181, 188–190, 197, 201–203, 211, 217, 218, 223, 224

Facebook meetings 18, 104, 105, 132, 136, 140, 162, 189, 190

Face-to-face 18, 34, 81, 103–105, 111, 136

Flat world 30, 31, 34, 40, 57, 82

Flexibility 4, 10, 13, 72, 111, 145, 211, 217, 221

Fluid boundaries 70

Formal 1, 10, 13, 43, 45, 50, 51, 79, 97, 161, 162, 179, 195

Formal budgeting processes 173

Formal classroom 220

Formal education 24, 25, 29, 32, 41, 43, 45, 49, 53, 56, 82, 84

Formal institutions 15

Formal instruction 203

Formal knowledge of programming bands 203

Formal learning 13, 49, 51

Formal processes 49, 165

Formal reflection processes 164

Formal structure 237

Four Walls Festival 6, 103, 105, 108, 118, 122–124, 132, 135, 143–145, 147, 148, 151, 154, 157, 158, 161, 163, 168, 170, 175, 179, 183, 184, 190, 199, 200

Freelance work 5

Friendship 52, 75, 78, 122, 182

G

Governance model 105, 138, 195, 205

Guide on the side 15, 27

H

Headhunt 181

I

Imagination 24, 68, 69, 71, 73, 82, 87, 212

Imagining 13, 65, 87, 103, 121, 122, 129, 169, 185
In-demand knowledge 40
Industry conference 36, 104, 214
Industry expectations 152, 167, 174, 180, 203, 221, 225
Industry professionals 6, 14, 37, 73, 101, 104, 107, 108, 118, 124, 129, 140, 152, 166, 177, 179, 196, 204, 222, 233, 236
Inert knowledge 36, 207
Informal 4, 14, 49, 50, 65, 79, 209
Informal learning 2, 4, 13, 18, 23, 47, 49–51, 56, 68, 78, 216
Innovation 10, 16, 41, 42, 47, 55, 63, 68, 71, 79, 87, 94, 103, 118, 130, 138, 185, 197, 212
In situ 94
Intellectual property 11, 126, 130, 204, 213
Inter-generational 68, 73, 202
Internal communication 132, 135, 137, 138
Interpersonal skills 56, 131, 137, 138, 140, 211, 216, 217, 219
Intervention(s) 7, 18, 94–97, 101, 103–105, 109, 112, 118, 145, 160, 201, 202, 211, 235

J

Johannisson, B. 84, 85, 87, 210, 229
Joint enterprise 65–67, 82, 119, 158, 191, 212

K

Know-How (skills) 84
Knowledge 2, 7, 9, 10, 15–17, 19, 24–31, 34–38, 40, 43–46, 48, 50–52, 56, 65–67, 71–73, 76, 78, 80, 82, 83, 86, 95, 109, 111, 119, 122, 129, 141, 161, 164, 167–170, 173–180, 183, 186, 191, 192, 198, 203–205, 207–210, 213, 216–218, 221–223, 225, 229, 230, 236, 238
Knowledge acquisition 24, 117, 203
Knowledge economy 23, 48, 53
Knowledge of marketing 121
Know-What (knowledge) 84
Know-When (insight) 84
Know-Who (social skills) 84
Know-Why (attitudes, values, motives) 84

L

Landscapes of practice 70
Learning 1, 2, 4–7, 10, 13–18, 24, 25, 27, 29–40, 47, 49–52
Learning about copyright 168
Learning about marketing 170
Learning about sustainability 186
Learning design 7, 10, 12, 15, 19, 31, 33, 40, 46–48, 53, 83–85, 93, 101, 203, 207, 208, 214, 216, 218–220
Learning ecology 34
Learning environment 7, 9, 10, 15, 18, 23, 25, 26, 28, 29, 31, 32, 34, 40, 41, 46, 51, 53, 56, 63, 82, 94, 96, 101, 102, 133, 208, 210, 215, 216, 222, 231, 232
Learning processes 19, 152, 208
Legitimacy 69, 127, 188, 222

Legitimate Peripheral Participation (LPP) 68, 69, 127, 169, 189, 202, 227
Like-minded 118, 119, 129
Linking capital 80, 81, 83, 87, 131, 194, 210, 215
Linking social capital 79, 83, 105, 139
Liquid 24, 26, 40
Little BIGSOUND 71, 104, 105, 108, 118, 120–122, 126, 131, 143, 144, 173, 179, 196, 212

M

Managers 9, 95, 103, 108, 123, 124, 129, 146, 148, 149, 152, 153, 156–158, 166, 169, 175–177, 179, 184, 204, 224, 233
Marketing 11, 42–44, 46, 99, 100, 108, 129, 131, 168, 171–173, 183, 195, 203, 223, 224
Marketing skills 45
Meddler in the middle 15, 27
Millennial learners 31, 223
Minimally-guided learning 38
Miscommunication 133, 135, 138
Motivation 7, 36, 37, 52, 84, 192, 197, 200, 227–229
Multidisciplinary 70
Multi-membership 68, 70, 72, 103
Multi-skilled 41, 209
Music business 43, 44, 110, 167, 173
Music education 10, 12–14, 19, 23, 47–51, 53, 54, 96, 97, 102, 112, 177, 180, 185, 208, 209, 223, 228

Music industry 1, 2, 4, 6, 7, 9, 10, 12, 13, 15, 17, 19, 23, 40–44, 46, 47, 51, 53, 55, 56, 73, 80, 87, 94–105, 108, 109, 117, 123, 127, 129, 130, 140, 143–145, 167–169, 173–180, 185, 186, 199, 203, 204, 208, 209, 214, 215, 221–225, 230, 231, 235, 237, 238
Music industry education 43, 47, 51
Music teaching 12, 19, 41
Mutual engagement 15, 64, 66, 67, 69, 82, 136, 139, 158, 197

N

Negotiating 72, 108, 143, 144, 150, 157, 160, 165, 232
Negotiation 13, 66–69, 109, 121, 144, 145, 157, 214, 229
Netiquette 33, 34, 218
Networking 13, 37, 42, 46, 104, 108, 109, 117–119, 122, 124, 128–130, 148, 185, 198, 213, 214, 216, 225, 229, 235
Networking skills 5, 117, 129, 131, 211, 237
Newcomers 45, 68, 69, 73, 189–191, 194, 210, 219, 227
Non-formal education 48

O

Observations 18, 35, 103, 104, 111, 137
Online music community(ies) 52
Online networks 32, 33, 52
Online social networking 29, 31

Opportunities 2, 6, 7, 13–16, 25,
    29, 31–33, 37–39, 41, 42, 45,
    46, 48, 50, 52–54, 56, 68–70,
    72, 78, 80, 85, 87, 97, 98,
    101–105, 107, 109, 110, 118,
    120, 122–126, 129, 130, 139,
    140, 160, 165, 173, 175, 177,
    179, 182, 183, 185, 188–190,
    192, 193, 195, 197, 199, 202,
    204, 208–215, 220, 222, 225,
    227, 231, 236
Opportunity recognition 5, 63
Organisation 6, 9, 17, 40, 43, 71,
    76, 77, 81, 85, 95, 99, 102,
    103, 108, 118, 119, 123, 125,
    134, 138, 140, 144–146, 154,
    155, 166, 178, 179, 186, 187,
    190, 193, 196, 197, 204, 205,
    208, 217, 225, 227, 232, 237
Out-of-school learning 48, 64

P

Participant-observer 18, 111
Participation 9, 12, 31, 38, 39, 51,
    52, 55, 64–66, 69, 72, 82,
    86, 87, 111, 128, 179, 189,
    191–194, 205, 222, 225, 231
Partner organisations 105
Partnerships 6, 23, 29, 35, 37–39,
    71, 73, 98, 101–105, 126,
    128, 140, 166, 168, 185, 195,
    212, 222, 232, 234, 236
Peer-assessment 27
Peer culture 31, 34
Peer-learning 4, 18, 27, 47, 53, 68,
    102
Peer networks 46, 129

Peer-to-peer networks 41
Peripherality 69
Peripheral members 73, 97
Personalised learning 12
Planning 28, 102, 103, 144, 145,
    158, 172, 175, 180, 188
Popular music 48, 56, 209
Portfolio 46
Portfolio careers 12
Practice 2, 13, 14, 17, 18, 25, 32,
    34, 36, 37, 41, 43, 45, 47, 50,
    51, 66–69, 71–73, 79, 87, 94,
    95, 101, 104, 110, 111, 127,
    158, 163, 164, 168, 177, 181,
    209, 217, 218, 220, 222, 223,
    225
Problem solving 10, 14, 83, 144,
    145, 158, 159, 217, 231
Procedural repertoire 198, 201, 204,
    225
Professional identity 147, 160, 237
Professionalism 134, 145, 147, 155,
    156, 158, 174, 178, 196, 204,
    220, 224, 225
Professional musicians 1, 12, 13, 48
Professional networks 45, 236
Programming 99, 107, 108, 132,
    180, 184, 223
Project 2, 4–7, 13, 15, 17–19, 31,
    33, 34, 37, 38, 40, 41, 46, 49,
    52, 56, 73, 79, 81, 83–87, 93–
    95, 97–100, 103, 107–109,
    111, 117, 119, 121, 122, 125,
    127, 137, 139–141, 143, 144,
    150, 152, 155, 156, 158–161,
    164–166, 170, 179, 196, 207,
    208, 211, 213–215, 218, 222,
    231–233, 235–237

Project management 14, 19, 117, 121, 137, 143, 144, 154, 159, 162, 165, 166, 195, 211, 231

Putnam, Robert 74, 77, 78, 80–82, 102, 104, 210, 212

Q

Qualitative research 35, 94, 112

R

Real-world 18, 38, 93, 95, 96, 211

Reciprocal learning 63

Reciprocity 40, 72, 74, 76–82, 130, 139, 140, 161, 164, 212, 215, 218

Reflections 32, 33, 66, 96, 101, 112, 129, 136, 154, 161–164, 177, 187, 192, 211, 219–221, 231

Reflection skills 161, 164, 211

Reification 66

Repertoire 48, 67, 69, 83, 125, 126, 129, 134, 136–138, 148, 158–162, 164, 166, 169, 170, 172, 173, 179, 184, 185, 189, 195, 197, 201, 204, 210, 212, 213, 215, 217, 222, 228

Risk-management 144

Risk-taking 5, 10, 14, 28, 84, 130, 181, 213, 229, 236

Roles and governance 187

S

Sage on Stage 15

Scheduling 144

Secondary school music educator 1

Self-directed learners 5, 25, 34, 56, 68, 231

Self-employed 14

Semi-structured interviews 18

Sense of belonging 82

Setting objectives 84

Seven deadly habits of pedagogical thinking 25

Shared norms 76, 78, 79

Shared practice 65, 66

Shared repertoire 66, 67, 82

Simulation 38

Situated learning 65, 66

Skills 1, 2, 4, 5, 9, 10, 12, 15–17, 19, 23, 24, 30, 31, 36, 40, 41, 43–46, 48, 50, 51, 54–56, 64, 65, 73, 75, 76, 78, 82, 86, 95, 97, 100, 117, 119, 121, 124, 129, 130, 133, 138, 139, 143, 144, 148, 155, 159, 163–166, 173, 179, 181, 191, 192, 194, 196, 199, 202, 204, 208–218, 220, 228–231, 236, 237

Sociability 81, 82

Social capital 10, 19, 63, 74–83, 85–87, 95, 96, 119, 133, 139, 141, 162, 165, 167, 184, 189, 198, 199, 202, 203, 205, 209, 210, 212, 227, 231

Social learning 19, 63, 64, 70, 83, 87

Social media 32, 38, 43, 52, 123, 131, 147, 172, 173, 218

Social network 18, 31–33, 52, 53, 65, 72, 74, 77, 79, 81, 87, 172, 218

Social network learning 32

Social relationships 74, 75, 85, 87
Social skills 84, 117
Social skillsets 141
Strategic/decision-making processes
    193
Street knowledge 46
Strongly bonded networks 119
Strong ties 125, 130, 140, 210
Succession planning 186, 187, 191,
    205, 226, 233
Sustainability 17, 68, 72, 167,
    186–191, 194, 196–203, 205,
    210, 221, 226, 227

T

Tacit knowledge 72
Teaching and learning 3, 9, 13, 17,
    23, 25, 29, 40, 41, 53, 208
Teamwork 14, 50, 63, 219
Technical skills 3, 144, 218
Technological disruption 41
Technology skills 45
Tools 38, 66, 67, 101, 157, 158,
    168, 183, 218
Transferrable skills 19
Transparency 25, 32, 33, 40
Trust 40, 76–82, 87, 110, 125, 130,
    138–140, 161, 164, 189, 212,
    215, 218, 226, 233

U

Unlearning pedagogy 39

V

Value 15–17, 26, 27, 31, 41–43, 48,
    57, 63, 65, 69, 76, 112, 119,
    127, 139, 145, 192, 194, 199,
    202, 213, 214, 218, 219, 229,
    236
Virtual communication 136
Vision 2, 3, 6, 13, 72, 102, 105,
    108, 126, 138, 141, 144, 166,
    187, 191, 192, 199, 200, 204,
    212, 229, 237

W

Weak ties 78, 86, 87
Wenger, E. 10, 13, 63–73, 102–104,
    209, 212
Work-integrated learning (WIL) 18,
    34–36, 208
Workplace learning 48
The World is Flat 29

Y

Youth 75, 81–83, 107, 108, 122–
    124, 131, 172, 175, 197, 199,
    231
Youth agency 80
Youth music 6, 9, 129, 214
Youth music industry conference 126